Operation: Gender War

Divide and Rule

Blair MacRae

Copyright © 2004 Blair MacRae   Chi Publications
All rights reserved. Short pieces of this publication for review purposes may be reproduced or transmitted in any form or by any means, electronic or mechanical, including photocopy, recording, or by any information storage and retrieval system.

First printing 2004
Revised   2007

National Library of Canada Cataloguing in Publication

MacRae, Blair, 1946-
Operation, gender war : divide and rule / Blair MacRae.

Includes bibliographical references.
ISBN 0-9733717-0-6

1. Men—Social conditions.   I. Title.

HQ1090.M34 2004   305.32   C2003-906485-9

Editorial consultant: John Ricker
Book design: Jim Bisakowski www.bookdesign.ca

Printed in Canada

Publisher contact:
Chi Publications
bond@culturebuster.com
www.culturebuster.com

Contents

Introduction v

I
Society Today

1. New Clear Understanding 1
2. Rooster the President 4
3. Staring Truth in the Face, Eating Popcorn 10
4. Zoo Glue 22
5. Cosmo 27
6. Progress Is Failure 28

II
Power and Female Sexual Attraction

7. Estrus Ardent 47
8. Red Mouth 64
9. Murder 67

III
Abuse of Rationality

10. Introduction—Reason, Rationality, Logic 83
11. Spice and Rodham 90
12. You've Gone a Long Way Baby 127

IV
Rebound from Victimization

13. Wrainbashed 145
14. Mad Donna 152
15. Mistaken Identity 181
16. 21st Century Foxed 194

V
The Feminization of Society Revisited

17. The Male Click Experience 213
18. Lash 216
19. Purposeful Incarnation 279
20. The Bomb 290
21. He, He 302

Notes: 305
Bibliography 313
Index 317

Introduction

I was taught that truth would be searched out and confirmed by human willpower. The light of truth, I was assured, would bring safety and benefit to human society and to all life on earth. But today it's *whose* truth, or *which* truth. Many people are uncomfortable, and when asked for "the truth," they either go quiet or fire rapid disclaimers about "who has the right, etc..." to determine what is the truth. They chastize those who would dare impose their personal opinions on another person's experience of "reality." *Operation: Gender War* takes issue with the trend to discount truth as just somebody's separate idea, spin and grab for power.

To say that present society, in this dynamic information age, can't get to the truth, can't get a decent grip on information, can't get the appropriate facts, is to say what must sound unbelievable. But it is often just this way with "popular" opinion.

We've lost the tool of our own language. Common language should be able to identify and hold the guilty to blame, but it often doesn't anymore. Our language has been co-opted. It has been hijacked, and its original meanings are being twisted out. Through propaganda, advertising and spin language has lost clarity and it cannot be counted on to protect against the abuses of power anymore.

Operation: Gender War is not just a gender-war book. The gender war is a symptom, not the disease. But the route to understanding is easier if it is seen in familiar scenes. By focusing on gender relationships, by being specific here, the general picture opens up. And then it is apparent that something has gone wrong. While rationality is being forced upon citizens as their guiding tool, the culture in America is also being feminized on purpose.

Feminism provides a front, a cover, for the tooth-and-claw, bottom-line disdain for others found in our society. And rationality is so conditioned into us and so overused that *reason* itself has been perverted. Reason today is actually destroying our *emotional, intuitive and common sense* response to the world. So the collective focus of many feminists, the focus on humanitarian values, has limited audiences and can only go so far.

Citizens are being raised and nurtured on *subjective* experience and are taught to derive their sense of *power* from immediate personal relationships. But the elite class thrive on execution of *objective* strategy and acquire their power through their growing world economic domination. The elite of America prefer the masses they have under their control to be subjective, and they foster their control through the media. People are being trained and told not to hold opinions about the external world because it is all going to happen "out there" with or without them anyway. Today a subjective individual is featured wrapped up in "personal" relationships, and *here* people's opinions are like rights!

Feminists brought down the highest values of Calvinism in the 19th century, and replaced them with an anti-intellectual sentimentalism. Their dissimulation behind a sentimental illusion would hide the class struggle in America. And this served capitalism. Psychological norms have been replacing religious norms ever since, meaning people are increasingly taught to focus more on what they should *feel*, not on what they should *do*.

By the close of the twentieth century strong faith is being placed on the power of psychologists to interpret events and make things better. People had learned to trust guidance purchased from "professionals", and to devalue traditional wisdom and common sense. Psychoanalysis has captured an esteemed place for itself in American culture, appearing to meet demands for theraputic and medical accuracy, without challenging or upsetting the social order.

"Feminism" was used to divide the Black Liberation movement and the Counter Culture of the sixties. Since then many forms of feminism have been a powerful force associated with the destruction of the traditional family. Today it marginalizes males and the male voice is being silenced. This could bring misery and misfortune.

Sex scandal, hunts for murderers, kidnappers and wicked weather all produce enough victims and details of personal suffering to fill people's attention with a subjective world view. The masses are also being trained to focus their critical attention on a media smoke screen and its plethora of subjective stories. These stories are about victims and personalize history. It is not the events that matter as much as the feelings of the victims. It all becomes about the preservation of the victim's world. That is really support of the status quo, for the way things *were*. There is no room here for any change of the external world.

In wartime, it's letters from soldiers to wives and lovers, and then it's the embedded journalists who only show the subjective experience of the small military groups they are placed with by the Pentagon. That keeps objectivity in the background. Attacks on the personality of world leaders out of favor with the powers running America are subjectively based, but this leaves the problems beyond the demonized leader's condemned character out of sight and away from accountability.

Not enough people are challenging the elites about the big picture in America. Political correctness *is* the status quo. When chaos and violence occur often the question of "why?" is being omitted. TV programs that broadcast subject matter that clash with "official" versions, like the *Smothers Brothers* decades ago or *Politically Incorrect* recently, are canceled. And prior to the 2003 attack on Iraq, *Donahue*, virtually the only TV program left that confronts the government's official versions of reality, is canceled.

New police powers arise. Dissent, protest, strikes and roadblocks may now be defined as terrorism. Oddly, it seems we're now living in the world that George Orwell predicted in his famous book *1984*, where war was peace, freedom was slavery and sexual behavior was used in rebellion against the *system* and its status quo. We're brainwashed and reprogrammed to official versions just like Orwell's people. Here in America, like in *1984*, ignorance can be seen being hailed as strength. There is denial of global warming, reneging on international treaties over world pollution, termination of the antiballistic missile treaty, undermining of the international criminal court and doctored evidence used to pave the way for war.

Telescreens, thought police and big brother are all a done deal today with TV, Hollywood movies and the media under corporate control. The TV trains our nation. In *Operation: Gender War*, I use the term "America" to refer to Canada and the United States of

America. It is basically the same North American culture, north or south. Canada rides onboard the ship piloted by the USA. The Canadian fate will be that of the USA.

I had to write this book once I began to understand how men, and their roles, are downgraded in North American society. Andrew Morton, who wrote *Monica's Story*, about President Clinton's mistress, has the nerve to say there is an "underlying misogyny" in the USA. He means a *hatred of women*. And President Clinton became, in Morton's eyes, President Butthead!

It's very weird how in present-day society our general beliefs lead to the claim of women as an underclass, as victims, as those who need support and uplifting. But look at the facts, such as the life expectancy of the male being *six years less* than the female, and the enormous quantity of statistical information that shows males are victims in the dumps, and a new understanding will arise.

I need to remind readers that my advocacy for an end to male-bashing cannot be justified without evidence that just such a climate exists. And thus, although some females and groups of females are held accountable for the anti-male subterfuge, my life experiences teach that women, in general, are valuable. And they own the right to decide the future of planet earth. Many are competent professionals who I would trust in matters of life and death; likewise I feel benefit in their abilities with my children. Great respect is held for the females that show up at protest marches and put their bodies on the line over social concerns. Whether protesting against the WTO, or doing activist work like that of Carrie Nation in the 19th century, who was out there actively protesting alcohol use and abuse, women are found in the leadership working for social improvement. I also have the highest regard for the accountability and the courageous brilliance of numerous female intellectual productions.

But men are also valuable, and I fear their collective voice is being obscured, drowned out in an overcharged and confused ideological battle. Best selling books like *Stupid White Men*, by Michael Moore, while shedding light on those who control America, derive much popularity because they bash males. And the author, Michael Moore, makes vile accusations about men that are simply *unfounded*. He gets away with it because America is proliferating as an anti-male culture.

Common sense is disappearing. People are reacting as victims now rather than creating solutions, as the genders lash out in subjective reaction to what they each perceive as abusive insult and assault aimed at them. *Schadenfreude*, a German word for taking pleasure in the humiliation and misfortune of others, is spreading. *Thelma and Louise* is chosen as the film to celebrate the twenty-fifth anniversary of the National Organization for Women (NOW). But while all the complaining between the genders continues, why does the notion of women's essential innocence still prevail?

The solution to the debasing of one gender—the males—needs a focus that reveals *men as victims*. This is to help expose the agendas of those who assault men and to spur men to begin to complain. Gender war in America and around the world is distracting both sexes from the "other," from paying serious attention to the whole, the society, the world. Once the big picture is captured, understood, then corrective solutions can be grasped and used to steer society towards health.

As a sociologist-investigator, as one who tries to stand back and see what it is that makes people behave in certain ways, to do this or do that, to decide how to live, I am attuned to the winds of social change. People who know me would likely admit that I have always had opinions and concerns about society. But I have experience too, wide-ranging at that—from my operating seat behind the wheel of my taxicab, here where I could easily interview the world at large as I drove the streets in metropolis, to the business world as a realtor and stockbroker as well and in the teacher's chair in the public school systems, I gleaned information. For many years I have been digging patiently like a mole through the darkness to search for statistical facts and evidence to back up what I sensed—that men are under attack.

There are more females in university than males today, and females have more sports teams in these universities than males. In all the media, the law courts, the schools and the universities I found men's needs are either ignored or debased. Even their families and homes are being lost, taken away. Studies show that *one-third or more* of all children born in America today are not cared for within a marriage. In African American communities the rate of unmarried moms can be over 60 percent. Single moms could soon be the group controlling the majority of the children.

Over the years I have pieced together the experiences and the facts. *Operation: Gender War* was set on its course to illuminate the truth and to expose the false and handy lies that are spread about "reality" today. Continuing seduction and betrayal of the human heart can only lead to a future that's just like our past, or worse. Our governments are sweeping men's issues into a corner. And they marginalize ethical behavior, concerned as they are for protecting corporate profit, no matter the humanistic degradation of the whole of society and of all of the world.

Operation: Gender War may offend some people. But I'll take the risk, because to ignite further thought, while it could bring anger, is better than what I see—the *doublethink* and *newspeak* politicians and the growing rip-off life lived around a media spin-world of untruth and fiction. As readers you are needed, because without your intentions to improve society, a lot of needless suffering will be accepted as normal. Otherwise we are on a course to make ignorance the crowning principle of our civilization. When our society has reached the present pinnacle of tremendous specific knowledge, this would be the great tale told by an idiot, wouldn't it!

Why is it popular for many females to cast males as evil? Are we? And what has caused them to have this judgement? Is the world suffering from an *overdose of testosterone*, as Sinead O'Connor claims? Are men redundant and nuisances, as Germaine Greer says? Referring to women's demand for equality and "all the privileges pertaining to the estate of the human being", hadn't Simone de Beauvoir claimed that "by and large we have won the game." In 1952! That's when her book, *The Second Sex,* was published and when she claimed women's victory.[1]

In the course of my research and sociological investigation I have become aware, so acutely aware, of the males' present plight. I found information that totally upsets today's media-formed pillar of consensus or "popular opinion."

All of one's attention is needed to understand reality. That attention and energy is distracted, dissipated by living in a fictitious spin world. The perception of the false as false is the beginning of understanding.

"The most dangerous situation for a woman is not an unknown man in the street, or even the enemy in wartime, but a husband or lover in the isolation of their own home."

Gloria Steinem[1]

I
Society Today

1
New Clear Understanding

Traffic lines, separate bumps of color winding around hills and stretching mile after mile further and further into the horizon. Huddled, stuck people hunch in colored cubes. Wheels stop, time reverses. Wheels move silently then, glunk, no more. Stare, space out, people can't have what they want, can't do what they want. And they hate themselves for being angry about it all. Radio distraction addicts. Without the music boxes, people would notice that the side streets and boulevards look like crash sites filled with cars dropped from outer space and sucked at random angles into a living earth. Did it have to turn out this way?

Chaotic patterns of hued autos: a light blue Pinto wagon on a grassy knoll here, and over there on your own block a rusted-out two-door burgundy classic leaded "pig", having blown its last big combust-fart and passed into history.

You may think you are nice, a caring type of person. But that may be only because you feel a tear explore your cheek when you're blotting out reality with Hollywood movies. A sentimental pervert, you deny the cruelty all around you, escaping into the moving picture shows. Dreamy, you mentally toy with the tragedies of strangers; the celebrities you follow like a vampire. But you are not on board. The networks ask you to send in your opinion, as if you could really know anything after watching their news programs, or that they really care. You are just a spectator.

Maybe you'd bloody rather watch your life on the telly, someone acting your part, taking the hits, making the decisions and getting the results you might deserve. Or maybe just an orgasm would smooth out the aggravation....

A beige Mexican hotplate glows at the end of an orange

sunset-laden alley. The men walk closer towards it. A cord paints a trail from it along the gravel and up over the frame of another poison-producing leaded "pig", down along the seat, and over, up and into the cigarette lighter. Power. They come closer and then stand in a semicircle around the glowing red rings of the hotplate. This was it, their destination. Night was falling fast; a cold wind came straight off the not-to-distant ocean. Big hands hung in the air around the appliance like those of the converted while giving praises. But their little piggies were cold, and these guys were without permanent residences. What's next? Well something has got to give. Where do homeless women go? Or is that a contradiction in terms? Perhaps a new clear understanding is coming. Perhaps people will begin to get the big picture regarding the men in society.

How come women claim they are like racial minorities? How come women in a group call themselves guys? Red Mouth is the equal of repressed, denounced and plodding men? Not very likely in this world!

When men can grow their own pets in their own bodies, when women don't outlive men by six years, when men's suicide rate isn't five times higher than women's (ten times after a divorce), when men aren't the greater victims of virtually all crimes, then the scales will perhaps balance out.

But hey guys, reduce your present emotional devastation by also getting a dog and carefully observing what it takes to love unconditionally. What shall it profit a man to orgasm in a woman? Julio Iglesias did—get a dog, that is. And then later dedicated his most famous album of songs, *Starry Night*, to his beloved pooch. At the time he was one of the most adored male singers, a handsome dreamboat of the highest order to his legions of female fans. He commented that his dog, in contrast to women, was always happy to be with him. He felt he could depend on its love versus that of many of the women around in the western world today.

Killer Consciousness

Conflict is what always drives the mind and the mind always fights to be right. We are all quite ready to defend where we are, to justify and explain everything we see as important within the fabric of our lives. We think we know what is right, and that we are where we are because of facts and events that led more or less straight to our present positions.

If some people are living in ignorance and illusion but do not know it, what is wrong? And how is it possible to live life like that? How can these people be so confident that they understand how things are?

There is pleasure in hatred and envy is satisfying.

2
Rooster the President

"Nobodies got a lock on the truth."
Bill Clinton from Ho Chi Minh City, Vietnam, 2000

So things *seem* to be moving along as expected, watching the network's broadly painted canvas of international *news*, and at home the *news*, except for the moral and "personal" dilemmas, is being painted by short info-bits with little depth or significance. Pot, porn and illegal immigrants all have expanded their market share and are now big factors in the American economy. And two hundred people of the power elite control forty-one percent of the world population's wealth. While their stock markets bring in free money from the casinos revolving in Wall Street's orbit, the public is snoozing and tuned right out.

The people are not interested in going after anything but obvious criminals, so the *longhairs*, the professional spin doctors and their media machine apply socio-political paint and hide the sins of those who pay them. Yes, this business-as-usual works out just fine. The USA is running its imperialist machine with a perspicacity that identifies and denudes much, and soon probably all, opposition to market economics, democratically elected governments and the like. IMF Group. The Rad.

Soon maybe a one-world government. Soon maybe criminals executed for today's petty offenses, for small stuff, as the rational rule of law finally wins out, and the rule of the average person is reduced to the channel-changer in hand. So, with a one-world government maybe *car*s will be taken off the streets, nuclear bombs sunk to the bottom of the seas, maybe all the weapons' metal melted into a huge bulk or perhaps shaped into a statue of Thomas Jefferson or someone else. Or a one-world government may at least make all the automobiles wear pollution controls, so that the filthy snaking highways that the people's tax dollars built are de-poisoned, their wretched cancer-causing environments toned down. It's viral! But, you gotta *say* that control of the whole world could bring a better *day*.

Consumers Beguiled

At home in-depth media is permitted to feed on sex exposés. The consumers in the democracy are allowed to take up sides in sexual scandals. Everyone is allowed to rage on, hurl abuse on those with differing "facts." The public here think they exercise their rights of freedom of speech and their right to personal opinion. And perhaps that is true, but it's ultimately of little meaning.

The subjects allowed public debate are far-fetched in relation to issues that affect the average person's life. And even if there were moral lessons that could be learned from an outcome of the word-wars and arguments, these scandals and incidents thrown to the public to fight over never have an ending. They are left unresolved, and people just keep up the arguing. Good distractions.

While the elite hunker down undisturbed and get the business of business done, the people wail with their words upon each other, divide into camps and eliminate themselves from the table. Anita Hill and Clarence Thomas, Bill Clinton and Monica-Paula, they never go away. The public is unsettled. The senate only puts on show trials. They have agendas other than the truth.

The Victim

The Pres, well, he is the victim. Born too close to a real whorehouse, what with the smells and the gaiety and the sexual signals permeating the *air,* Billy Clinton could not always *beware.* Like Big Bird he flapped innocently, sometimes clumsily, family alcoholism and sexually related dysfunction to him just everyday stuff. But the injury had been done, and to our ladies' man, some kind of nastiness became associated with some fun. Hurting as a boy, as the story goes, not because of mistakes necessarily made, but because of witnessing gross neuroses of others. Slammed into denial as the psychologists do say; the hot head, the flushing cheeks, the gut screaming to run and hide, as some cruel or violent scene plays out in front of young Bill—all this left markings, and perhaps late in life these marks lead to need.

The supposed solution to bizarre emotional feelings of entrapment is understood somehow as getting something. Consumers understand these problems—products and services are thought needed to satisfy or fix-up. So the Pres' product is female. It relieves past pains and drains anxiety, boosts self-esteem via service-attention, and the rage darts out. It's a cure, these women, for our *President,* and some may say it's heaven *sent.* To think of solving all the conflicts in Pres Bill's mind, psyche and body, and to attempt to cure his compulsive indiscriminate grabbing of the female, some most annoying and uncalled for *too,* well the problem is stuck right up in his generation's attachment to productions dealing with the *sex glue.*

Sadomasochistically, because of being caught, trapped by the ads of sex signals that target male culture, and catching pleasure from trapping images, the guilt for males arose. And the females' guilt filled internal caves through them using below-the-belt strategies, while faking a Victorian female moral superiority.

President Clinton's boomer generation—the balled, enthralled Dionysian conscripts of the 60's—became ashamed and put in their place by church and drug fatigue. Then the handy raging orgasm disappeared –

> *From being free, it's said*
> *'Cause girls can't handle this liberty*
> *"Without getting paid"*
> *So marriage (again) was the key to getting laid.*

But more than guilt or gluttony, Pres Bill's unwelcome pawings were leading to supreme courts around the land having to host and sit through listening to his BC Spin Band abusing the English language—causing a national *rage* as millions see the big Pres as an animal to lock in a *cage.*

> *But mercy, is there mercy for the guy,*
> *The one who can't seem to stop pulling down his fly?*
> *Keen interest of his sort,*
> *Why in females' company is he so desirous to consort?*

This female fan might be like others to whom the symbol on the washroom door with the legs apart—this image only sends signals to this sort of female spread-open vulnerability. So walking away every other day to the other door, then a figure with a skirt gives the head the red alert! Is Bill one to whom woman-openness signs are readily sought and *seen*, but now stinging reminders of goofing-up force him to split the *scene*?

He is the boomer pres and his early education reading *Peyton Place*, and *Lady Chatterley's Lover*...and the *fashion* pics that soared.... Bill's libido must'a kicked in and on roared *el presidente*—all through life and into his twenties, the naked pictures there were plenty. Big screen movies obsessed on sex and the James Bond of the times deserved Pussy Galore, preferably shaking while stirred. The feminists took off their bras—now that was kind of nice—and why should women be afraid to be natural? So on the feminists went, but soon only nipples pushing against cloth were the visible segments, and the "boss-female" mind seems to get angry 'bout giving it away—in *Penthouse, Playboy* and on the street. So Bill's stimulation was begun, but soon his constructed needs had to go underground.

Getting the stuff out in the open is the solution for the popular males needing willful crucifixion upon erotic female flesh to quell their ego-sex confusion. That's to help them to confront and overcome neurosis, sexual obsession. But many sex *therapists* work upon the needing males with hands hung with sharpened nails. This Bill was raised in very liberal free-sex times that said: *if it feels good do it,* and *why don't we do it in the road.* Free Love! These words ruled. In the late 60's and into the 70's, everyone getting loving and naked was seen by many as progressive, as a good means for overcoming a violent, selfish world dominated by *capitalist pigs* and greed, etc.

Later, with the rise of third-wave feminism, "love" became seperated from "free". "Love" became sexual politics, with "personal" agendas and "personal" grasps for power. Thus poor Bill had to suppress his natural personality. And repress his needs.

Victimized or Disgraced?

Pres Bill could have used a better society to grow up in, but, hell, where is the perfect world, eh? But if missiles crash into third-world countries because the Pres wasn't getting *proper* poontang, then perhaps he should have retired and bought a whorehouse, where his needs may have been more easily met. And if taxpayers must keep forking up the dough to pay his propaganda spinning hirelings to paint a phoney aura around this *Bill*, maybe a less greedy-needy obsessive-compulsive should be raised onto *Capital Hill*.

Why was Pres Bill a disgrace to so many, and a victim to others? He is a boomer; he went through the sexual freedom decade; he is used to lots of satisfaction. But as President of the United States he was getting himself in some boiling hot water. Just sex? Well, if you're the Pres in secret liasons with spies, foreign agents dressed as females—some don't even undress—well, some say, what'ya got?

> *Have women from a distant planet set a trap,*
> *And this guy Bill was getting a very bad rap?*
> *But why was his weakness so strong,*
> *To take him where the nation doesn't want to belong?*
> *For the love of light,*
> *Why couldn't our man just get it right?*
> *What is behind the real story*
> *That has lost him the grand vizier glory?*

The round face and his big eyes easily lend him our inner trust. But now that is all just a vapor trail, as Bill's media-painted image in the big blue sky sways, distorts and is brought down to earth in a valley of angry retorts from the irate, those that vehemently thrust in a chaos of free-speech, scratching at this, the public sore of scandal. The upon-high seated bigwig owl righteously attacked because of owly lust, forced from his nest, rebuked as a low-life *with talents for low intrigue and the little arts of persuasion.*

Yup, this William Jefferson Clinton didn't have a dad around when he grew up, so living around and in a matriarchy became acceptable. What else was there to do, especially with a very strong mother in charge? Grow up and marry your mother-type, of course, and then your world stays normal. What normal is *is*—what you are used to. Right?

Young Bill lived for a time with his gramma too, and she is said to have physically beat up on Bill's grandfather. So what must the young lad have seen? And the sneaking around, well it's a hangover from Bill's early life at home in the matriarchy. Slip out and get some service, get back and empathize-spin with the female-run household, learning to drink from the cup of emotionality, the empathetic involvement gleaned from out of the gynecocracy surrounding.

But now the former Pres has to come home to a career-focused, obsessed wife, one whose perceptive reservoir is inundated with the false-consciousness contemporary females endure. These women have been forced to reconstruct their vision of themselves upon deconstructionist rhetoric, endlessly their treasure being pulled apart thread by thread and now the results—a battle, a societal gender-war twister. Full out in the open have crept the once-whispered anti-male criticisms and jibes, the blamed now publicly named, the meme-ideas set in motion.

> *Packaged propaganda " tacts,"*
> *Paid-for research cooks up facts.*
> *The reactive rational salivate and look for the kill,*
> *But a claimed victim status brings the big chill –*
> *Even by a man, this Bill—stimulating orgies of defense,*
> *Lobby lists of the gay, feminist and black civil*
>   *libertarians built his filter fence –*
> *All bleed into the media feed*
> *To keep their man out of court and freed.*

Yes, and it's worth listening to, especially for the single soccer moms who've got the boys at home in their private materfamilias. And maybe this Bill will seem the success of them all. But tall stories circulate about those driven to *de-sublimate,* the ripping their revenge against a *matriarchate.*

3
Staring Truth in the Face, Eating Popcorn....

"I must break away from beauty and sentimentality."
                                                    Piacasso

It's becoming ever more clear, ever more certain that the best bet for the future is for ignorance. The culture of ignorance suits this information age. Just as good attracts evil, happiness is balanced by sadness, or peace is contrasted by war, so insight is muddied by false information. Ignorance can lead to blind belief and to prejudice.

North-American society is in the cultural grip of feminization. It has been for over 200 hundred years. It *is* a feminized society. All the while, all the noise claims the opposite! Virtually no one even thinks this through.

Most accept various accounts of women's liberation as a progressive and recent event. It isn't at all recent. The hegemony over the culture that has been garnered by the feminine ethos in the past two centuries has both served the elite capitalists and sacrificed the male population.

Ann Douglas, in *The Feminization of American Culture,* brings water for the desiccated, withered masses, the victims of the present information age.[1] Her facts sponge the vitality of accurate knowledge back into today's wizened souls. A Parr Professor at Columbia University, a teacher of American studies at Harvard, Princeton, and Columbia, she goes back into the Victorian Era to find the roots of our present North-American culture. What is dished up is revealing.

As women's usefulness diminished during the industrial revolution, women sought to create an *influence,* says Douglas. Power they desired through this "influence". It was a moral power they wanted, almost religious, to portray the female in terms similar to her close ally in her power quest, the ministers of the church. In the nineteenth century these two groups, the ministers and the "ladies," would destroy a Calvinist, male-oriented culture. They would establish a feminized society and provide a sentimentalized smoke screen under which capitalism, tooth and claw, first took control over America. Today capitalism is in the intermediate stages of taking global command.

Today the feminist spell that originated in the early nineteenth century America is cast on western society. As well, the long-haired spin doctors aim the sentimentally charged and feminine nurturing value of compassion for the underprivileged at those who are now receiving market economics and democracy to make them *free.* But it's women's nineteenth-century obsession with nostalgia that revealed a yearning for former times, before capitalism became the dominant force in America.

Isn't the charged verve of the nostalgic, dripping hopefully with intense feeling and sensitivity, still women's claimed territory? All who enter here are her's. Today nostalgia for non-competitive caring-sharing values, ones that would help socialism, are displayed in Hollywood movies, where everybody is guaranteed a sentimental tear or two, so they can connect to humanity. And this may be many peoples' only way to get deep emotional connection today—at the movies.

The nostalgia for positive *helping* values, that reach out and comfort, really only highlight their lack today and the resultant inhumanity that exists everywhere. Because the total effect of all the cruelty in society today is just to make people expect more of it!

The dominance of capitalism, and its violent splitting of the whole world into small elites of *haves* and massive hordes of *have nots,* is muted by all the feminism around. Feminists usually align with sisterhood, with a feelings approach, and with inclusion rather than exclusion. This gives the selfish capitalist system its counteragent. And this may be therapeutic for society, and help heal some of its dysfunctional neurosis—this feminine refuge sought, free from the brutality of capitalism. Females dissimulating behind their freedom-from-capitalism banners, where there's a claimed empathy and inclusion for all, ignore the real world of the bullies in charge of society. But it gets the women a special treatment, to be identified with the liberation *values* of anti-capitalism. And it assumes they have the power to distribute their healing *female touch* on those they choose. It's like star power!

Female focus today is mainly on the "individual" and his or her needs, tastes and relationships. This focus can create a wonderland of biological and even psychological awareness. This is so subjective, whereas the historical, objective perspective gets ignored. Objective clarity isn't simply about debate, being right and taking a dogmatic fighting position. No, but *mentalism* is about rhetoric (ideology) being used only to win, for winning. The truth can be another matter entirely. Mentalism suits capitalism, with its conflict, comparing, like consumer shopping and then the bottom-line competition towards winning. This breeds separateness (the individual), and isolation from others (competitors). Communal feminism is an antidote to capitalism. But it's not capitalism that usually takes the hit today as responsible for the terror around. No, it's the men!

As they rage on about "male" violence, men's cruelty and men's imperial conquests, the feminists and the culture they have brought into being allow extreme display of the persecution they vilify.

The intelligentsia's failure to acknowledge America as a class society, instead recognizing official propaganda versions of egalitarian democracy, has left the masses blind to their true circumstance. At home, it's women's empowerment and reproductive rights, sympathy for the mother and her children and support for development of an education system that emancipates "feelings." But away in the markets of the world, a bottom-line conqueror sets the agenda for the nation, for reasons the future *bought media* will surely entertain.

In the early 1800's women and ministers began to draw together. Both groups were without political power, and they sought *influence*. In the main, men were the ones working—the income producers. The women painted their role as providers of men's refuge from capitalism. This was through men's access to women's humanitarian and morally righteous, "spiritual" personality. And through her control and directing power over his believed panacea to the competitive world of capitalism, the sanctuary of the *home*. According to Douglas, the "Pink and White Tyranny" was "the drive of nineteenth-century women to gain power through the exploitation of their feminine identity as their society defined it."[2]

In the nineteenth century, women "comprised the bulk of educated churchgoers and the vast majority of the dependable reading public. They were becoming the prime consumers of American culture. As such they exerted an enormous influence on the chief male purveyors of that culture, the liberal, literate ministers and popular writers...."[3]

After 1833, the disestablishment of the Protestant Church meant that ministers couldn't count on public financial support, and thus they had to put themselves on the *market* too. They couldn't ignore their female customers.

The ministers and the ladies became the "central agents in the process of sentimentalization."[4] Their influence was moral and psychic. It promoted sentimentality and nostalgia. It was exerted in the growing mass medium of literature. The women and ministers promoted themselves in the most favorable light, and they exercised an enormously conservative influence on their society.

It's not the female values—nurture, acceptance, and the culture of feelings—that are the problem. When reading Douglas it becomes obvious that it is pandering to *sentimental* rather than matriarchal values that is the problem. From their "sentimental peddling of Christian belief for its nostalgic value,"[5] through Sunday school and their focus in everyday sermons and in popular fiction, the minister and the lady "provided the inevitable rationalization of the economic order."[6] There was no other way a young America could endure capitalist-imperialist culture, except through nostalgia for a past that was innocent, with a yearning but amorous focus on sentiment. Sentiment yields values and emotions that make one's internal world come alive with what actually could *not* come into being in capitalist society. Sentiment may briefly re-connect the heart's feeling with the mind's conceptualizing. But that is usually all that is accomplished, for only a brief period. The "real world" is soon allowed dominance, hegemony, over all life.

It is frightening to think that a country may glorify just the thing it doesn't have or do. But the appeal of compassion, fraternity and communal warmth is not part of the market-economics mind-set. Calvinism was "largely defeated by an anti-intellectual sentimentalism...."[7] Sentimentalism can also be used to protest against power that one is supporting, such as sentiment in books and movies for the victims of imperialism. It's a perverse way to get the heart to open. It always borders on dishonesty, this sentiment for *your* victims.

With the "masculine" conquest, expansion, and industrialization of America, the "business of the globe" became portrayed in anti-female terms, as against the feminine ideals of nurture, healing and inclusion. The problem was that the feminizing force slid into mere nostalgia for what was felt lost and unretrievable. Sentimental themes arose and became idealized. They helped people connect with a vision of life that had included values not found in the real world created by capitalism. But they left people in illusion, with the home and the women in it raised up into a heavenly refuge. The real daily lives of the people were dominated by a bottom-line capitalism that drove compassion out. Empathy was thus thought to be found in the home, and through the women and ministers of the day.

The female of the nineteenth century surrounded herself with sentimentality, as did the ministers. "The minister and the lady were appointed by their society as the champions of sensibility. They were in the position of contestants in a fixed fight: they had agreed to put on a convincing show, and to lose. The fakery involved was finally crippling for all concerned."[8] Sentimentalism aided self-evasion within American society. The veil of sentimentalism hid the class struggle in America. It brought "the cultural sprawl that has increasingly characterized post-Victorian life."[9]

Young middle-class women in the Northeast, Ann Douglas says, were trained by conservatives and reformers alike to:

> "serve their male counterpart, not compete or
> even participate with him; her significance was
> to lie in her connotations rather than her
> actions....The ideal woman...was to exert moral
> pressure on a society in whose operations she

> had little part, and to spend money - or have it spent on her - in an economy she could not comprehend. She was in embryo both a saint and a consumer. Naturally the lady and her advisors underplayed her status as consumer and overplayed her status as saint. Middle-class women...preferred to stress their moral and religious 'influence' rather than their evolving importance as highly socialized and expert shoppers. In actual fact, however, the two roles, saint and consumer, were interlocked and mutually dependent; the lady's function in a capitalist society was to appropriate and preserve both the values and the commodities which her competitive husband, father, and son had little time to honor or enjoy; she was to provide an antidote and a purpose for their labor."[10]

Throughout the nineteenth century America was feminized by the alliance of the women and the ministers. Calvinism, a strict religious code, became diluted and replaced, as church-going turned into basically a *social* function. *Popularity* became the gauge for a church's success, this an early example of an aspect of the future consumer society. Feminized values were replacing strict belief, as Christ was assigned a sentimental appreciation.

The woman-element began to dominate in Christ. To desire to fall into God's arms, to be pressed to the breast, *like a child to the bosom of its mother*, became acceptable. God then became personalized, and was thought willing to enter into personal *relationship* with each true believer. This contrasts with the Calvinist God, a God whose truth and whose actions had often been thought *beyond* mere human comprehension. Sentimentalism did much to gut Calvinist orthodoxy.

Ministers were swept up into the feminine ethos. They had to become "subjective", an approach that put great demand on a minister's sensibilities. They had to *professionalize the personal*. The minister lost his authority from and connection to the *impersonal*, to the transcendent word of God. Like the malaise of many women at the time, the ministers dwelt in a soap opera, in a *claustrophobic private world of over-responsive sensibility*. Douglas: "Cut off at every point from his masculine heritage, whether economic, political or intellectual, the liberal minister was pushed into a position increasingly resembling the evolving feminine one."[11]

The minister and the lady dominated the reading markets. And although women were not generally known as writers at the beginning of the nineteenth century, by the end of it women were established and very popular as writers. The minister of the eighteenth century had been a serious reader of philosophy; by the mid-nineteenth century ministers had become lovers of fiction and poetry; they proudly became *light* readers. Women would eventually dominate the reading market and determine the product. Thus America became swamped in sentimentalized fiction.

> "Between 1820 and 1875, in the midst of the transformation of the American economy into the most powerfully aggressive capitalist system in the world, American culture seemed bent on establishing a perpetual Mother's Day."[12]

Feminized literature actually could be said to have ended history. Ann Douglas writes about how the writers were "bribed" by the feminine populace to "invalidate" and sabotage the masculine experience. Male accounts of history as a series of external events, of times and of actions, were replaced by an internal, psychological type of history. Devoid of events, there are now only objects and emotions. A biological consciousness replaces historical awareness. Dates in time lose importance; instead it's births, marriages, aging, illness and death that mark the important points in time. Here the average person's life cycle is of greater importance than any achievement. The minister and the lady contrasted the damage that "male" values (capitalism) brought—separation and open hostility—with *their* promotion of "feminist" values. But they never interfered with the actions of the market!

The Hegelian history of energy, enterprise, virility and direction was dumped. In its place a new history, without events, but now with objects and emotions, arose. A major flaw in this type of personalized history is that it assumes the individual as already, in essence, a determined entity. There is only the question of validation or preservation of the individual's internal, psychological order, but no genuine change.

The ministers' and the ladies' writings would substitute *space* for *time*. The *relationships* between characters and the main subject of their writing was paramount. An account of the Civil War was produced without a single soldier or battle! No military history here, but outrage can be turned toward those who wage those battles. Masculine, objective history has continued to disappear ever since. In 2003, Hillary Clinton's book says it all. It's called *Living History*!

In recent times..., after the World Trade Center attacks, the media always focuses on the victims of the attack. For months, it's all about their suffering. The why—the historical context, the events leading up to the attack—is at depth ignored. Then there is the hotly debated O.J. Simpson murder case, years after a mountain of fact, submitted as evidence, failed to convict. It's all gone so subjective. Here is where personal opinions count, and everyone goes off babbling their own spin. Oh, how the *longhairs* love the herd engaged in "sharing", sharing points of view, that is. It's why all these talk shows are broadcast into your homes by the corporate owned networks.

Arguing and separated, each citizen is imprisoned in the turmoil of his or her mind's ceaseless conflict. In debate the mind seeks only to win. Just like in the hyped-up capitalist mode, with its competitiveness and conflict, there is supposed to be a future in mental competition. People are taught to see a future, and freedom, in this conflict. But, again, the *truth*—that could be a totally separate experience.

Women's magazines have generally been anti-historical. Their focus is mainly on domestic management and romance. Victorian women reading novels for leisure were in a mass dream like the TV-viewer is today. Intimate and chatty, sentimental, psychological and biological, the consumption from many of these "worthless novels" left the reader light-years away from the world's events.

In early America, the home itself became the female area of direct control, became *heaven,* a place of healing and respite away from the pain of a worker's toil, a refuge away from busy competition. The home became so sentimentalized that men saw it only as a zone to aspire to; it became like their savior. The women dissimulate behind the heavenly image of the home, and with their added socially recognized moral influence, have even more power. The power to distribute to the chosen ones the grace of comfort and security away from the fury of capitalist society is a god or goddess-like quality. The home was nostalgically claimed to be where the heart was, and the lady was assumed to be naturally in this home.

Ann Douglas states that by the late 1880's and early 1890's "...many men, and women, were becoming deeply concerned about the feminization of American culture and the closing of the frontier, actual and metaphorical, which it suggested."[13] Then in reaction to feminization, Jesus Christ began to be described in more macho terms by ministers such as Billy Sunday. Christ became "the greatest scrapper that ever lived."[14] Muscular Christianity rallied men against becoming sissified by feminism. Great concern was also raised at the time about the overwhelming majority of *female* schoolteachers. But the political powers owed much to the female culture, and gradually the feminizing forces reclaimed their authority.

> "The forces of feminization were significant enough—they had tapped the increasingly formidable processes of industrialization, commercialization, and mass culture deeply enough—so that any opposition, even that waged by a Harvard graduate like T.R. [Teddy Roosevelt], had to be conducted on their own terms. Certain forms of deprivation and exclusion had made middle-class American women, the readers and consumers of the nation, and the men who imitated, flattered, and exploited them, logical heirs to the anti-intellectual tradition in American culture; and they had conspired willy-nilly with changing historical circumstance to make anti-intellectualism the tradition in American culture."[15]

18

Irresponsibility reeks out of the feminized and sentimental observer found in the magazine culture of America. A romantic vision wants change, and would want to make right the wrongs of society. The romantic reformers would use history and political and social understanding to promote their cognizance of a better world. But this is missing from the sentimentalist view, where social change is not the issue. Sentimental masochism attaches to passivity and entertainment. But the minster and the lady were to pay the price for their duplicity. Ministers lost respect and status. The church would lose a great deal more of its power. The lady, however, is another matter.

Ann Douglas refuses to identify what price women have paid for their dissimulation behind the sentimental and the nostalgic, obtaining power by painting themselves as the righteous possessors of healing morality, and as the "angels" of the heart's moral oasis, the home. Their high-level seduction of men allowed capitalism to flourish; it hid the visibility of conquest. Sentiment functioned as a spiritualized form of acquisition, whereby the women coerced and co-opted the men. Sentiment became the nurturer of dysfunction and neurosis. It created a huge reservoir where more and more neurotic *Insurance*, people's acceptance and expectation of evil, could grow.

Douglas says women, too, have paid a price. But she won't define it. The ideological dominance of today's politically correct feminization probably scares her. She knows her academic, responsible, well-reasoned remarks could be misunderstood. She does say, however, that "my ongoing interest lies with the various forms of intellectual and emotional dishonesty American culture has developed and exploited...."[16] Like her heroine Margaret Fuller, she demands, "Give me truth, cheat me by no illusion."[17] Violations of honesty bring suffering, says Douglas.

> *"All my scholarly research, all my personal experience indicate that we Americans, as individuals, and as a nation which has invested heavily in the notion that the truth shall set you free, suffer when new violations of honesty occur—whether the intensifying sentimentalism of the middle-brow culture of 'influence' in the*

> *nineteenth century or the far more ominous creation of a secret government in the apparatus in the FBI and the CIA in the twentieth."*[18]

To read Ann Douglas is to see through the *popular* smoke screen that inhibits understanding of the past and the present. The value is the light that is shed on reality, and on what reality could be if the distortions were removed.

> *"The discourse of power, how it advertises and disguises itself at different moments in our history, is my ongoing subject, the ways in which its self-expression 'goes bad,' in Hemingway's phrase for a new generation, alert to the lies of their predecessors if inevitably blind in part to their own."*[19]

Today, in a time of political correctness, blindness to historical accountability distorts both an understanding of the past and of the present. Sentiment must be seen as itself a nurturer of more negative *Insurance*—a location that ultimately reinforces negative, dysfunctional assumptions regarding the failure of humanity and its inability to trust in itself.

Sentiment also allows people to be distracted from cruelty and evil. But that only allows dysfunction to grow larger and larger. People thus expect more of it. That is the *Insurance* - the "knowing" that there's more and more bad news and anguish, torment and tribulation, coming. It feels guaranteed! When it comes it gives the assurance that one was right-on to expect humanity to fail, to mess up and destroy all that is precious.

Today popular music and the movies provide some feeling connections, and they distract from "reality". Sport spectatorship also provides escape, but much of it still ends up basically worshiping competition (capitalism).

Politically correct sympathy and acceptance of many *sexual* behaviors may allow some to think there is a general acceptance for all in society, but this is not revealed elsewhere in society. Sexuality is today a location where many people escape their personal devastation from capitalism, and they can call this freedom, but it is freedom to escape, not to grow in one's own chosen manner. The elite are only too happy to see the plebs burn out relishing their "freedom" to have sex!

It is feminism today that is most like the sentimentalism of the 19th century. Brute force, imperial conquest, interventionist wars and virtually inhumane treatment of the working classes originate in the same society that boasts of women's liberation. But a lot of the "liberation" is just another smokescreen, blocking sight of the ruling classes' behavior. "Popular" feminism pulls at the heartstrings, claims a moral authority, asks mercy for the victimized and the marginalized, obsesses on equal treatment for all in the collective, and aims to set-up social safety nets to aid and to protect some citizens. And all the while it seems violin music is called for. Feminism, in many of its present day forms, may seem to be like a modern antidote to capitalism. But it can become just an escape from reality (capitalism), that can actually support the status quo and bring little hope for change.

> *"The love of a woman is not sentiment, as is a man's, but a will that is at times terrifyingly unsentimental...."*
>
> Jung, Carl   *Aspects of the Feminine*, p69.

4
Zoo Glue

Life is a power play.
It doesn't matter what you say.

Postmodern murky-gray malaise. Watch TV. The pears you buy at the market give you heartburn. They've been picked too early, sprayed with stuff to ripen them en route, and frozen. You're suffering and can't trust, a maladroit consumer.

Twenty-five cups of coffee and the looney orgasm. Stay in your cave, where you can have your stuff and be what you want, where it is safe and where things are on your own terms. Watch TV. Soul sleep. Carnal mind.

Alienated but vain, cynical but persuaded into paralysis— you're ever-seeing but often not perceiving, ever-hearing but often not understanding. Between the illusion and the reality is glue. The television falls, crashes the humans' hypnotic trance.

Zoo glue (entertainment glue) binds people into mere observers. Can't see their true situation, and it seems like they don't even want to. Just wanna watch TV. Nicotine, booze and television chain the spirit, subjecting citizens to the spectre of soul robbery. Emotions and ideas become interchangeable. Stunts your growth.

Freedom to Be Confused

Michael "media-manipulation" Jackson, the one who married Elvis's daughter, not the accused fornicator of young boys—it's the way the media presents reality that counts. The image rules.

And the image-makers, the powers directing the media—who are they? Well, one day in 1995, CNN and *USA Today* inundated the population with the results of their poll: the American people, asked which man in the world they most respect, chose none other than their very own president, Bill Clinton. Makes one wonder. Anyway, before this *poll* was taken the congressional elections of '94 wiped out President Bill's Democratic Party, and that was just a few months earlier. So *then* he became our hero? But the next day after the poll it was announced that President Bill wouldn't have to stand trial on sex assault charges until after his presidential term was over. Nice packaging.

Psychology embraces illusions with never-ending applause. Females love psychology for some reason, maybe it's their feelings. There's something there they love. Our world is overrun with psychological explanation, a never-ending juxtaposition of pretend, analysis and desire.

It's been discovered that what people *imagine* is at the heart of what they will believe. Well, they just heard the news 'bout Bill. And how he is huge: Pres Bill is the most respected man in the universe. And this is then believed, and while it is in fashion *some* of the stewards of power then released the President of the United States from sexual assault charges, although later supreme court judges would reverse this spin success.

The same TV network that released the poll about Bill would one day say Bill's political partner, Al Gore, won the state of Florida in a presidential election. This was announced way before the polls had even closed. It wasn't true, but the false information may have influenced how many people would vote and the error may have helped determine total votes for the new president of the USA. And years ago the most recent image of Michael Jackson counted. He had married—a woman. Soon some people doubt the accusation that he assaulted young innocent boys—after all it was never proven!

Images are allowed to rule. Consumers are dreaming multidimensional fantasies and trying to stuff them into real life. Meanwhile, real life is being manipulated by thought-control, brainwashing and propaganda evolving from the offices of the power elite—the zones that manage the country. Twice removed, local losers *learn* to groove on ugly, a result of their educational dementia. Power wants to stay in power and can be forgiven this desire, a natural-pronged intention. It's just that the broadcast news needn't be taken for reality. Much of it only reveals the reality of interest groups that control the media.

Perversion rules: promotion everywhere, building a case, selling crap. An agitproped angst lies deep below the affirmation-trained smile of the nation. Cheerful robots with wiring problems believe in things they do not understand—like "the market." But they are bombarded by commercials like the rah-rah, "I believe in the market. I believe in me." They are spoon-fed, controlled and mistreated. It might as well be the Central Intelligence Agency sitting in their living rooms, reading tuned Ph.D. doctoral scripts while background music grabs pieces of their defenseless soul. Who produces these drama scenes broadcast to look like freedom of speech and an individual right to express individual truth?

The educated TV heads debate. But it's all duck soup in the crossfire. Freedom to be confused! They're all members of the same gang, and if things really changed they would be out of jobs! It sounds like the land of the free and looks like the home of the brave. And having an argument may be called freedom, but debate, and seeing only black and white, leads to seperate egos at war, without consensus, and keeps people stuck in "personal opinion." Divided.

Like animals, people will defend their points of view. The mind is all about conflict. Panicked by all the aggressive promotion, most people lose a desire to actively participate. *Zoo glue* splats brain, explodes human will into gumbled chunks. Fractured minds—have money, will buy.

Images are now reality. Presentation is everything. Why do we believe what is presented to us, what is seen, and allow it to override the underlying truth? It's as if a symbol, like Michael Jackson's marriage, or any marriage, causes extremely deep things to register in us. Marriage overrides the accusations. The most respected man in the world a rapist? We are under the spell of the public-relations sultans of signs, the artists of the apparition and the makers of image.

Apocalypse Curse

The warnings had gone virtually unheeded. All the normal men were either incredulous, not believing what they heard, or they were unable to assimilate the information and use it to their advantage. Thus fear again prevailed.

Meanwhile, alone, her right hand touched the golden tube to her lips and then started to spread the color. Ever so controlled, and with a knowing patience, the colored arch proceeded all the way up and through a little U-dip, and then down to a stillness at the mouth's corner. She exhaled, as someone would who had just finished an important task. It was done, but only the top part. A confident hand finished the bottom lip. It was easier, what with the flesh being thinner, and because the teeth could be used for support.

She cleared her mind with the next long exhale, cast her eyes downward and for a time was in a meditation. Like an athlete she was still, loose, just trying to rest into her body. A game it was all right, with an adversary, an opponent, her enemy, the threat she perceived in real life, the one her premeditated will sought to entrap and neutralize.

Seducing the Male

Centuries of abuse, years of defending, of worrying, of learning to know when and how to defend against the monsters always about. Nature, tooth and claw, snakes, tigers, millennia of savage lust-rape, mammoth mutilations in total disregard for the preciousness of life—this brought response!

Pink flash that's some stash; paint it smartly,
    don't be rash.
Lips, lips, labiate, floating in a world of hate –
Zonk the male, bring him down, prostrate prisoner,
    toady clown.

Painted, red, pink, anal brown, they all work effectively to derail any male mania. And then the "monster" goes around thinking 'bout honey. The sight of her colored kisser neutralizes his aggression, and she gains personal power. And today, lotsa cops and telephones keep tabs on the beastie ones. It is like she's *dressed naked, but claiming innocence.* Today men always have to be thinking sex. She just paints it on and pretends nothing has happened. The real *guys* have no choice, now they are *penisheads*. The real male genes seek visual information. Inherited male genes are like those of a hunter relying, trusting in instant visual clues, with sight so closely linked to life or death. Now nihilistically numbed, he evolves into her *love puppy*, but without the strength of an earth hunter. No, that has been replaced by the gentleman in pursuit of a favor. In fact, said favor has become a *chief pursuit*.

Constantly derailed and pulled into visual side roads, men gradually come to believe that they are naturally seeking sex in response to nature. But, alas, *human nature* has again got its meddling curse involved. Psychology justifies illusion—the earth's darkling plain runs amok with painted, rounded, fleshy, labially conscious beastesses.

She had flushed rouge on the cheek when aroused carnally. This was a sign. She's hot! And he saw surrender to desire had rushed this red-blooded, hot-vital passion over her curved skin. So he felt he knew that she was his true partner, could see her involvement, physical response: her commitment to do, her bond to deed, her lover's trust. Signs for all to see! He was wrong, it was a hoax: painted, stroked, cheeks sport a blush-on hue to coax, to fuel her grab for power.

Men are caught, trapped in a drama they can't understand. Props almost. Seduction holds on to them, clings like an electric pad across the shoulders, gripping like a screw placed into their guts, turning-burning. Daily passion has consumed them. Sexy stimuli ignite zealous wanting and flames a fevered addiction to female body-parts. Everywhere is woman, the fashionable feminine—all sex, all spread over the streets and sidewalks into supermarkets and down lanes.

The men might equate this sexy splash as just more entertainment, but they would be seriously mistaken—they are being set up. Promises of respite from insecurity and fear, and a seeming invitation to escape into pleasure, spur men to jump onto the ship of erotic fancy. Smiling colors and smells, floating fashion "dolls," veering tangents of erotic flesh, all cruise by, swirl around, walk away.

Men's biological, procreative mission in life teases at them terribly and tension builds. But they *believe* solutions can be found, attractive solutions too. In elevators, bars, behind cars, along beaches and over the hills, all about in parking lots and tunnels, solutions appear. It is endless: a boon and a bane, a blessing as well as a curse.

Could life be more without women constantly making their presence a challenge, a come-on—an attraction of more significance than appreciation?

5
Cosmo

Cosmopolitan magazine boasts and brags and flaunts the statistic of running over 200 pages of ads in one monthly issue! And the country even believes this is success—so much of a manipulative-laden personality has seeped into the social body. Rationality rules, it's money that matters, cow farts cause pollution and voter turnout remains low.

Everyone is alone, power hungry, self-interested, attempting to present themselves in an individual style that kicks butt: T-shirt, chains, Polo, Ralph and Tommy, tattoo, buzz-cuts and piercings....

But further alienation sweeps the nation, and into seclusion hobble the hordes entranced with popular illusion-delusion, drinking the drug "beer" and thinking about shouting: *I am.*

Buy it, shop for it, search through the garbage cans lined along the mall. Then paste on your identity.

Inside the costume a computer runs—endlessly winding streams of words, phrases, sentences that attempt to bring coherence to the present, to give direction to the future and to facilitate understanding of the past. But it's become a big neurosis focus—as distracted citizens figure ever more furiously, probing for answers to wordy questions; their skulls resonate until media stupefaction blends a social consensus.

Nothing interferes with the *elites'* syllabus! Coprophagous brain wired to *words*, it's brought the country the manager *nerds*.

6
Progress Is Failure

"The business of a woman's ordinary life is things in general, and can as little cease to go on as the world to go round," so said J.S. Mill in 1869.[1] In the mid-nineteenth century the tasks of women were crucial, said Mill.

He also noted that "a woman seldom runs wild after an abstraction," begging conclusion to the questions of today: what is money, what is the market, what is consciousness, what is romantic love, what is much of today's education, what is advertising, and what has come of you, dear woman?

To Mill some females possessed "lofty enthusiasm" and were capable of a sustained excitement (spirit), their strong feelings intrinsic to the development of strong self-control.

"Progress" Since the 19th Century

> *"You live, you learn."*
> Alannis Morisette

So after all the progress of the past century or so, females sell cars, boats, microwaves, stocks and bonds. They hostess for bucks, fly B-52 bombers and professionally represent for pay. They have the energy and self-control to show up and work, and they may also bring some of that "lofty enthusiasm" to upgrade the work environment, benefitting all around. Although many had seen this lofty enthusiasm as a birthing out of "the greater nervous susceptibility of women," Mill claimed that for a nineteenth-century woman "much of this is the mere overflow of nervous energy run to waste." And he said it would cease with a different upbringing, one in which women were brought up to work for their livelihood and to participate in physical exercise. Mill argued that women of the higher classes were raised like:

> "a kind of hot-house plants, shielded from the wholesome vicissitudes of air and temperature, and untrained in any of the occupations and exercises which give stimulus and development to the circulatory and muscular system, while their nervous system, especially in its emotional deportment, is kept in unnaturally active play; it is no wonder that if those of them who do not die of consumption, grow up with constitutions liable to derangement from slight causes, both internal and external, and without stamina to support any tasks, physical or mental, requiring continuity of effort."[2]

Excessive nerves without jobs and physical outlets could negate well-being for the pampered. But women's domestic work was detailed and essential and emotional. Women were trained and actively involved in feeling comprehension at some level, something that is *still* their forte, their heritage.

But to Mill the singleness of purpose that the male had for a *particular* job was lacking in females, as well as the physical regimen necessary to quell emotion and to remain focused. He said it was literally *learning* that was needed. And exercise! The female casualties of moral Victorianism needed to break out of their overprotected exclusive gender meekness and its demands on their behavior.

Learning was the route 130 years ago, but women are addicts today. Now there always has to be a reason, a reason for everything! Or maybe excuses, as strings of words are grouped in special order to explain away anything, everything, to instruct, destruct, re-instruct and deduct. It's like baby talk, but women are told to see a future and power in information, rationality and reason. But all the thoughts and considerations give a false sense of security.

Dark forces are feared and reason is upheld as their protector. Because of fear of uncertainty, and because uncertainty is basically non-rational, the use of reason to find security, answers, is embraced. So fear motivates the exclusive use of reason with its isolating and self-interested characteristics. Then when looking for personal reward, reason becomes connected to function. That is logical. But everything that works is not necessarily good. Everything that could work to make one's life an individual success in a competitive society couldn't be allowed. On its own, practical reason can leave people alone and frustrated. Value, ethics and humanism, if left out and not incorporated into reason, will strand society in wasteland of inhospitable and deadly competition, each person alive only unto herself.

Same with nations that live on "rational ideology." Belief in market economics ideology is based on pure reason, a reason that doesn't have to get its hands dirty in the real world. It's like belief in religious explanations. Selfish logic blocks greater understanding. That's a weakness of rationality. Many nations want to keep people stuck in the word glue. Imprisoned in their rational *jail*, here the plebs aren't so inclined to *wail*. Rationality will often eliminate doubt. Uphold the status-quo. Otherwise, using common sense and intuition people may revolt.

Are these women today overreaching, trading their natural emotional wisdom, intuition and common sense for some mental constipation? What they want, and what they need, isn't going to be satisfied by reason alone. The teacher rules and her purpose is to keep learners in wonder. While you're busy, stunned and studying, the teacher's boss, the corporate government, is mucking-chucking your human rights asunder. In his second term Bill Clinton even promised more education: two more years of what some see as state-supported human-to-robot construction and alienation.

Learning is big business, runs for profit, trains today's contestants learning as they must, market economics' lessons one by one.

Rationality removes compassion, as *rules* rule in the law, as some of the most "educated" countries in the world have become the most ruthless police states. And rationality is dished up like it's going to (yes!) save or improve the country. Using the schooling methods forced upon citizens today, people won't get much benefit from their rational training. Just like all the technological advances that haven't helped average Joe and Jill financially in the last thirty years: more work, less income, less full-time or decent jobs. For many it's become part-time service industry third-world MacJobs.

"It's a tough world," a CNBC anchorwoman exclaims as Tiger Woods spurns MasterCard to sign with American Express for $30 million. The deal is even concluded while Tiger is playing at a tournament sponsored by loser MasterCard. When will the people not be duped? When will they not be told that the future demands their worst side if they are to survive? Disappearing down the drain at wee-little per hour while chanting affirmations, smiling, in their temporary, part-time, loose, sublime lifestyle embracing poverty. Does it make their life *so* challenging, *so* gripping—this the lifestyle that's taking millions out to learn humble-pieness and gratitude for small mercies. *For a job!*

The lesson is rad but will be forgotten, usurped, faded into a closing scene begun by remote control—the pulse bringing the finger through the button, producing the bullet of continuous audiovisual hallucination.

The nation's nervous, edgy, but ready to suspend conclusion and escape into the curious moving pictures—like wandering stone-agers fascinated by mirrors for the first time. The movies and TV are often far removed, however, from reflecting anything close to people's real self or image. It's simply the entertainment they're all so used to. Movie reviews are now reported like hard news, as if they were major external events!

Mental Masochism—Expecting Less

> *CNN, Bob Novak: "No, I don't have a social conscience."*
> Capital Gang[3]

In 1970, Harvard sociology Professor Daniel Bell had said it would take about ten years for social change to improve the crises in American society. He said the resources were there, especially after the Vietnam war ended, to solve all the areas of concern and to "finance the public needs of society."

The external problems, however, were at the mercy of internal moral values, said Bell, and so far *liberalism* was messing up

American capitalism. He said: "American capitalism has lost its traditional legitimacy which was based on a moral system of reward, rooted in a Protestant sanctification of work."[4] Bell blamed *anything* that stood in the way of American capitalism and its adherence to the "principles of economics and economizing: on efficiency, least cost, maximization, optimization, and functional rationality."[5] Oh, sacré bleu! That functional rationality be denied! Expert pleasure sadists—the tooth and claw gang—would evolve out of adherence to Bell's principles, saying the same thing. But because something works won't guarantee that it's good. Fascism and imperialism make up the corporate business model.

Greed and selfishness became rationalized as core pursuits, as life was painted as a jungle-market, with predators seen as pervasive and hanging from every branch of every tree. Fear spread everywhere, and soon the heart center was corrupted. In an impersonal bottom-line world, the heart feels the hurt and the anger and becomes tormented by desire for revenge. When power is believed a "personal" issue, people (consumers) seek to fortify themselves. The cold reality people find facing them in a competitive market run by mammoth international corporations scares them into selfish strategies.

Back in the 70's Daniel Bell said that technocrats, the "rational priests," and their management techniques, were the answer. Rationalism and technical education were to rule, he said. Liberal value-oriented intellectuals were to be replaced by technocratic policy-oriented intellectuals. That may be logical. Will it produce ethical behavior? Logic is not reasoned necessity. It is *logical* to want maximum profit, but improving workers' conditions will cut profits.

Thoughts of material abundance and ease and luxury were to be replaced by the moral sanctity of a job. Making sadism moral, Bell rams the intelligentsia's head back up its tuchis. Many of them feed on cold clarity, order, taking good fare and turning it anal, reassured by travesty. Average people without the drudgery of bleak employments, who act like the upper class, who enjoy leisure, sport, etc., they are demonized. Liberal layabouts.

People's expectations from democracy were beginning to be purposely shut down by the big-business owned politicians and their policies. People, they determined, needed to expect less from democracy, and they were ready to focus people's attention away from the questions of *value* to those of *function*.

A marketplace became promoted as the function of democracy. Function is practical. Usefulness is logical. These characteristics have been top motivators in our science-oriented society. But over rational obsession will not satisfy mankind's needs. And just because something works does not mean it is good. Many government policies exist only because they work for small groups, like corporations. Functional, yes, and useful to some. They are justified rationally. One of the results of scientific advancement is the narrow world of function predominating, regardless of the *value* to the whole of society. Function is mechanical and demands rationality. It easily turns the world over to the rationalists. Value, and ethics, that's another story!

Value, like social programs and social safety nets to protect citizens, along with most policies associated with left wing humanism, became demonized as creating nothing but debts. It was a lie (most accumulated government debt is from interest charges on the debt and from tax breaks to the wealthy), but it worked. Most people rolled over, asked for less, expected less and got just that. Even health care is cut back. By 2003 CBC TV in Canada will broadcast that the fourth leading cause of death has become hospital admission, people contracting fatal illness from just being *in* a hospital!

Power of Truth and Memes

Reason eliminates doubt. Puts everything in its place. Humanism, on the other hand, says more can be done, life can be improved, all is not in its place.

Vanity, egotism, conceit and vaingloriousness may be cockily portrayed as self-reliance, but they lend wings to descent into purgatory. There are trivial truths, and there are ultimate truths. The opposite of a trivial truth is plainly false. The opposite of an ultimate truth is also true, like Jesus' Sermon on the Mount—*Blessed are the meek for they shall inherit the world; Blessed are the poor in spirit for theirs is the kingdom of God, etc.* When belief supports doubt, *allows* doubt to exist, as it must in the presence of an ultimate truth, then self-understanding is operating.

Would you rather be right or be happy? It depends you say, on the situation, circumstances, as your rational training (hazing) kicks in, and you start to justify, analyze, construe, make-up, bullshit, defend, protect—you become part of the problem, using memorized responses that you've learned and been taught.

Memes, *thought groups*, exist and want to rule. And they're powerful, potent and nurturing. That is because the mind is cunning and ambitious. The mind is also acquisitive and envious. In its vain search for security the mind may grab memes and ideologies and feed off them like the addict who desires the superficial rather than face up to true circumstances.

Memes will take your world and color it any number of ways. Pragmatic-democratic-socialist or reactionary- puritanical- conservative—it doesn't matter. Fascist, commie, feminist, Christian, monarchist, Stalinist, collectivist, born-again Muslim, anything soever which! Many true believers line up for thought fortification to bolster themselves against the "pathetic" life offered in the sweatbox called society.

It's this addiction to knowing in words, that is the crutch that one day will be taken away from the craggy crippled society, a society racked and paralyzed by its own stiff and unyielding dogmas. Now so many layers of false-consciousness twist the dysfunction of its monstrous existence that the behemoth is near to topple. Envision it snapping, as a billion splinters deploy isolating all the believers, those who have built their house upon the faulty ground of rational ideology. Heavyweight boxer Tyson bites off an opponent's ear, gets out to beat the heat. Non-rational? The act of biting another person was called "inhuman". The Rubicon was crossed centuries before. Now we are unable to recognize the crucial instant. O.J. got justice?

There is also a psychological darkness surrounding average Joe and Jill citizen too. This dark stuff relates to the unconscious and gives some unaccountable females room to operate. They use the answers dished up by the Psychology Industry to escape responsibility for their anxieties and neurotic behaviors. And the psychological message is usually that problems are from internal causes and are exclusive to an individual, and are not caused by the external world (society).

Memes wizz through space giving all sorts of psychological reasons for failure and dysfunction. But it's chaos, as soon everything becomes questionable. Then too many psychological excuses cover up abuses.

Decline of American Capitalism?

Liberalism was *blamed* for a lackluster lifestyle —this the 70's barbed-missile *meme* (thought) spin sent to a dizzy middle class in desperate need of accountability. And seemingly ready to punish themselves. And jumped all over by their boss-sadists, these everyday masochists lined right up for the goosing.

Pleasure-seeking liberals demanding government spending for social programs and "instant solutions" were said to exemplify "apocalyptic moods and anti-rational modes of behavior." Americanized psychoanalysis defined psychological problems as unique to each person, eliminating consideration of the broader social contexts that influence people. Liberals could be demonized as lazy, irresponsible daydreamers. American psychology tends to ignore social reality. Thus, those complaining about the external world are simply seen as personally projecting their individual neurosis on the society as a whole. Problems, and their solutions, were to be found in one's self, and not in the external world.

Liberalism, Bell stated, had promoted growth in the economy as a means to provide the resources to raise the incomes of the poor. Growth, in an affluent society, had been seen as necessary to finance public services. But Bell claims growth only brought the "spoiliation of the environment, the voracious use of natural resources, the crowding of recreation areas, the densities in the city."[6] Liberalism, the professor said, was getting away ideologically unchallenged because "the corporate economy has no unified value system of its own." So growth caused poverty and pollution. Had the hoped-for solution, growth and increase in money, just produced a hungry, dirty beast? Or, maybe the corporate economy's lack of a unified value system reveals a *no-values* system. And this lack hints at what happens to morals and values, as well as what ends up on whose dinner plate, under the God Market (GM)....

Of course, it was hard for the new liberated woman hooked on learning to resist submergence into the popular ideas of the day. Everyone is used to grabbing the new, the improved, the technically up to date. So the latest and greatest media-generated ideas about reality garnered big audiences. And things that had a mystery, like the *unconscious*, and things that were bigger than an individual's life, like *supply-demand*, had a presumed depth. They had an almost mighty force and were related to emotional healing or to money. These things (ideas) were eaten up by the needy minds, the modern and postmodern minds addicted to the electro-shock of information. The popular ideas of the day used to be subservience to the Will of God, or to astrological omnipotence, or to myths, or to the Gods of war, of beauty, of the sea. Whatever!

Now *market economics* (ME) is believed responsible for generating whole societies, and every detail of human endeavor and all human relationship.

Some women using "new and improved" information have been blaming men for all their negative *conditioning*—the root of the problem for many suffragettes is said to be found with the opposite sex. Memes flare insinuating that slave-maker males, a woman's dearest dreams would derail. Why was it so easy to get women turned against men? Sexy stuff that gives rage its ring, the calling of guilty fired at the men, those who could actually bring pleasure tonic to the women for this life's suffering. Do the angry females realize they may soon lose their lovers, their traditional support base, the men? But the ladies were actually being abused by those who sing the praises of the *free-market thing*.

Today progress is totalitarian, the market economy run by a manipulative, insensitive, untrustworthy bunch of managers, working for the sadists above and giving orders to the middle-class and the mass below.

> *Forward into feudalism all the serfs do swing,*
> *But nutt'n really matters, it's the TV thing*
> *That scatters—babysitter, propagandizer,*
>   *automaton-maker extraordinare –*
> *The owners scuba dive, eco-journey down*
>   *the Meta,*
> *While their chattel peons watch sit-com canned channel*
>   *laughter.*

The Past Rules

The past and its worship of *rational organizational structures* became the *habit,* and the ingrained message—a separate, competitive critic—became the everyday medium of experience. People feel stranded, alone in their wordy heads.

Rationalism withholds abundance, because of the *conflict*

inherent in *memory*. The mind is always comparing, tearing apart or building an attack. Never at peace. The Gods it makes up end up restricting life—they make up a devil or a darkness to resist. Restrictions abound. And memories just force comparisons, and that's more conflict.

One word stimulates, ignites even more, and the mind chases its tail. Language rumbles and grates along the rooftop of the plebs' heads, setting them up as victims—as reasons birth out of living sensations, and slice reality via independent clauses with prepositions followed by blatant nouns. Then more adjectives are dumped like boiling urine onto anything you can make up a name for.

The mind, when used for rational action, is all about conflict. It reacts! The mind has the habit of *exclusion*. The people have repressed their resentment and anger at being forced into mentalism, and hating themselves for their participation and in way over their heads, the people are easily led. Sadomasochism is assimilated. In fact, it's free and guaranteed from the moment a child shows up for grade school. Exposure to TV fast-tracks the process, as pre-school children are turned over, given up to the networks.

But the people are grateful for some kind of freedom—for the devilish "free market" meme that rules them, that big lie allowing them freedom from *responsibility*. Everything becomes the *markets'* fault! But left behind while they escape their responsibility is the *challenge*. Instead an answer has fallen, and mediocre man arises.

Today, it may be shocking at first to understand the manipulations that go on in the unhealthy, slagheap-slopped, debris-cluttered junkpile society around us. Men and women compete in a voluminous viral smog. Within the tempest, the whole of society and all life's detail has been mentally cut up into pieces. These pieces are then randomly glued by each person into their isolated "personal" worldview. The chaos of their competing memes blocks communication and is the real work of the rational "priests" and their educational system. Now the true consumers, the moderns, can't separate the illusion from reality.

New Right Kingpins

To the *owners* people aren't even thought of as capable of recognizing beauty or of voting for the right political parties. People aren't trusted, so young adults get the message—go internal and try to figure it all out. Now if the information isn't easily available to get upbeat results, then the *process* of analyzing will only get the majority out of the way—and maybe for the rest of their lives! It is said that the New Right kingpins are massive liars. They don't have faith in human beings, and some not even in themselves. And they don't give a damn about perverting the language as long as the results are favorable, the bull crap is believed (eaten) and the people are sedated, unwired. Success is money, and public relations is manipulation, a smoke and mirrors, S&M thing. Owner rape: *all-day TV commercials...feeding 'em the boots, take their money, give 'em moving pictures, whatever!* Nothing but ads is a screwing with the very synapses of life—hardcore because the power is over people's behavior itself. Once a human being reconstructs his or her reality with the ad's tools of reason and rationality, then consumer belief becomes the secret mask that an exasperated average citizen wears. In fact retail therapy, "shopping", has caught on, many rushing out to the circus mall to get a fix or just some fiddle fun, like an evening on a beach, reaching and rushing after winged moths in the firelight.

In the big picture, frightened consumers scramble till they drop on the sadist's spinning wheel. Getting modern, civilized, progressive, the educated are stuck. They are fast-fried by the age of seven, stripped of their unique creative powers by high-school graduation—*can't talk when the television is on nearby*. And then the stunned are further frozen into selfish consumers thinking disgusting lies (affirmations) about their freedom and choice and advanced life spans, many without vital connection to an organic functioning soul. The chopping block they started slicing the world up on in pre-school became a runaway train.

> *The blizzard of the world*
> *Has crossed the threshold,*
> *And it has overturned*
> *The order of the soul.*
> —Leonard Cohen, The Future

Rationality Becomes Boss

People thinking in corners, trained since birth to dive inside, go figure, their mental machinations equivalent to scratching at scabs—it's not going to fix the problem and will probably make it worse, but it's so painfully, angrily addictive that everyday masochists can't resist. And so it is with many people's jobs, with life in the cities, with people's bad-health habits and relationships with many of the opposite sex, as well as some same-gender antagonisms. People are *used to* dysfunctional living! They can't escape because they can't understand it all. They are trapped in their disorder. Using their rational education they've got their heads in gear. Many of their learned memes and understandings are faulty, therefore, their lives must be weird. Ignorance is like an invasion of *dysfunctional bacteria* into their social and emotional life, as sequential meme invasions of propaganda infect their soul and then ultimately torment the physical body.

The values that commercials attribute to toothpaste or deodorant are difficult to imagine when using a dictionary to understand the meanings. Can products act like living people giving protection and love, or bring health, well-being and popularity? Surely the words are broken away from precise accountability. By focusing on a product a person's subjective impressions are touted in relation to only the product. Words like "save, liberate, equal, power, popular, fair, honest" are losing their significance in political and social life. Rationally, a case may be made for products to "save" something or to "liberate" some small aspect of a person's life, but the advertising culture has trashed accountability. Reality does not match the wordy claims of those prostituting the language to sell their items.

Rationality has now become reason. Rationality impersonates a means that was to bring the *cure,* but when average Jill and Joe's heads start to smell *manure,* spin doctors will soon be tackling that meme, that's for *sure.* That means order, with everything neat and tidy, structured to defend against any disorder, as if life is now supposed to be like rationality. Authority itself is believed to be the outcome of this rationality. So people obey, follow what they are told to do.

Waiting for the nod that may never come, educated "robots" may one day only run on word group order, any other messages received thrown high overboard. Witness subdued citizens without a healthy common sense in their angry desire to receive the masochist's *delight,* and through pain and suffering to teach others what they think is *right.*

The owners even tell most nations what to think, what to debate, who to kill, how to live (eat), and basically what is going on, day by day. TV networks, radio stations and newspapers absorbed into the web of the ruling elite can make it nearly impossible for anyone wanting a particular attention to truth. For example, in the 1990's France tottered on collapse, almost fell, but the historic event is unknown to almost all. No coverage. We're not informed.

Distrust of Language Leads to Unaccountability. The postmodern distrust of ideology, whether voiced in nationalism and the expected lying words from politicians or through the unaccountable claims for consumer products, has brought a distrust of words themselves. This distrust would be healthy if people could think things through. But the effort needed is awesome, and most people cannot find the time to muster it. Instead people are allowing themselves to be seduced into an anti-intellectual, subjective and feminized culture. Feminism thrives today in our subjectively trained culture. It's a passive culture, a "now" culture of feelings in the present moment that looks to be protected and entertained, rather than to be accountable.

Spin may be seen as the new thing, the catch-all word that sums up what citizens now expect to dominate their lives. That is an identification of reality and is positive. But in Singapore the results show that *spin* can become the meal each is to eat every morning. Until they believe! The very thing the moderns had learned—to distrust ideology—is returning with acceptance of spin.

Somehow the answer to spin became non-resistance and giving up the righteous demand for accountability. The people, running on the various word groups in their heads, may really be giving up on intellectual solutions. Without a reliable rational grasp of their world, the moderns are easily lined up and led into pleasing sensations—much ado around plays, fiction, movies, and video games—the stuff that takes them out, but leaves them also feeling kind of groovy.

The subjective use of rationality, through affirmations, through focus on intentions rather than on outcomes, through focusing on the "now" and on the details of interpersonal relationships rather than focusing on history, the big picture and the accountability of actions, hinders the objective use of rationality to reason. This subjectivism has brought chaos to intellectual understanding.

Educated jackasses boot the poop around, go blind calling slavery freedom, calling freedom "nothing left to lose," then die breathing polluted air.

How much car pollution before the dimmer switch in the sky can't be readjusted? In 1948, the County Air Pollution Control District in Los Angeles, with a staff of 200 – mostly engineers, chemists, physicists and field inspectors – and an annual budget of 2.5 million dollars, set standards that had to be met by "any fume-producing enterprise before it can get a permit to operate." Very rational. A reasoning people naturally assume solutions will follow. But today it's chemo-radiation soup-du-jour in the sky, as filthy motor vehicles putter up the anal-like corridors of the City of Angels.

Politician A. D'Amato from New York says in 2002 that there will be "$50 billion a year in health costs in the USA from pollution." Media sources in 1996 relayed studies that said 6,000 people would die in Los Angeles from air pollution that year. Are these studies reliable? Couldn't the disease caused by the poisoned air really be even more pervasive, affecting all people's quality of life and neurotically affecting their expectations of how long they might live? "Malaria" was a word that originally meant *bad air.* Today the peoples of the world live in the aftermath of a global automobile marketing triumph. And most suffer with the malaria. People think about being trapped, poisoned and ignored while the owners advance to more organic habitats.

Cigarettes kill about a half a million Americans a year, but one of the longhairs' educated men, a *presidential candidate,* declares that "nicotine is not addictive." Then a few more years down the road this pro-nicotine presidential candidate's wife stands at the Mexican border, and now *she's* one of a current crop of newly minted "fake" candidates for another overblown spin production of presidential competition. She begins to dole out her platform. And it rests, you can bet the ranch, on the war against drugs! So there it is: complete unaccountability and disdain. Beaten to a pulp, the public is force-fed this diet of worms.

Despised public will you turn the other cheek
And not get these bilingual rapists of your wakefulness
  off the street,
Hiding in the hallways of power discrete,
Not ever accountable to whom they have fleeced?

Progress

Is progress just another word denying any success at living now? It's old, this notion of advance-development-improvement. It's the Judeo-Christian heritage, and it's behind Marxism and capitalism too. Western civilization has been buying into it for over 2000 years. So drop the progress on Hiroshima? Or interview millions of citizens, and ask why there is world hunger. You hope their answers will reflect the gain in maturity and behavior, the gain in understanding and the gain in adapting to the world that *progress* has brought to them.

Is progress the ascetic, solitary ideal incarnate? That is, is it the belief in the overthrow of the present and its main problem: you? Progress could get *you* out of the way! Improving what? Yourself, the problem seen as begging solution!

Look to where the *will* to truth, or better, to where the separate *truths* of cults, bands, clans, gangs and political groups leads and see why many claims for dignity through rationality are way off base. If caught in the light of day, rationality is seen flexing its muscle of utilitarian control. Its spin within the syntactic sentence structures can actually block true communication.

In progress, the present is excused, and the promise of the "promised land" overtakes consciousness, so the soul slides along and waits for resolution. Years later, the television commercials start replacing themselves and parodies of some ads re-run on the screen, aiming for a consumer audience grown older. Where did it go, the time, the years? It's then like the older generation had said thirty years earlier: it would be too late! Waiting unto progress can *suck*. The present-day subjectivity and chaos, without a positive and a realistic direction for society, is in the end the failure of the purpose that reason was for—to organize the best possible world for all persons.

Women and the Marketplace

"The marketplace is not always right."
J. Stiglitz (former World Bank CEO)

Nurturing babies while trying hard to maintain aggressiveness in the marketplace has got many women of today emotionally needy. But they don't complain about corporate manipulation much—the methods of the elite. Nope, many just bash males instead. Frustrated, some females paint pink and go look for victims, just like the owners do.

Anchor newswomen were getting pretty well naked in the mid-90's, flashing seductive skin segments and radiating sex charisma, but today the *owners* have decided that it's better they mainly resemble smiling low-IQ cheerful robots. Political correctness stuns. But simultaneously, elitist parvenu masturbation has swept the nation. Women are encouraged to love their pleasure. It's become like business. It's results oriented—it's controlling, physical. And men can suffer alone. So welcome to the level playing field of unanimous hating replacing caring. The plebs desire affects, venting—it's the rock 'n roll of market economics (ME)!

Why does the world smile favorably on feminine women? Why do so many women want the right to be ardent psychopaths? Do they try to copy what they think they see in the men?

Does femininity give women a competitive edge in the present economy with those in government greasing their wheels? Walk into any government office and scan the faces nesting at the desks dotting the work environment. Zoom in on any male skull in these pools. Is there any to be seen, to even begin a count? Schools of mermaids swim all around, smelling interesting, shampooed, directing attention (often into a cozy happiness, these lofty enthusiasts) unto the senses. These are the students of Lombardi, famous coach, and for too long do his words still ring: *Winning is everything!*

Fifty bucks a day is a start, but fortunes aren't going to be grabbed very often in this world economy. Instead it's the grab the job environment—where it's usually warm, there's company to share your hyper-modern life with, and TV will get you home and into bed. Or many a single mom may just escape into after dinner play with their offspring. It may be *day care for adults*, is what it boils down to, for those showing up for the stressful *work glue*.

The female of today has access to jobs and is encouraged to

exercise. Good news. But they are brainwashed like the rest of society, and much they are taught to believe in is going to disappoint them. If they rely too much on the rational process, used by schools and the TV programs they have been captured by since infants—pausing to think things out and constantly learning "how", many won't be able to "do" what they may need to do for a full life of their own that's filled with integrity and purpose.

Without *exercise* and *understanding* many females can be manipulated to vent their "excessive nerves" on males. Being constantly told that our society persecutes females, and that patriarchy means slavery to men, drives women to see men as their enemy. They can become reactive victims of the popular anti-male propaganda filling today's media. And those that think their venting is "progress" have unfortunately been misinformed.

II
Power and Female Sexual Attraction

7
Estrus Ardent

To begin: when a female anthropoid is biologically ready for sexual relations she enters into an *estral cycle*.

She's in heat, and it's for offspring—
There the focus of her system does swing,
Into attract-match scenarios seeking male genes,
And the future to bring.
At the peak of estrus she's so popular!
The guys, well they can't help but know,
It's like nature has got to show,
What demands life here on earth must prevail,
Without obedience said life form shall fail.

So it's serious all right. Attraction of a sexual partner is now necessitated by biological demand. At the peak of her estral cycle the female is most fertile and males are alerted, libidinously lured by strong direct signals:

Enchanted, enticed, beguiled spark-of-life chain-gang
  volunteers,
The males relate easy with their peers,
Seeking mutual solutions to biological survival fears,
Procreating worldly children as the future nears.
Planet work responsibly done, its part of the customs,
The price paid by survival efforts on Earth through
  weighty doldrums.

An event taken away in swollen currents, riding it out, in the night, big anthropoid hunkster does his natural duty.
Now this work was not intended as full time anyway, and so it's, like, only when *she* calls is he to accost. Then the genital wrestle starts. *Solicitation in the jungles of Earth....* Don't call us, we'll call you, leave your application on the desk.... Ancestor anthropoid's system: female signal, male alert. It's all about control, what works, thank you, sir.

Truth and Inequality Among the Sexes

Emotions that underpin feminine and masculine constitutions flow from separate biological identities. Different biologies. In every society a bedrock male motivation is the feeling that the women and children must be protected. To a woman the truth is that the weather changes. But by using the feminine means that nature gave to her, a woman commands much.

Female hormones are not bringing in all the same channels—each with its own truth—as those that the males are immersed and motivated by. The details of the many truths can vary, as they are processed through different channels on the Human Being Network—and that includes all humans in every possible state of mind, body and soul.

The men have got the testosterone that builds the muscle to protect the women and children, and to hunt and to kill for food. The women have the estrogen that enables them to stockpile reserve food in their body fat for emergency use, for them and their children when there isn't anything to eat.

So the simple truth is *variable* depending on the hormones. There is a specific *neuro-endocrinological* composition for the experiencer of the "truth" itself. If hormones got stuffed aside and denied and repressed, somehow their release of truth would be interfered with. Thus many want to know just what is happening when females trick their bodies by ingesting birth-control pills?

When directing attention and focus upon notions of *equality,* the truth is then being overshadowed by ideology. The gender feminists, with a perceived oppressor, and a combative *strategy* based on having as equal an arsenal as their enemy, make their fight unequal. Women wearing male masks are not biologically equal to their objects of annoyance. She can deal with the most powerful of men and succeed using the hormonal built-ins that are her truer nature. To deny this, or to accept popular lies about equality, etc. cheats life itself and its basic instincts—this, when impulses are divorced from basic natures.

Like an addict struggling to avoid the pain of withdrawal, present society has virtually inbred the lurch towards word solutions, the grabbing of rationality, intellect and ideology to soothe the wound of human alienation. Disconnected from their intuition and disturbed, frazzled factions seize answers.

The weather may be changing, and so are female bodies, subjected to atmospheric-climatic transience during the monthly menstrual cycle. It's a training course in vital shifting, as physical differentiation brings internal mood shifts, an oceanic overtaking of female consciousness. It should make one wise, this ability to endure change, to develop patience through the knowledge that the shifts return in harmony with nature. But it's unpopular—the emotional queen bee—and thus now the equality package is sought. Now the big enchilada, androgyny, is heralded to lead the victimized into the promised subdivision where females get what they *should* want, a fifty-fifty share of everything.

It makes sense, these thoughts, ideas like—sharing, equality, shared responsibilities. It also makes sense to stop murdering, stealing and lying. Many women point the finger of female moral superiority (FMS) and shake their heads after catching moral no-no's. Mankind's abuse of mankind is still being reproached, but growing numbers of men don't lend more than half an ear to these types of women today. "She" may soon be toppled off her righteous throne. Buying into "competitive market economics" and into democratic blandness—the forces funneling all into desensitized rationality, sameness, into the distracted consensus—her moral claim to power can not survive much longer.

It scares women to not keep up with the prevailing fashionable images of themselves. The ghost of their mother's tears and the assumed passive-aggressive weakness that is believed to have been forced on her, spurs on women's leap into reason away from her compassion. Power here is not feeling, it is seen as information. And who has got the information?

Equality makes sense and sounds delightful, but in the beginning equality is only an idea, born of spiritual desire and incorporated into the rational structures. In the end perhaps it's only an idea, signifying delusion. If men and women have separate, unique biology and experience the world through their biology, how can they be called equal? Left brain, right brain, hormone changes, all the differences are weighty baggage. DNA estranges the two genders and overturns the equality blender. Two sexes equals two motivations and two strategies.

Sex Among Baboons

Baboon harem-worker males are always on call to mate with a female whenever her colored posterior shows red-vulva readiness, estrus imminent-ness. Courtship is female friendly, and in some primate communities at no time does copulation occur without a prior solicitation of the male by the female. That's normal action, Jackson; stimulus-response heritage, the controller and the controlled, as these primate females in estrus actively initiate seduction, flashing for a future. It's nature's "red flame." Lips sink into depth activation, male motivation. No problem to read those lips, in the Kingdom of See!

The guy baboons bring food for estrus-involved species members. He instinctively wants offspring; it's big time in survival-focus forces, one of the strongest drives, the innate need to procreate, successfully bring forth genetic replication. So, if she's going to provide sex, he'll provide food. And in times of scarcity and hunger, the ability to provide sex could be a real lifesaver for the female and her infants.

Survival necessitates behavior; impulse and compulsion drive to support and promote success at survival. And if a female could provide sex all the time, conceal estrus so to speak, wouldn't this just be the *cat's ass*—a master stroke of manipulative genius, a skill the able and adept could access, facilitating continued living. Kids would then live if they had sexy moms, and this sexiness would be passed on along to them as a competitive skill.

Act like always she can copulate, and upon fresh meat they *all* can eat! Although sexual intercourse is rare for some animals, the cunning and deception, and the manipulation of the facts by today's primate descendants, the non-fertile human females, works for their continued survival.

In estrus just everyday,
And in the bed it seems she'll play,
Addicted to sex, hiding estrus,
The two tango.
Life is like at the playboy mansion with his everyday sexstress!
Hoopla and pomp parade, the cosmetic fandango!
So it goes....

Herstory

Something happened back on the farm when she was young.[1] The kid watched horses. An image hypnotically consumed her; the spectacle witnessed through cracks, between soft and weathered wood slats nailed at intervals to sturdy fence posts. The flesh and poise of stake horses swiftly challenging life in a big, strange world—she loved their determination, control, and individuality, capable of running in wild tenacity. Attracted to a force that yielded to rebellious instinct, towards freedom—here she grasped intuitively a symbolic incarnation. It was a reflection of how she would dare, how her unbridled will would spur her success in the business derby—and her mind and soul attached for life.

It was power that she would get, of course, and this power rode warlike—skilled, competent, but with a dark side, the devouring aspect of unleashed passion. With her, strength and power were willfully assimilated, related to, and raised into obsession. But her murky philistine instinct was at odds with a law-driven society such as twentieth-century America.

A revolutionary empathy, this her life's work, needed an unusual strength and focus. Beautiful horses, especially thoroughbreds, and most particularly championship race horses, upon these *backs*, Elizabeth Arden claimed victory, literally, as a stable owner whose horses competed, and won, at the most prestigious of racetracks. And figuratively Arden rode her own personality to victory as a corporate icon with an inexorable, competitive ardor and proclivity.

Elizabeth Arden changed the world. A revolution was facilitated via her marketing strategy, and today's world must grapple with the consequences. Irony, that meek teacher of mankind, had it that it could be someone rather bereft of physical sensuality and sexuality that would rise to what today would be billionairess status selling prodigal seductress stuff.

"When people think pink, dear, they think Arden," she was wont to exclaim. Her doll-like feigning and child-like unprepossessingness were one personality used to get this former Florence Nightingale Graham her way. But more commonly, the overlord, Elizabeth Arden, a hard-nosed businesswoman, commanded. The peoples of the planet came to identify her enterprising company name with a familiarity shared by only two other corporations: Coca-Cola and Singer Sewing Company.

Elizabeth Arden re-created the annals of female beauty. Beginning around 1910, she rode a wave of liberationist feminism for big bucks! A twisted tale it be too, but, once upon a time a successful marketing campaign managed to inculcate in the female a visionary perception that liberation could be attained through becoming a certain kind of an *illusion*. Heretofore any smart girl wouldn't be caught dead with cosmetics, so *obvious* a sexual statement, this the immoral stuff used by actresses and prostitutes. But somehow a new generation was birthed and the judgement overlooked, a new look they took. The smells and colors of the whorehouse somehow began to appear in the home.

In 1912, *Vogue* magazine announced to the world that the discrete application of a small amount of paint would enhance a lady's appearance. *Signs for all to see.* But soon even puritan women began to appropriate pigmentation emancipation and joined the flapper daughters of the middle class, and they reached out, and bought!

In 1912, Elizabeth Arden raised her prices. She liked to overprice, appeal to snobbery. She had shrewdly, and astutely, linked upward mobility with beauty. She liked the association: high society and the beauty business. Arden delivered her charges, the great swelling masses of women emerging in the early twentieth century as independent consumers, unto the competitive fields of American capitalism—armed with beauty.

And the charisma culture was buzzing, with around 10 million single women working in the USA then, and, like the men, wanting fruits from their labors. In capitalist culture, the ethos of the individual intones all about. Everywhere everyone wants to rule, take possession of some self-reliance reward, become a winner by learning how to coerce domination and mastery in the marketplace. But if any one person was not able or willing to personally battle to the entrepreneurial pinnacle, some thinking to capture the fruits of financial success as public evidence of God's favor, then at least respect was readily bestowed and due to the one who moved up.

By amassing wealth, salespeople (excellent liars), merchants (mark-up artists), stock manipulators (magicians), and promoters (hypnotists) can become white knights. So what's to stop a girl from using a little allure in her own covert operations? The chaps don't usually even know a strategic operation is going on. And, depressingly, some of the dames don't either; they'd figure things were as right as rain if all the females were just born painted, silver-lidded, rouged and baby-doll wide-eyed—a bunch of Dolly Partons all pinked up, puckered, cross-your-hearted, big-boobed, calf-shaved and all; natural-born heat raisers attracting sex vibes.

Autocrat Arden

In 1914, Elizabeth Arden brought mascara into the US, signifying the origin of the *outbreak* of the mascara massacre of males. Arden next promoted health and beauty as though they were equivalent, and pressure here from the manipulative "masteress" coerced women to choose both, or at least to look like they had. Fabulously, health and beauty became a women's *duty*, sensually thinking to be happy now she's got to be a *cutie*.

> *Slick chick with talcum, rouge,*
> *"It's war paint honey, we'll never lose";*
> *Devastating, ravishing-dazzling dudes*
> *With twenty-four-hour-a-day lust alludes.*

Liz was a control freak, a dictator at the office. She would link beauty and loveliness with health and prestige in the same big-lie slime selling that governments use to baffle the naive and the preoccupied anxious: like "bombing for peace" or cutting social programs to *help* society get healthy and robust.

Cosmetics were "sold" by the industry as a means toward liberating women. Throughout the 1920's unrestrained cosmetics promotion-propaganda brought access to this "liberation" to everyday women across America. Looking *healthy*, plus looking sex-receptive, it can be deceptive as much as downright *stealthy*.

Arden would not humble herself and take directives from

anyone, either in business or in marriage. For years she had falsely identified herself as married, as a *Mrs. Arden*. She, in fact, did not marry until age thirty-seven, and this marriage was to a business partner. But being alone with husband Tommy was fearful for her; her chiseled rock ego wasn't easily forsaken for intimacy with the opposite sex. In business, not bed, Liz found satisfaction.

On company trips with Tommy she would often bring another employee, a woman, who she could relax with. Sleeping in the same bed with a same-sex employee was commonplace for Elizabeth. For years many different women would accompany Mrs. Arden around the world. Liz wasn't too enthusiastic about males, unless, of course, they were race horses. She admitted judging a woman with the same criteria as she would judge a horse: all rear ends, legs, and face.

Arden did join the suffragette movement, but this was merely another political move aimed at promoting her business and to expedite getting closer to some of the movement's high-society membership, the blue bloods of the elite ruling class—those she so much desired acceptance from. Never did she sink her teeth into the platforms of the women's campaign, but nonetheless did network with many of the crusade's upper-class power people.

Understandably perhaps, numerous lesbians hung around the female emancipation movement early in the twentieth century. And it is very possible Elizabeth Arden was a same-sex lover, or latently so, and that she spent a lifetime suppressing it. Constantly surrounding herself with women, traveling, working and sharing her bed with them, it is rather obvious she preferred their company. But the architect of social change, as commander of the cosmetics revolution, she who conjured afresh the image of womankind with a cosmetic allure of sexual salubriousness, flushed-cheek consent and readiness, she herself, was maybe without a real inclination towards sex. Arden was probably not much of a sexual creature! Not physically anyway, and so painting on the signs were a compensation and a way to power over men. And in later years, she probably was never deeply involved sexually with husband number two. He sent for his boyfriend on their wedding night.

The Rise of Authoritarian Women

While Arden's cosmetic crusade swept America, in Europe

D.H. Lawrence was heard storming around, contending about women being "on the move," predicting a coming persecution of men. The "dynamic polarity" between the sexes, according to Lawrence, had swung around and men were becoming feminized, assuming sympathetic-sensitive roles, while women became active, effective, authoritative. But it was all a fallacy and "they are only playing each other's roles, because the poles have swung into reversion. The compass has reversed."[2] But it would right itself again, in time, he said.

Lawrence went on to contend that at certain periods, "such as the present [1920's], the majority of men concur in regarding women as the source of life, the first term in creation: woman, the mother, the prime being."[3] Man is still a doer, Lawrence says, but only in the service "of emotional and procreative women. His highest moment is now the emotional moment when he gives himself up to the women, when he forms the perfect answer for her great emotional and procreative asking. All his thinking, all his activity in the world only contributes to this great moment, when he is filled in the emotional passion of the women, the birth of rebirth, as Whitman calls it."[4]

After men begin worshiping "pity, and tenderness and weakness, sensitivity escalates, feelings exasperate, and he wavers." Woman meanwhile becomes the fearless, inwardly relentless, determined positive party. She grips the responsibility. "The hand that rocks the cradle rules the world. Nay, she makes man discover that cradles should not be rocked, in order that her hands may be left free. She is now queen of the earth, and inwardly a fearsome tyrant."[5]

Elizabeth Arden accelerated this insurrection of the early twentieth century by giving women a tremendous ability to increase their center of power. And the heart of female power now lay in beauty and its sexual-emotional overpower. *For shine is the power and the glory*—managing, goal-setting, getting predatory.

> *Men got to boil,*
> *Cosmetics delivers the broil,*
> *Brings on burning turmoil,*
> *No uncertain benefit, con amore,*
> *To the signori,*
> *It's all simply hunky-dory*

For women's vainglory!

Real news here; it's bad news. Women were reaching out for greater responsibility and equality, to participate to their fullest extent in an industrialized society, to shed "archaic, redundant roles" that they thought didn't match up and fit the reality of their modern lives. But at that moment, somehow, the means to achieving a new selfhood and social worth was presented through transformation into a beauty object, to attract and control men. To get more food? Liberation through manipulation of male services. A callous maneuver, stratagem of the apes, this the launch of the new twentieth century equality.

Sentimental Beauty Stays Home

As the world plunged into a brutal bloodbath and World War I revealed the corrupted natures of the beast, the ruling class marketed freedom, honor, patriotism and applied peer pressure. Men were slaughtered in an obscene, naked belligerence. As Lawrence said, it's man the *fetcher, the carrier, the sacrifice, the crucified, and the reborn of woman.*[6] For the surviving troops, back home there's another throng that awaits their labors, for to build her homes and bring home dough. Then she'll give them out heaven's great reward, sex and beauty where the cuddly cosy spasms brew, this for the slave gangs of modern men—they now history's all time great "retards."

Destabilizing the Sexes—Susan Brownmiller

Turning girls male-carnivorous helps destabilize any effective union of the sexes for the purpose of getting after the criminals responsible for our third-world country status that the Bought Media tries to obscure. Man-like rage was the result of feminist provocation and manipulation when Susan Brownmiller's big hit of 1975 re-interprets the history of the world. *Against Our Will: Men, Women and Rape* was the pill Susan administered to the growing, protest-conscious female consumers, as the hood Tricky Dicky Nixon was about to be impeached, escorted out of the White House, and sent into mafia-retirement oblivion.

To Susan, one of the most important discoveries of prehistoric times, along with fire and the first crude stone axe, is that male genitals could serve as a weapon. Is she a control freak with *penis envy*? Or perhaps a projecting sadomasochist, claiming *rapists work for all men* by keeping women under control? Or maybe it's just her vanity, as Susan herself states: "feminine vanity is the ultimate restriction on freedom of mind."[7]

Brownmiller is also writing about the cosmetics industry and its cruelty, leaving a woman feeling unworthy, dissatisfied, guilty, and "never free of self-consciousness because she is forced to concentrate on the minutiae of her bodily parts."[8]

But to develop the rape scenario as the basis of society *grinds anger* into the mind. Reactive thought will protrude, and its brain-bingeing brings vengeful ideas down upon, and destroys accepting, the unbelievable softness of any moment. Any goodness of the present experience of the moment, of the *now*, could be denied, pushed aside. The positive texture of time is banished by worry and becomes wrapped in coils of phrase-fretting, in burdensome-wording and in lashing-out at an enemy.

Rape as Insurance

> *"I learned how to fight dirty, and I learned that I loved it."*
> S. Brownmiller, *Against Our Will, Men, Women and Rape*, p. 403

Can women's masochism be explained as a hangover from the early caveman days? Clubbed on her way home to her cave, male genitalia finish the assault, keep women under control and in fear? After getting used to this abuse, to some the resulting masochism becomes flashed as an excuse.

Brownmiller claims rape became "man's basic weapon of force against women, the principle agent of his will and her fear."[9] She figures men "discovered" rape and then used this finding to control. Gender warfare is promoted in Brownmiller's scathing attack on supposed male intentions. Rapists work for all men by keeping women under control, dominated by force, says Susan Brownmiller, and "men who commit rape have served in effect as frontline masculine shock troops, terrorist guerrillas in the longest sustained battle the world has ever known."[10]

There it is: Rage against their protectors! Used to complaining to get things done, it's bitching gone modern, deliberately ugly, even invoking within the females the killing rage claimed aimed at themselves. Here the meaning of rape is connected to the concept of women as property (capitalism), and rape is also the *secret* of the patriarchy, claims Brownmiller. Perhaps fear of rape would keep women in fear, controlled, predictable, just as guilt, competitiveness and the market do today.

> *Everyday masochists looking for order,*
> *End up screaming-blaming their husbands for*
>   *the disorder.*
> *Meanwhile fleecing foxes, crazy but shrewd,*
> *Give lip service to fairness and the protection of the meek,*
> *But only rake in profits for the power elite.*

Susan Brownmiller figures rape is *normal* in our society. A conspiracy to get women to want protection, meaning a need to get a man in their lives. Rape supposedly serves the male psychology of the conqueror. The male "ideology of rape," says Brownmiller, "is nothing more or less than a conscious process of intimidation by which *all men* keep *all women* in a state of fear."[11]

When attacking males, rape is used to build a case that depicts males as monsters. If some people are hurting others by raping them, then that allows for more cruelty as revenge. So rape scenarios ensure further meanness. And the gender feminists, like Brownmiller, are agents that provoke more cruelty. Her rape-as-male scenario guarantees viciousness will continue. Her scenario is just more bad news. It depresses, perturbs, and then its real damage—it makes sadism an everyday expectation. Bombs will rain on Afghan and Yugoslav citizens.

So Brownmiller got the women's movement of the 1970's excited about a male monster that lurked all about ready to rampage, assault, even perhaps kill the opposite sex. Then a line drawn in the sand began to separate the genders. The hatred became deep, furthered by Susan writing that, in war: "a female victim of rape is chosen not because she is a representative of the enemy, but precisely because she is a woman and therefore an enemy."[12]

Are the kids Brownmiller's generation will breed and bring up going straight into drugs and lesbianism? Where else is there to go except into ideology and church in an imagined fearful rape culture? Susan's aggressive sociology inculcates disunity among the genders, a schism duly exploited by "the market."

And hate-rage returns continually, until Susan's sisters are driven to attempt to control the male. Even men's sperm don't venture eagerly or with singleness of purpose when Brownmiller speaks. No, they move at random, undirected, and are transported up the female tract by *female* secretions, cervical ligaments and muscular contractions along the passage.

Femininity—Fear of Failure

But standing back and taking another hard look, it seems Brownmiller has another wee agenda that's giving her fits. She calls femininity a "compelling aesthetic" and says that "the fear of not being feminine enough, in style or in spirit, has been used as a sludge hammer against the collective and individual aspirations of women."[13] Throughout the centuries she says women have been nostalgically objectified: "women as symbolic aristocrat, women as humble servant, and women as glamorous plaything."[14] But this seems nice work if you can get it. Because the men have been objectified as laborers, soldiers and breadwinners.

Brownmiller rails against uncertainty, the fear of not knowing how to live up to the scripts—"the embedded contradictions leave every women uncertain. Is she correctly following all of the instructions?"[15] Please, what is this continual deferment to authority, the obsessive need to be taught, to get instructed, to learn how? To be catered to as the under-educated and weak *stereotype* that most feminists revile—this is sick!

Asking for certainty, she's afraid of *doubt,* can't understand what abundant living is *about.* Wanting it ordered with protection and assurance, like a classroom in grade *school,* these uncertain citizens are asking for the treatment of an ignorant *fool.*

Make up your mind with the pink sludge hammer of the Revlon Revolution? Paint, spray, shave, *deceive* and into your bosom serf-laborers do *cleave,* working and dying upholding your *compelling aesthetic.* It's easier to manipulate because this society is *pathetic?*

A woman is expected to depend on tricks says Brownmiller, and "...appearance, not accomplishment, is the feminine demonstration of desirability and worth." But the luxury of catering to the beautification that Brownmiller describes plays on feminine vanity, and she, herself, says this will result in "the ultimate restriction on freedom of mind."

Now let's see, the ultimate restriction of female freedom of mind, according to feminist spokesperson Brownmiller, is vanity. The itch for the praise of fools, it's a self-interested, egotistical, arrogant, self-worshiping, immodest, autoerotic, stuck-up self-sufficiency that leads to a peacocky pride, an aggressive bumptiousness, a perky prima-donna vaingloriousness and a conceited swelled-headedness. Vanity denies true human connectedness. It is a dishonest "showing up". A woman, says Susan, "is expected to depend on tricks to prove her feminine nature, for beauty, as men have defined it for women, is an end in itself."[16] Real men do not trick themselves out to be pleasing Brownmiller adds, and "have rarely tampered with their bodies at all, historically, to make themselves more appealing to women".[17]

Female Cosmetics as Symbols

It seems credible that war paint could be used by a conniving female to attract and snare an unwitting male. And so it was that the vamps and sirens of early movies had worn heavy mascara and lip paint when portraying wicked, manipulative *bad girls*.

But by 1940, Hollywood glamour had incorporated facial make-up, false eyelashes, phoney nails and dark red lips. Hollywood had fantastically got women believing that glamour was cosmetic icing and polish as much as it was an attractive physique. By the 1950's lipstick was part of the American way of life (meaning?). Femininity may have endured an identity crisis, as Brownmiller says, when the powder puff (shiny nose) was turfed off the vanity table and merged into history, but Brownmiller claims that "lipstick has been the all-purpose, the modern expression of the feminine soul."[18]

People in the late 60's looked for the truth. The women's movement rejected artificial beauty and asked why a woman needed to "fix herself up" with camouflage, etc. The honorable feminist then shunned the gussied-up, dolled-up pulchritude that Hollywood had been promoting since World War II. Instead, women made an effort toward sexual honesty, and understandably they had an anti-make-up bias. But people's rational thinking really only works to facilitate further organization, and then the thinking itself will *structure a personal take-over model*.

Modern education forces the learning of management principles and rules. These weigh on behavior and anti-rational forces are fought off. And so, the isolated human, the pragmatic spacewoman homesick for quarters, talks herself into waiting upon almighty progress and rational solutions to fix all up. But she is waiting too much for others to do the actual heavy lifting – the experts, the government-funded groups. The belief in progress has freed the will of man from responsibility, has curbed warrior action and now indigence festers. Similar symptoms, evidence of the current freedom constriction, are observed as the myth of truth in art is replaced by the myth of *value in objects*. Results, and separation, are the guiding principles. Strategy seeks control and cosmetics bring it.

By the 70's, female masochism became such a mammoth swelling tide that Twiggy became the supermodel of the globe. At ninety-two pounds, this five-foot, seven-inch anorexic—no breasts, no hips—was seen as a rad incarnation of female excess. Anti-estrogen (fat) jingle of the time wangled that you couldn't be too rich or too thin. Ugly beautifulness romped with the white-mushroom-bomb eyes against a darkening sky. Jumping schizoids needed escape into the preposterous, the unbelievable, hoping magic or something would pull them out.

The true feminine soul may soon be disappearing or may not be recognizable to the women of tomorrow. The mental construction going on today doesn't have a healthy emotional base in reality, for it thinks itself into reality and is then supported by a propaganda culture. The mental construction is stricken with a postmodern consciousness lacking resolve. This consciousness is overwhelmed by morals and a male incapacity to complain and criticize. The result is *disunity*. Soon it's holes to be drilled through tongue, cheek, nose, nipples....

Flipping

So many points of view exist today, so much promotion of value, but the fruits of following other than consensus concerns are portrayed as forbidden. Enduring the confusion, calling it rad or modern multidimensionality, society today, beset by troubles from all sides, flips into *denial* and then posits a politically correct model of modern society as one that doesn't even have any problems. In this conception society's *confusion* is celebrated as *excitement* reaped from a technology heading into limitless outer space. This mental model is promoted as dynamic, electric, fabulous, overwhelming and unpredictable, and in such flux that perhaps in a month from now *anything* could happen.

Unfortunately, this modernism of agitation and excitement is oppression, and being told to groove on it because it is awesome won't do. By the 1980's, life in the modern social world was painted by Marshall Berman as:

> *"the sense of being caught in a vortex where all facts and values are whirled, exploded, decomposed, recombined; a basic uncertainty about what is basic, what is valuable, even what is real; a flaring up of the most radical hopes in the midst of their radical negations."*[19]

So, to Berman, it became like *purgatory*. Watching your politically correct rear-end in a zoo. Strawberry Fields, forever. *Nothing* is real. The soul deserted, forgotten, as cosmetic megalomania helps everyday masochists fight back, attempting to imitate the masters and get some sadism into their own act.

Women as Slaves to the Cosmetics Industry

Susan Brownmiller confesses to placing herself in "permanent bondage to Elizabeth Arden."[20] Over many years "my feminine insecurities changed with each new style." From lipstick it was "an easy jump to fooling around with foundation, powder, and rouge, to compacts, tweezers, eyebrow pencils, lash curlers, liner, mascara and eye shadow, to moisturizers, pancake and liquid bases, eye creams, night creams, glosses, blushers, nail polish, perfume, et al."[21]

She calls her made-up friends "defiantly pleased with their feminine tricks of beautification...brave and chic, women on the go."[22] Brownmiller would come to "detest the stuff." But she was shocked and confused when many of the "sisters" continued to walk out of their houses with stuff like eyeshadow on. She found them "pitiable" and dumped these friends and their "conjurer's art." She was appalled about insecurity, failure and inadequacy being played upon to induce their consumption of disguises. Surface phenomena, like cosmetics, as they become familiar, grow in the human mind into essences. But these essences are made-up. Cosmetics, Brownmiller says, "are proof, if anything, of feminine insecurity, an abiding belief that the face underneath is insufficient unto itself."[23]

She blames men, of course, for all this because a woman's face "has responded to the age-old injunction of man to woman: smile."[24] Corny yes, but it's true men want women's happiness. It's a sign that fills a man's heart with the courage to fight and to delight in the majesty of his life, shared successfully with an approving female. But check out the scowling, angry runway models—the isolated, bony, tight-lipped fashion goonesses from the late 80's and 90's, and grok the vanity and anger happening.

The woman's movement at first turfed greasepaint as oppressive and demeaning, as material that promoted the very opposite appraisal of womankind than the free, liberated, self-actualizing view they fought for. Brownmiller says lipstick is being used because of a lack of men, that competition for men sends sisters into the war paint. But Brownmiller pauses to give: "congratulations to the cosmetics industry—they weathered the storm. Make-up doesn't have to be natural anymore. Women are proudly celebrating the fake."[25]

Isn't it ironic?

8
Red Mouth

Red Mouth is a threat to be taken seriously, by both guys and dolls. Red Mouth's aim is control, and she owns a mighty seat in the boardroom on the way to "hell". Maybe look away, forgive, have pity. But vamoose, take off, blitz, chow, whatever, but say good-bye, be gone, make it history ...*sufficient unto the day lies the evil therein.*

Since the death penalty was brought back in 1974 in the United States for convicted murderers, as of 1994 only *one* woman had been put down via capital punishment! Recently a few more (Karla Faye) have been put down, but it's the men who are executed by the hundreds. Look at the facts and it seems obvious that if all the murderers were caught, women may be found to have committed more than half of spousal murders![1] In the US approximately 1,900 women commit homicide each year, and almost 90 percent of their victims are men.[2] Women commit the majority of child homicides in the USA. And infants are murdered by women at a higher rate than women are murdered by men.[3] Thus maybe soon someone will begin to hold females accountable, and perhaps execute them for murder too?

Red Mouth is maybe one of the bad guys, you know, and, like many of the bitch priestesses, she could be sensual. She may be a wicked nymph, lusting for power to placate her fear of her own nothingness. Living awash with pains and sorrow, blood and decay, "she" intuits it shall remain so for all her days. And she bends until she realizes she might lose, fail to get ahead in the jungle-out-there, and then conforms to the pack, the female school of fish she has been chucked in with. Her society promotes women's power through presentation of herself as a sex object.

So to trap power is complex and demanding. She will hone her skills over many years. She will paint her face, rub odors over her body and pay endless hours screwing around with the hair on her head. Paint your toes? Well there are lots of tricks, learned to glean power from men's attentiveness. But it is really architecture and mathematics. Hard-wired ape-man instantly is raised into sexual focus, helpless under certain visual clues—a cakewalk under the waterfall for her! And perhaps one of the origins of culture itself?

Now here is something reliable in a topsy-turvy world. When the "beautiful" maiden rests her tender rose-blushed and brushed cheek upon satin pillow and ever so gently closes black mascara-handled blue eyelids, she can let sleep surround herself secure in the tremendous knowledge of visual manipulative strategies.

Gelada—the baboon—shows genital pink to: (a) get sex and have babies, *and* (b) get aggressive males redirecting their energy. Storming chest-thumping guy baboons can make a mess of a lady's jungle hen party. Just bend over a tad, raise a sly thigh high, blast a hot pinkie into his eye-brain and kaboom! He's in a different stimulus-response scenario:

> *Genital snap shot,*
> *Use what you got!*
> *Raise the thigh*
> *Control the guy,*
> *Strike the pose*
> *And the deal you'll close.*

It's a sexual advantage. It works! Male aggression is paralyzed; the baboon guy thinks pink, entertains notions filled with emotion. Now if everywhere a guy baboon went he was exposed to these reddy-pink flashes of ascending labial mobilization—a conscription, an exhortation, a banzai bugle call to respond biologically for the life in him, he would be just as "retarded" as *modern men* are. That is it. Dazed and confused, sucker-punched. Jumped and psychically raped in a combat zone many a man doesn't even usually know he is in. "*Turn Heads in Your Direction by Keeping Lips Lusciously Lubricated.*"

A smile and the eyes, the perfectly etched eyes. Sculpted presentations framed by goddess-like colors. Here too Red Mouth is adept at absorbing male energy. It came from the testicles, if you knew how to attract it up. Windows of the soul. Not: mascara massacre! She'd just absorb it all. A walk across a crowded room at a dinner party and she was full, filled with yang. Adept at using these energies. Good becomes bad, then bad is good, as form and content both vaporize into the vamp's melodrama, the one she invented to give death its due.

9
Murder

Just what is being flaunted on the street?
These wedgy slinkers draw heat.
Like hawks are drawn to the center spot where beats
The heart of their prey,
Males instinctively respond to their DNA.

Seductress wanton nymph bum-decorators. Jaws-labia sweetly puckered and painted come-ons, wolves clad in baby sheep's clothing. Rend you to death. Fear and boredom bolsters the urge today, allows the victims to buy in, line up for the big ream-out. Excited they are by sex, a packaged deal flagellated to a conclusion, allowing unconsciousness and respite from their frustrated melodrama. Life? Perhaps the American life for many, but in America men die six years earlier than women.

She-beast hunts for money. Phallo-dough. The secrets of the pyramids are one thing, the power of thigh spread another. And she's on her bike in rush hour in heavy traffic, one lane all to herself, and she's giving you the finger. That's it! Or else, see you in court.

Heat and vapors, choking auto exhaust, the metal and the weight they don't compute, within the dirty city's chaos and insanity, future skeletons yearn for fluid, fruit. But it's stacked decks. She's flaunting a way out of the concrete jungle. Suprafrustration. The air is blistering with millions of broadcast signals. Television, radio, cell-phones and all the rest of the high-tech transmissions are piercing brains and bodies, causing an overload, making people escapist. People don't know, don't even want to.

On his car radio whines a John Denver tune: *Just give me one thing I can hold on to; to believe in this life's just a hard thing to do.* Overcrowded, cowardly Homo saps, uncertain to breathe air, skeptical of the drinking water, gotta little problem: *like* everything is broken. The animals look better off for future possibilities.

Aghast angst can be trundled into an exciting alienation—a hell party for carnivores and others addicted to carnal passion. Hit *live wire* switch.... Electric sex! Maybe heaven is spread all over the face of the earth, but many people just do not see it....

Sex as an energy field to play on. The key to unlock the prison that progress has imposed? Expeditiously seized! *Fucking pressure is everywhere now man.* Summon up the thundercloud, ride the sexual current, be the sexual energy in the universe. Then peace comes dropping slow in an aftermath slicing orgasm, wrenching the displeasure out of the participants, the suffering meat-clothed skeletons. A forced surrender. Gnawing jaws book off.

North American culture had locked itself onto adolescence, hadn't aged—it's cult of youth promoted a pubescent fascination around sex. But too many explosions of rage now erupt along its yellow brick road, here on the darkening plain that man's science may one day turn into glaring desert.

Scapegoats are mates. Orgasms nuke. Wipe out your sex partner! Mate blown up, controlled, exploded, imploded—now an appetite almost professional is fed in bed. So here we have come. Bosnian, Viet Cong, Iraqi, Kosovian, Afghani women raped by shattered-up, dysfunctional soldiers. Missiles and orgasms, war and sexual intercourse.

Industrialization, whizzing technology, boozed-up parents and the big-D (denial) rattles the youngsters. The young mammal clawing to get out, get some breathing room, some air, and then frustrated, turns back on itself. The wanton urge to explore the electrical-overload orgasm-circuit sensation becomes a freedom, a means to close away a hostile environment, and a cheap vacation....

The Hook

Ego barbarians left without a war to wage, no decent, righteous cause left to serve and protect, to kill for. It is illegal, particularly out of the question nowadays. And men's frustration attaches to aching ballocks of fire. Their energy used to be needed, and it was respected. But today it is all tied up by the entertainment culture's images. It's not much demanded for survival in hostile wilderness or in combat.

The male's very being and energetic force is now screwed, overly transferred, to an incited heat-rage that begs for sexual targets.

Then there's the guilt! Sex is important to a man's self-understanding. It's something like what emotion and psychic relationship is to woman. But today many guys are trying to settle for orgasms without sexual partners. Masturbation, however, could be lonely, perhaps guilt-ridden. And the mood could be sneaky. If the guy figures he is *weird* masturbating, but has also bought into the popular notion that orgasms are wonderfully great achievements, then he's going to think that *maybe* a good place to do it is with a woman. That'll terminate his guilt. So he'll marry someone to try to terminate guilt.

Rage, stress-mess, gender judgements, and addiction to excitement all pulsate within a high-tempo emotional-sexual state. Would we have let our society get so frantic, competitive, electrical and mean, driven to apocalyptic sensation, riding-the-wave-of-any-second-now oblivion, without a way out—a guaranteed personal off-chucking package, something to cop us *out?* It's the Big Release. President and proletariat alike can be puffed, popped and spent as their consciousness dives into the cool pool of *not...* consecrated to fastidious nullity. Then nothing matters any more.

The samurai warriors held women subordinate, perceiving the female nature as dangerously over-inclined towards jealousy, silliness and discontent. Protect them? Shield them from themselves? Die for them? Stats please: Naam, World War I, World War II. How many dead, wounded? Gotta know. Every hero, every Fire Department human being—all 343 who gave their lives in the World Trade Center attacks on September 11 was male!

Being a hero is a life-threatening role. Millions of dudes dead. Women know in their heart of hearts that *he* died thinking he was protecting them. Right? He surged up over the earth, a body rung by passion, Battle Hymn crescendos filling each cell in his body completely. Vibrating wild, his thirst to set the world right, the bombs bursting in air.

Beckoned via a call to glory: the hero's pathological obsession to be worthy of love. Propagandized. In the twilight's last gleaming he's a slave, cannon fodder, disposable. *Piece of lung splattered over a broken wooden cross; bumpy, gooey greyish specked with red spots. Tunnel through his chest, cylindrical opening dug right through, now frontal cavity, grass growing on the other side.* Devastation so final it's almost impossible to reach inside the side pocket, withdraw a leather wallet, let it flop open against the thumb. Pictures of this man's living family back home, somewhere safe. He's dead, baby; just more shit lying in a muddy field, just garbage; something to get rid of, make disappear, like voodoo or something. At home, they'll get some money; they'll be helped out.

> *He's nutt'n, one stinking carcass in the bags.*
> *Do the "bitches" outsmart the buttheads lads,*
> *Wiggle their promised ass,*
> *Get them to do the fight'n for the brass.*

Promising sex, is that the sting? Wacky ways...dying for SEX? ...training given for low self-esteem: purple hazing, military torture training.

How else can you motivate a man to not value his life, to give the utmost while denying all his potential earth time? For who do men do this? Women! He's disposable, a replaceable item discarded at random. He dies, so she can learn to love? And women? They're always working on self-esteem. It's a big deal; she takes courses, workshops; help sought, government helps allot. Choose the life you desire, follow your bliss. Focus on visualization, affirmations. All try to focus on a woman's worth, significance, potential.

Woman? Fire department, police department, special rescue teams. Gotta know: Any woman risk her body herself? Most women don't do dangerous jobs, even though the wages can be better than jobs in safe work environments. Women value themselves (self-esteem), and most are not interested in any threatening circumstances, even for money. Physical threats to them are definitely freaky, and constantly they are alert to threats.

Obsessed by an instinct towards self-defense, a woman has a built-in personality that promotes what she needs. Physically-bodily-safe-societies are her desire. Men have lined-up for centuries, silent like ghosts, receiving their marching orders for combat.

Males are taught not to complain.

She's adept at getting her body protected, and she fades into a shocked puzzlement when asked if she is conscious of dressing as a sex object. So used to going to the wall in defense of her physique, she's speechless when crimes are attributed to cosmetics. Anyway, she *is* used to being elevated up beyond someone who commits any crime. She is used to being protected and being worthy of said protection, her body *a temple sacred by birth, and built by hands divine.* Many women claim to lack power so they can remain *unaccountable*, which is exactly how they want it. Behind the mask of an endangered species she wedges her plea to all society—for *her* benefit.

Capital Punishment

Greedy individuals abandoned in the supermall. Reared as consumer pioneers, the would-be princesses have become nervous, distrustful and isolated, thinking they need courses on how to create their own meaning.

All that school was just so much mental training, forcing many of them into their minds—and they became mental cases. Stuck alone in the corner and figuring things out—with words, endless syllables of blab twisting through their mood. The medium is once again the message, and the means is again the end. Dumbfounded, word phrases keep flaring, igniting further linguistic focus. This dance of affliction drives these confused citizens into alienation, from themselves and from society. Forgot what they need, want everything.

With wealth, some escape from the tyranny of public education is possible—tennis, holidays, summer retreats (from what?) and consumer-spending-championship power. But even the wealthy are made mental. The system scares kids.

Ever since the gang that President Reagan fronted for boosted interest rates in the early 80's, it's been strictly rule of the rich. Who else could survive 20 percent and higher interest rates? The wealthy just put their money in the bank. Easy, no brains really needed. But if you've very little money it's scary. There is an army out there on government assistance, and another making minimum wages. Literally millions are in jail.

The deficit isn't the average person's problem. It is an *idea* worked at and featured. Governments want to make it seem a personal debt, a personal responsibility to humble the populace with the burden of debt. Keep them off balance, some guilt glue. So they use the deficit as a threat to the average Joe and Jill's lifestyle. Then people will fight each other to sweep *dung* for minimum wage.

With the people in distracted passiveness, the big money absconds out of the country. Free trade, a lot of *dough* hits the road, like into Eastern Europe, South America. All around the world our guys are putting their money. Corporate New Nations (CNN), the bodies of great authority thriving without the constraints of nationhood, interact. Beyond borders the real power zones—*NIKE, IBM, SONY, GM, ETC.*—network. The middle class disappears into a Grand Canyon, where they serf.

The market itself is trusted to rectify injustice and produce employment. *More ideas.* If only reality could be crammed into ideas. The market doesn't care about people, only profit. That's it; your town pump drains your dough, legal tender; it's there only to get profit. It certainly won't aim to create more employment as humanistic policy. No, it will only crave cutting jobs in its fanatical obsession with bottom-line profit-making. *Excellent companies* get lean and mean, right? The results force some to see a blood-thirsty nation of "rats" and "sharks," bourgeois entrepreneurs, darting about desperate for a kill. And shrinking possibilities under *cop-rule* just make it hotter, raising the temperature. Is greed enough? Propaganda mush is fed into citizen's living rooms through the boob tube. Why all this *budget-cutting*, deficit deceit, while *elite* groups wallow in unbelievable wealth and claim their place in the sun, tucked away on easy street? Exhausted from fighting each other, citizens miss the point.

Capitalism does not work *for* a nation. The Great Depression proved that. But it's just like 500 years ago: rule by those kings and barons, today's corporate chiefs, with the politician-flunkeys taking their orders from below. Can't blame a girl in this world for trying to escape the wretchedness of middle-class serfdom. If it's routine for the governments to use dirty tricks to keep themselves in power—espionage, wire taps, propaganda, assassination—then what's the harm in a little lipstick?

Trial of the Century

Lawyer sits in the television screen; she's talking hard and fast. Attractive too. She's ranting on about spousal abuse and scolding that it's never too late. But everybody knows the jury let the killer go; her client's sister is dead; justice for the celebrity murder is unrequited, dismissed. No quid-pro-quo solution here.

But she is out for a pound or two of flesh from particular male bashing, a huntress onto the evidence needed to conjure up guilt and to dump wagonloads of crap at the feet of men. Her retaliation demands a reprisal against the assumed force in the world that is guilty of causing the crime: *inhuman male destructive violence.* Indeed, her client has been leading a rag-tag band all over the country, whipping up fury, aiming at capturing women-beating men, playing a blame tune, escape the goon boon.

The Illusions. The lawyer, well she's all dressed up in expensive clothes, attired professionally, and is alluring or trying to be. She is still marketing attractiveness at middle age and aiming to win points through intimidation: coiffed locks, a wide smile and lotsa teeth. And the blush-on cheeks, hot highlights raising attention up and then into watery eyes framed by the etched, painted eyelids put on for power purposes, an attract-and-control agenda, embroidering nudeness, captivating soul segments from the oppressed. Surrounded with deluxe (carved) eyebrows—the Lana Turner-Cindy Crawford- Brooke Shields fantasy look.

Pluck, wax, whatever it takes, shave 'em off and paint 'em back on:

> *"Intensify brows with Brow Shape—especially at arch—to balance the deep tones on eyes. Brow Shaper in Shaping Taupe. Dust Blusher high onto cheekbones, and sweep up toward hairline. It's a tenacious formula...."*

But the coup de grâce is her mouth:

> *"Intensify delicate shades with mouth-maximizing liner and eye-catching sheen. Think of bold lips as a kind of accessory. Wear them anytime*

> *you're up for impact—on their own, or paired
> with equally strong eyes. Just remember: color
> this strong needs precise application...."*

It's indubitably a head turner—the luscious, ample red lips are enough to steal attention away from almost any hard issue.... And she's going on about this immature brutalization of innocent human beings: how we've got to start doing more to halt the victimization of so many; how education is urgently required to help us all understand what a critical issue we've got here; how we have run out of time and it will be too late if we delay tackling this problem any longer; and how people should not have to suffer treatment of this sort from others, especially from those that they love and think worthy of their trust.

Illusion would prevail in this trial all right, but it was the professional smoke-and-mirrors type, conjured up by defense lawyers that eventually baffled the jurors so they could buy into the fantasy. So does that justify living off illusion, making one's life a deceitful manipulation of facts to get what one thinks will bring satisfaction and happiness?

In the trial, as in today's life, fallacy succeeded, nothing so startlingly new:

> *"Eyes appear flawless—not at all 'made up,'
> and are a natural for any time of day.
> Better-than-bare eyes are about quiet enhancement."*

So to pretend, to act, to fake and manipulate reality to the extent that "natural" is really unnatural, well, this is the basic training given to many modern women by their mothers. And it's dysfunctional, abusive, a form of oppression not often noticed. The women look angry in many advertisements, shot this way purposely to reflect a determined individuality and liberated strength. But women's anger needs better direction if their lives are truly to become free from subjugation. The vanity encouraged is beyond worldly beauty. It goes into control, of first the mind—*make up your mind*—promising to give confidence and liberation. And then it goes into dominion, since the ego can dominate and compensate for a myriad of insecurities.

> *"Dazzle them. Maximize lashes with two coats of full potential mascara!"*

It's a popular lifestyle, but unfortunately not openly admitted as strategy. Mentally using cosmetics to control the physical may actually cause energy to dissipate and diffuse the magnetism between the sexes. And as women go physical in this mental manner, combining cosmetics with a politically correct front of denial, the resulting spin and swirl is distracting our society from progressing beyond the abuse of its members.

The Orenthal Version. Like many protagonists, Orenthal had sought revenge because of rejection by a woman. It's an old story, and one that has made the rounds. But this is the Orenthal version, and its setting is the modern American culture that's invading so much of the world.

He couldn't bear the insult, didn't carry on, go forth, fix the problem—recognize, get help—and let go of the captivating domination of hate. His attachment to her as his selfish, personal source of comfort and love and as an ego-boosting possession led to his anger and jealousy. But this is what most people that *think* they are in love today are going to have to face too, if they don't understand what love really is.

When the source of pleasure is removed or not available then the rage builds. When the comfort is not available at the snap of a finger, then the frustration and blame begin. Stuck loving their problems, humans live in their zoo like caged animals, but judged as worse. Despite having the capacity to elevate life for all, humans believe in scarcity, individual ego, and fallenness—and in American culture life is sold as a challenge to swim with the sharks without being eaten alive.

Both protagonists were addicted to sex, and a certain type of sex: exactly a fearful, trapping, ego-loving, hate-controlling, heart-devouring, common-crucifixion type. And in the expedition through the waters of affliction, in a furious feasting on the other in the white-water wrestle, the dropping duo end together tied unto extinction.

Then he wants out, but her lascivious game she plays out in front of him—hetero-and-lesbo libidinous carnality—and he's not handling it, not making enough effort to forgive her the experimentation. She's driving him crazy, so cleaved to this jealousy-enraged love has he become. He has to win, thinks he must triumph. She knows his buttons are all pushed, that he's terrorized, that his *big-boy* ego is being trifled with. Then stir in their hidden, sexy, guilty ghost-guessed secrets only the heart could confess. It's obvious these participants are afraid to confront projections—what they are really *using* each other for—as the *shadow* in life blocks true understanding.

A *time bomb* ticks while daily life passes amid smiles and greetings shared, waved, conferred all along the busy sidewalks of the malls on warm afternoons. The currents of human experience flow and mix together, an interactive collage filled to the brim. Human energy abundantly flows into the cup of life and through a cornucopia, the raw potential capable of moving mountains. The human will directs both the propensity to horror and the predisposition toward love of a creator. But here it's a case of excess passion, from the Persian *passion*: "to suffer." And these "suffering," hopelessly attached, heart-breaking, ego-ordering, possession-type and user-for-pleasure-while-tripping-out relationships, they are products of cultural dysfunction.

Greed and Superstar Athletes. Capacity exists within people for honor and respect to be given to each sacred life, for all to be supported and readily encouraged to become their highest and best *selves*. But is this goal getting the attention it deserves?

Greed for big dollars does not pay off, if it's humanity that is to profit. Corporate nations are always on a war footing. Survival success may be for the slick-willie ruthless, the inheritors of capital, or the lucky lotto-fluker, but that's it. No one else is getting into the lifestyles groove in greenback Gomorrah, the money-lusting land where gluttonous souls are found yearning for falsely advertised panaceas. Natural-born mercenaries attempt to destroy competition, take away, deprive and thrive; this culture sets people at odds in killer-competition.

Meanwhile athletes, the physical ones who could most likely be victorious in a group slaughter—a free-for-all butchery special, winner-take-all skins game—those born with top-formula body machines, well, this culture pays them up to a hundred grand a game, then watches, idolizes and elevates these unusual runners and jumpers, hitters and hurters, throwers and catchers, these athletes that could so easily outdo the watchers in any natural setting. A nation with an inferiority complex has its head stuck up the toob, while the TV networks claim it's paradise. And that it's only the athletic *excellence* they admire! This nation keeps order through intimidation, separation and exclusion. The brutes get most of the loot. Superstars don't give much hope, only promote an awe at human physical aptitude. Superstars sell *product*, get billions. Fans give money, buy stinking running shoes, go home, watch TV. They are in the land of the lost and losing, their brains washed with cable, their taxes used to fund a massive global military that is hidden away from their sight.

> "There must be some kind of way outta here,
> Said a Joker to the thief,
> There is too much confusion,
> I can't get no relief."
>
> —Jimi Hendricks

Hate love, love hate, claiming that the sex is great? Drugs of course are here involved…as the creatures de-evolve. Mismanaged sex and pride parade across these desperate lives. Society, for all to see, isn't helping children to be upright and to learn how to leave, when evil cleaves out the virtue of compassion and forgivingness.

Working together, the done-up lawyer and her client's man-battering blitz sweeps the nation. Soon many women feel victimized by abuse and find shortcomings in society and in other people, and they rage against these abuses. And this rage will eventually define their lives, becoming fanaticism spread sensationally, in hyper-explanations of who has done what to whom.

Sundry women are corrupted by the male-abuse campaign and swell the angry gender feminist ranks. They are informed the future belongs to them. Unfortunately, reduced expectations is the only medicine that's going to keep them from total let down. They were educated to believe a patriarchal society has a grudge against them. Then using anti-patriarchal *ideology*, combining it with positive thinking, they start anew, rationalizing their world, and it comes across like male macho. Mental male macho, the aggressive use of wording – sequences of sounds made into words and then aimed at desires – creating reified environments, those that exist *only* abstractly but are now mentally sucked into dangerous emotions. Nattering brain syndrome: the results are poor, and these women basically create the very opposite of their goal. True believers, our culture forms, and then sends these "feminists" into no-man's-land. So strictly driven, these rational true believers are running after abstractions. The mind can explain and justify diabolical strategies. Mix in some psychology, and anybody's life can be seen as dysfunctional, victimized and abused. *Ideology boils rage.*

Talk shows spend all day stoking the flaming hate. Sharks feed on bleeding humanity, attack the males. Anything that helps build a case is seized upon, and the egos swell. Egotism can soon be marching around, but dressed-up as moral goodness. Just the *facts* that *promote* the patriarchal victimization-reality are rationalized. Each one increases the rage and the belief in victimization.

The Psychology Industry turns people into victims. Victims are relieved of the burden of dealing with complexity, facing things beyond their control and accepting personal responsibility for their behavior. The victims become reactive, and lose their own creative power that could help solve their problems. They get co-opted into the blaming game, stuck in the blame glue.

Life as hate. Quite a pleasure, to hate, to blame for life's unsatisfactoriness. It puts the responsibility for one's own shortcomings, faults and fears on other people or institutions. And the exposing of yet more presumed injustice serves to bolster moral righteousness. It's like life as a *reaction* to lawless forces that *have* to be put down, exposed, defeated. Then ignorance triumphs. Ideas begin to replace emotions, responsibility is denied, suffering is mistakenly justified. Life becomes a blaming-reaction to uncontrollable forces, and that equates to a life of being the victim.

Blind Love

She did it for *love*, in Canada. Karla Homolka says that's why she and her husband killed three teenage girls. For love, she says she was driven by love. Her fifteen-year-old sister was their first victim. They both raped her. Later she died from poison they gave her. Homolka claims she had stupidly loved her demented husband. Well, she's struck a deal with the feds, took a twelve-year sentence in return for her testimony against him. Doesn't the system ever execute women? Soon she'll be walking around your neighborhood, probably hoping to fall in love with someone. This woman, she's into relationships you know. She says she will kill for them, and the courts seem to accept it....

> *"And I find more bitter than death the woman whose heart is snares and nets, and her hands as bands: who so pleaseth God shall escape from her: but the sinner shall be taken by her."*
> —Ecclesiastes 7:26

Power Love, Love Power

What does it really mean for a woman "to be taken"? Of course there's more to it than male abuse.

In popular oriental philosophy it is commonly believed that yin absorbs yang. Thus female surrender can be a tactic as well as an emotional instinct. Males respond to the submissive invitation. They will serve and protect. But claiming total equality today, then asking to be dominated on demand may get a woman labeled as crazy. Some may think women are *always* masochistic. And that women crave what a man usually sees as torture and punishment—submission, chaos, fear. They may also wonder if this is the heaven this wiggly, curvy creature is yearning for? At wits end, it keeps them guessing.

> *Female porno is bamboozling our America,*
> *Bringing a lot of dysfunctional hysteria.*
> *From the supermarket halls,*
> *Around to the romance novel stalls,*
> *The fantasy turns reality so murky,*
> *Can she somehow be this quirky?*

Passive algolagnia (i.e. masochism) embraced as a life style? Best seller: *Sweet Savage Love*. Look around, check it out. Romance dramas have been almost *half* of North-American paperback sales! Adultery, rape, incest, dysfunction and abuse surround a heroine's upward mobility and grasp for power. Generally, in these books men get eliminated; women get wealth.

Power love, love power. Who's on first? Our minds, our minds have rationed up vitamins and schemes. Is it the plans that might put an end to us? Or is it the lack of belief that plans can be made real when society is told that cutbacks on spending must continually occur? Most of society is becoming obsessed with simply escaping into entertainment. Not enough people are paying attention. Feminization is flaunting feelings, the subjective experience, over the intellect and its accountability and objective plans. The schools barrage the intellect with too many facts from all areas. Here unconnected memorization pieces can only frustrate the grasp of the big picture.

Mental monster youngster turned gangsteress, so mad at being forced into brain sap trap, rationalizing, memorizing in a corner, heel! Figure it out (school), out-figure it. Use your head darling. Then most buzz brains, even those with great potential, plug into television, and it's basically over, finito. Tall walls are built using all the useless information. Two or three hundred thousand Iraqis push-buttoned. Press another button and soon it's *Sex in the City,* seven thirty, channel four.

Sex in the World

The presidents gather in Washington. They're signing the peace treaty: the Saudis, Palestinians, Egyptians, Israelis, Russians, Spaniards, Norwegians. Some other kings and front pieces are there to facilitate the historic signing. Diplomats for peace nest together, feed, and after dining the various leaders arise and speak. "Peace shall prevail and the world shall benefit," these words rise up, surround the gathered, and go out via satellite around the world.

Applauding in the front row, many of the presidents' wives, distinctive women, skirts and dresses yarded way up thighs, their legs attract a focus; they showcase creamy-curved, shaved, silk-like flesh. A definite turn-on, and, yes, lugubrious painted lips signal the biological message of readiness, imminent ability and desire—an unchallenged declaration, coupled with those brushed-on, blood-flushing, *in-heat* cheeks, raising expectation, an advertisement beckoning. For peace? War is scribed onto these bodies—calls for aggression, thrustful purpose and pleasure strategies, the taking of selfish joy, temporary amusement, escape. Conquering through deceit, diplomacy, the pro-sorceress of the apparition is setting the stage—the earth held hostage to the femme fatale.

III
Abuse of Rationality

10
Introduction—Reason, Rationality, Logic

Fascism and Stalinism and the logic that grew the law,
To many feminists today they all contain the fatal flaw –
Replacement of what an individual feels or a mind could draw,
With strict belief, sciences and the law.
What is missing in female grief is communication you see,
Because life here exists only in relationship between I and thee,
So law squashes particulars of the human scene sublime,
Where the fems do say there yields the truth divine.
Women intuit the needs of Pres Bill and Monica L,
And the law of perjury can go to hell.
It depends, depends on relationship between human beings,
Not on the strict laws like some machines!
It's so frightening to be left all alone
That these women empathize right to the bone,
All this logic-law must seem like some mystical hallucinatory power,
With stern attention and the raised eyebrow it does tower,
But good-natured female needing and humanness, will it devour?
If the point of law is to separate truth from what is subjective,
This is the field the female may have neglected.

The logic of empire, church and *state* is esteemed throughout history, carried on high by those who *legislate*—basically males. Men, they had turned to logic because, the feminazis say: *men are lonely, socially retarded and sentenced to violent death because they ache for an intimacy they don't know how to fulfill, and because they are unable to satisfy desire and are always tormented by the presence of women.* These men, the "femzies" say, turn to cold, detached, predictable, eternal logic and thus the law.

The men are deemed by the *feminazis* to have bought into and to be hanging heavy with the logic system. They are seen as *regaling* in a weighty *certainty*. The men are thought of as egotistical and pompous from believing they have all the answers through their law, with its rules, accepted credence and certainty. *Just following orders,* that's said to be the male outcome of allowing logic to mutate into rules that have an absolute power to coerce the citizenry. Soon violence and cruelty can simply be given carte blanche to further support the law. Personal responsibility is then often shrugged off easily.

Men are said to manifest an indifference to suffering in their strict strategies—like creating embargoes and sanctions and bombing to further diplomacy. And striking-out in court three times in California now means jail for life. Is this following of rules and the using of word-logic over life itself repulsive to humanity? To humanist-subjective feminists, aren't words spoken for the ears of another? And where is the other, the whole, feeling embodiment of another human being, when laws are written in a book?

It's said males respond too well to logic. Some claim they are so emotionally, subjectively insensitive that they grab the word *glue,* believing it can pull them *through.* Western society set up the rational-logical hierarchy as the perceived road to progress and success.

Plato and Aristotle, from masculine culture, one separated from the generative life of the household, were like most logicians. They established basically, but not entirely, male influenced worlds of reason, where the written word and its code became the highest judge. Here society chose to place its most honored ethical guardians. Masculine egos fought throughout the *ages* in universities for their right to grasp truth in its *stages,* to conceptually seize the meat of moment and then to try to change the structure of society, to eliminate any *flaw* simply by following their new-made logic and *law*.

In the ancient virile logic-culture women were mainly excluded, along with a focus on subjectivity. Interpersonal, emotionally significant sensual relationships were not hailed as the be-all and end-all route to satisfaction and further understanding. They were not front and center. Logic separated women and men, in law courts, in official assemblies and in hierarchical bureaucracies where rational discourse prevailed. The female lived in a somewhat illogical feminine household concerned with reproduction, child-care, household tasks, and emotional healing. Their duties developed social harmony—not rules of law for debate. Not in the sundry sciences could women see a *future*, let alone a place fot *nurture*.

The Greeks identified reason as the guiding trustworthy principle. Reason was believed a virtue, and thus rational action would be expected to lead to the greatest good. Or so it went. Back then it was believed the reasoning intellect could decide the truth on its own.

Women and Logic

Ever since the enlightenment of the eighteenth century there had been further trust in liberation through thinking things out, through rationalism and logically structured scientific investigation. Did women feel left behind—in their world of fertility, pregnancy and birth; in the world of the flesh; in the world of emotion and change?

The rational *concepts* that rallied women of the past—freedom, equality, maternity, society, and progress—are without the same meaning today. The concepts have become so messed with by so many self-interested groups that they are disembodied from original meaning. These concepts are used anywhere, to promote anything and are often attached to business commercials, complete with musical jingles. The concepts are now just like verbal cosmetics, circulating in formal rhetoric. They have no definite, dependable meaning and are just masks giving credence and respectability to a horde of selfish actions. Because rational approaches are used to sell consumer products, people distrust the wordy spin cycles that bombard them constantly.

But today logic constitutes words of power that promise success in market economics, and many females have gone mental. To many women wanting to get into the employment Disneyland of today, their female need is to learn this logic language of the patriarchy. But by ingesting the mental-logic world view must she then *submit to domination of a paternal state bureaucracy* that the femzies say is *more oppressive and dominating than a husband?* Logic some call the *language of her oppressor*, saying it has enforced boundaries and limitations between her and men.

Some feminists claim this logic is a project of male domination. By assimilating this logic-language today, in universities and in the business world, females look for reward. But will they lose their emotional intelligence, in their flirtation with this claimed "oppressor"?

> *Are angry women with bleeding hearts lamenting their lot,*
> *As humanism becomes categorized, cast away, forgot?*

"Dumb" as a Route to the American Dream

Forrest Gump consciousness is the major downer of recent decades. In the film, the hero Gump believes because he was told to, and that is the end of it. Whatever the official consensus opinion, Gump will buy in.

In the movie, the character Gump will make himself a doormat for women, and he will kill anyone that someone with a uniform on tells him to. He is neurotic and escapist. He idealizes a drug-addict slut as a heavenly angel. He believes in God "cause his mommy" told him to. He is putty in the hands of the military and is frigid, alienated from natural sexual activity. He is a neurotic psychopath who is blessed with an elitist superstar Ping-Pong playing skill. He gets lucky, makes millions in the stock market, gaining it through other's bad luck and misfortune.

The movie is really just about more scarcity consciousness and reduced expectations, like the ecology spiel and market economics sadomasochism. Depressing and realistic. Realistic, like the *nausea* surrounding the lives of the desperate characters are "real" – not as in normal, but "real" as in what *one is used to*.

Just following orders, Gump may even think he protested the Vietnam War because he passed by an anti-war protest. This guy is a mark for women and preachers and politicians. And he is a bleeding heart, a good democrat perhaps, trustworthy to the middle class because he too feels their pain and because he is a little stupid. He lucks out, capitalizes on disaster, becomes mega-rich. Is it luck as the lifestyle of the rich and famous?

Follow orders, blindly *believe*, and yours will be the chest to which reward will *cleave*? This guy as a role model means consensus opinion, the *official* cultural conversation, has no opposition because Gump's structures of tacit pre-understanding are perfectly tuned to being told all about the meaning of existence. He jumps to follow orders, but his appeal as a non-rational hero fades when it is realized that he has dumped thinking to the point of letting the official version of events rule.

Is Gump an American hero of today? He is about sadomasochism because Gump gets to kill "bad" people while belittling himself. He probably would be a *pawn* for any women who paid attention to him, as he convinces himself that he is in love with Jennie, a women who can't stand him. Later on Jennie can handle the billions Gump got. She's dying of AIDS anyway, and her son will be looked after. She is a real user-bitch. Gump thinks it's love, and his, of course, is the romantic cavalier-type dedication to the one-love soul-mate stuff. Did Gump ever have sex more than once in his life? Marrying the aids-infected leech, is this a good idea?

Gump would kill for a Coke if someone in authority told him to. A *male mark* extraordinare, cannon-fodder for the military, to see him adulated is more than scary. The movie audience is manipulated by a sentimentalized shared pity, with a big blast of fear from viral AIDS, as war and financial failure mushroom into its male-demeaning theme.

This movie is falsely promoted today as portraying the radiant triumph of the little man with a big heart in a bigger ugly world. But Gump has little depth of understanding, and he is like a child-man who cannot comprehend the real world. He is brainwashed. He keeps running and running, away to nowhere, to escape the organic knowledge he'd find if he could only look inside his own heart. But he is a systems man, programmed for limited abilities, partial understanding. What he is told becomes his reality, even if his instructors have coercive hidden plans. And his rational abilities keep him stuck on the same page, parroting out streams of memorized words, as if they produced his only real meaning in life. It's sad to see a human life running mainly on the "owners" logic and spin.. His mental responses are like his rapid response as a Ping-Pong wizard, like the stimulus-response of those who have been tortured into repeating answers on cue.

But little citizens smarter than *Gump,* they too must submit to a life directed as though in an illiterate garbage *dump.*

The Ideology Gymnasium
All the "laws unto themselves" driving around burning oil
Are seen as Pavlovian dogs to foil,
Guinea pigs and mental cases to derail,
And grasping their attention the longhairs begin their tale–
Rehearsed, tried, tested and true, they got notions of just what to do –
And average Jill and Joe is getting put right through –
Into the ideology gymnasium, worked over, frisked and flipped,
Broke on the wheel of spin, stripped,
Pummelled, drubbed, taking their cue,
And their scourging, maybe even minus a clue,
Unsure to which exclusive club now everyone crawls,
Democracy is politics, painting the walls,
Creating reality, those elected, their truth selected
And the plebs in their stalls
Shall be affected.
The Opposition members prick
Up and throw reason poop around, very slick,
Bewildering (sickening) everyone not hip to the trick –
Kicking the pits out of the plebs, rapid assaults right on their heads,
Constant gunk, glue and more and more information making their beds,
And somehow accepting this indoctrination of confusion,
By all accounts plebs have solemnly learned to paint their disillusion
Into a personal dysfunction – but unfortunately this Dysfunction has now become their "special" seclusion.

Women Expose Logic

Some women have been leaders in exposing rationality, its logic and ideology as alienating pursuits. When the claim of rationality to be reason as well as common-sense and the only route to truth and knowledge is unopposed, then the *Vagina Monologues* and the three minutes of only moaning correctly may salute the misogynist project to *refute*. Logic, the suspected project of domination by males, has *some women* looking for avenues outside of logic today and, while leaving the strict thinking to the men, what *logically* could be called anarchy and chaos are sort of being welcomed back in. Reason needs to be balanced by other ways of knowing.

But the world just won't stand still. There's so much survival work to do that the female dreams of consensus and democracy, and time for each to talk things through, may be only another fantasy that can't be realized. Relativity to female needs is relationship itself. They want not just the words, but *who* they were said to, what *state of mind* they were spoken in and what kind of people spoke them. Words themselves, for numerous females, cannot alone tell the truth; they must be spoken by somebody and originate in a social relationship. Many a female looks past words and, through her subjectivity, searches for ultimate truths.

Rushing now to today we see the female lawyers in some kind of weird disarray. It's not likely for the truth that they attempt to convince judges and juries of positions that are most likely false. Clever girl bamboozles all, wins for criminals—as forensic evidence becomes only rhetoric that briefly gets in the *way* of modern heroine winning the *day!* Words as cosmetics. But danger arises if women's subjectivity is severed, and women become inhibited by all the word glue. Losing the female's emotional intelligence would not be good for society at large.

11
Spice and Rodham

In the ancient Chinese practice of the bound foot, to become a concubine a young female would have her feet wrapped tightly so that they would remain small. This was considered sexually attractive, and it also meant that a woman who had bound feet could not easily run away. She needed protection and had to submit to her protector. To be called a concubine today is an insult to many a "feminist" woman, implying a failure at self-sufficiency and a situation breeding low self-esteem.

Nowadays the revolution is *Spice Girl* perfect female flesh standing up on awesome high heels stretching toward the sky. And these women with the resilient pop-back flesh fortressed-up made tall, they are now extra vulnerable on high, so defenseless, so tied to their thick soles and elongated stilts that protection is again mandatory. Like there's no life like it!

> *Without male security or hired guns these Barbie*
> *dolls would tumble,*
> *And the enduring dream of being saved by prince*
> *protection could instantly crumble.*

Female Sex-Guilt Glue

The bound foot has again emerged, and, with lots of *police* protection, the girls feel emotionally safe enough to splurge. It's a running over of the liquid cup of female sex glue. Here emotion, cosmetics and dress-ups all relate to exciting the sex urge, and fuel it and rake burning coals from out of the gut up and all over the mind, the soul and even down onto her centerpiece—the butt.

With high-heels comes elevated and more curvey calves and the now more rounded buttocks, so what about their mother's equity feminism? Who gives a fuck!

> *It's your ass mom—ya, take that morally*
> *righteous feminism*
> *And stick it where the sun don't shine.*

Geri Halliwell may reveal neurotic girl guilt glue when she refers to her Spice Girl role as "that wicked streak in me." It's so perverted, using sex and cosmetics to paint on sexual messages that are lies: harassing, causing chaos, getting power through weakening others and knowing you're a manipulative witch to boot.

It is, you say, for the loot—treading on little boy snakes, wiggle and lick, lipstick shimmers, then give curvy butt the teasing hip, all the while asking for protection, like a baby deer lost in a concrete jungle surrounded by speeding traffic, danger swirling-driving by.

Still unaccountable, females today frolic as emotional roller coasters like the everyday-fantasy of the Ally McBeal TV role model. Compulsively seeking, she is shopping for the right male. She is sexy, fashionable, but a cheerful mess, a frivolous neurosis—meanwhile her phoney lesbo threats tense up the sex close to the modern tightness of denial, while Camille Paglia adds fizz and hisses memes like *female sexuality is humanity's greatest force and male lust is the energizing factor in a culture.*

Today's feminists, what do they say? Well many of them are upper-class types, and they can afford to dabble their egos in "daring" private enterprise, or take college degrees and get some socially responsible management careers. For the rest, female opportunity that only leads to being a minimum-wage "loner", this is false opportunity. Books like *Living Alone and Loving It, A Guide to Relishing the Solo Life*, published in 2003, make much ado over escape from traditional relationships and trash marriage as a solution for loneliness. But it is really sadomasochistic for most women to walk away from marriage and relationship. That's why spinsterhood was so feared before. Women, told by government and the media to expect a world that is *so* different from the past, are buying into the coming social disaster.

Many people soon put up with less. It's the culture of reduced expectations. Failed marriages and single or lesbian motherhood are becoming social realities. Maybe that's why McBeal is so nervous. But in addition to their new jobs, many women have still got housebound duties, once the major source of complaint. Is this the liberation their mother and her sisters brought? And some just stay at home and slice open government's baby-breeder dole. Just get pregnant and someone will have to pay! *Why we are angels, ladies sweet and straight, you know full of sugar and....*

Meanwhile divorce from men is promoted by many feminists. Indeed, divorce from men is cultivated in America! The woman's side almost always engenders sympathy in the media. Nicole Kidman gets the biggest spread in the Women of the Year Special by *US Weekly*, "for making it on her own." But it's because of her divorce from mega-star actor Tom Cruise. Everyone is supposed to pull for her. It's popular, this male-as-villain scenario. And the basketball mega-rich wife of Michael Jordan, who began divorce proceedings, she must be the envy of them all. With 500 million US dollars on the table, this marriage-as-strategy for upward mobility will get divorce some good PR too.

America does not reward marriage. But in Mexico, the government gives financial incentives to marry and have children. So their divorce rate is lower. However, America encourages women to break free, self-actualize and to do so without regard for a man's life. The powers-that-be see advantages in dividing male and female, and in encouraging the female to get out front and center as the electoral force they will cater to. But divorce brings single-motherhood. Many children will suffer without an organic parenthood. Flaming rebuke has been hurled upon men in America, and when launching a divorce the married women can easily characterize them as mean, insensitive and inattentive, and the women win support.

Frankenstein

Beat and berate
The husband all should hate!
Blame him for all the world's woes,
Then grab a settlement and off he goes.
Or teach the twit to be like a feeling woman as well,
Like how Bill Clinton found (hell) he could cast his

> special spell.
> Bill is basically a testosterone male,
> Can this alone land him in jail?
> Early years under single momhood somehow just
>   made him come undone,
> And take knowing advantage of the female in
>   circumstances when he should have run.
>
> The single momhood is everywhere these days.
> Teenage boys enduring the mixed messages, lost in
>   the action-jackson rage-haze
> Of driving-force testosterone fuel,
> But their single moms' emotional vulnerability at
>   home is to a man so uncool;
> Makes a cagey critter, maybe a little frustrated and
>   even bitter.
> Homophobia could soon become a valid concern –
>   dissimulation - all the feminist garbage, boys are
>   here forced to learn,
> It's being breathed and born into young minds unable
>   to defend,
> And they too must therefore grow up and pretend.

Today's male-hatred by radical feminists, many who are from the baby-boomer generation, has helped the *masters* keep society from changing to benefit the middle and lower classes, as men and women are sunk into a hate pot and the *out-of-control* type movies are re-enforcing the false-consciousness, with phoney female roles now the macho roles—unbelievable. Men painted as ugly, violent rapists, like naughty boys that should be locked up and dominated sexually. *The English Patient* gets societal top grades, even though the men are stepped all over, ruined, killed—treated as pathetic by the cheating bitch. And in the blockbuster *Titanic*, the cute boy-man, he sinks to the bottom of the icy sea while baby-doll floats on the small buoyant scrap of wood only one can share. What is this sacrifice, and why does it go unnoticed? Many men love women beyond conviction, but they bring them much too much misfortune. They are manipulated sexually, and somehow have bought in, and see a sentimentalized sex object as the answer to their life's suffering.

Mouth Pieces

The Vagina Monologues and *The Girl Lawyers* will never ever come to peace. How can non-rational three-minute moanings of orgasm in *The Vagina Monologues* be compatible with those using rule-bound logic to delineate society—the newest swarm of legally trained females who use the law.

> *It's the commercials some may say,*
> *That has driven all the real truth away.*
> *Many minds have been blown right out, indeed,*
> *And upon the billions mind-souls float critically while they bleed,*
> *The ads keep incessantly rubbing in just what they need,*
> *Words used with impunity to sell shampoo, broken free from truth*
> *Then flog Tampax, vacations, shoes and the tile on the roof.*

Advertising is gone beyond graffiti and won't be caught. Any and every mainstream cultural force is co-opted into the bullshitting, the scheming to make the people keep jingling with envy, dreaming, thinking the solutions only need be bought.

But the abuse of the words themselves leaves so much room in which the longhairs can get away—while wedging in acceptance of *any* impending doom. Words need listeners, alert and processing minds, participating in mutually worked-out plans, the solutions and challenges together to be met. Instead giant teenagers simply crash on couches, fed on tampered chemical meat relished with additives *discrete*, with *everyman's* television at their *feet*.

> *The network's children seeking refuge,*
> *Sprayed with meme flares*
> *And sent further into deluge,*
> *The flicking light hypnotic,*
> *Big brother's machine narcotic.*

The bombardment takes away resistance to lies and unaccountability; deceit makes victims of the subterfuge.

> *Raising all the kids with lying machines,*
> *This is bound to make them somehow mean*

And mad; TV's abuse of them is so sad,
Removing the trust for others they might have had.

Disgrace upon the merchandisers who rape minds with words twisted only to sell to the teens and tots raised in front of this phoney baloney. Who knows what the political swarms of hacks can achieve, make the prisoners of the twisted television symphony believe. Words sung and logical sounding; rights and claims ring with bells and music too.

Citizens have become stooges held weighted on their seats,
Boob-tube flying images totally over their lives does creep,
Fading them into the democratic egalitarian zombie sleep.

Lies are now acceptable. They are understood as attempts to get consumers to purchase merchandise and amusements. But a culture of deception is now functioning—one confusing personality with character, that follows celebrities partly from inferiority. And consumers are told daily that unemployment, pollution and fairness here at home, well—it's just all great.

Hillary

Hillary thinks of herself as feminist. She's upper class, university-educated. To her it's rad to be *gender-powered and self-centered,* and anything that promotes getting respect, jobs, protection and government assistance for females is basically OK.

Clinging to feminism in a society of alienation gives
*   some punch,*
Even if the context can be way out to lunch,
But when the going gets tough, females merely switch to
*   fluff?*

So some feminists motor-mouth on about *freedom to become self-actualized* (to be sane), and carving personal territory *free from male abuse.* But then the pomp and fury of their claimed victimized circumstance—where they are claiming a gruff roughing by a huffing, muffling patriarchy—works to once again paint them in simple suffering!

Hillary is being groomed to be the first female president of the

US. So who is she anyway? Hillary Rodham was the one chosen to give the valedictory address for her graduating class at college. It was 1969, and she had received her first degree, from Wellesley College, the very college where the gender-equity *experts* have cropped up more recently. It's they who believe that gender is indeterminate at birth, that boys and girls are *actually* equal. Wellesley is where the notion of growing beyond gender is now pursued. It's where an individual's gender is seen as taught, as an identity learned, not one inherent. Gender is *learned* between the ages of *two and seven*, they say. No hormones, no biology.... Here Hillary had studied in her early academic days, before going off to get her law degree from Yale.

Hillary, like Peggy Sue, got married. Marriage was her choice first and foremost, and she delayed her law degree and her graduation to follow her husband around. She had the right stuff for her own professional career. A sturdy mid-westerner of high intelligence, strong will and ambition—she had wanted to be an astronaut at age fourteen. But she threw herself into the role of the subservient wife. Did she think she was in love, or that she had to tone down her individual ego? The pose for competitiveness isn't usually like the attitude that generally invites an intimate marriage contract.

Snidely known at Wellesley as "Sister Frigidaire," because of her platonic opposite-sex relationships, she yielded to her man's career path. And her later defense of his philandering drives home an aspect of her personality not to be ignored. Whether it's masochism or defending her meal-ticket, it's off-balance, showing lack of any principles other than personal chauvinism. Gennifer Flower's, who had a twelve-year extra-marital affair with Hillary's husband, Bill Clinton, was reported saying Hillary has been with more women sexually than even this Bill Clinton!

Hillary and Anita Hill

In 1992, in a speech at the American Bar Association convention, Hillary praised Anita Hill, who was part of a shady left-wing conspiracy to get at Judge Clarence Thomas for inappropriate sexual behaviour. Although Thomas avoided being professionally destroyed, and nothing was ever proven, the gender feminists and their advocacy research teams pulled off a propaganda victory as a result of their Thomas harassment spin. After the Senate "show trial" was over, and Thomas was acquitted, public perception remained vaguely suspicious of Thomas, while Anita Hill swept the country like a heroine, giving speeches to enthusiastic audiences about "gender issues." She was seen as clean.

Sexual harassment lawsuits would skyrocket after 1992. That is because the media became alive with female outcries: patriarchal, male-dominated politics had failed to take Anita Hill seriously! Everywhere up popped the blamers, and soon Anita Hill was the poster girl for female abuse in a society said to be run by misogynists. She was featured in *Glamour, Ms. Magazine,* on the cover of *Essence.* She was on *60 Minutes,* the *Today Show,* and the networks ran dramatized and sympathetic versions of her story. Awards were given to her at every turn, and soon loud calls were heard for Anita Hill to be on the supreme court, or to become attorney general. She was being well managed by those looking for female-over-male patronage, and by the divide-and-rule longhairs. So well handled, in fact, that sex allegations skyrocketed. By 1998 Mitsubishi Motors had to pay out thirty-four million dollars to women on its assembly line to settle a sex harassment suit

The "Anita Hill Effect" resulted in a record number of women being elected to public office in 1992, and may have even influenced the presidential race where the gender card brought Bill Clinton victory. By 1996 Clinton would get 16 per cent more women voters than the competition.

Using Anita Hill, the gender feminists had pulled off the usual, a smoke-and-mirrors obfuscation of the truth, invoking sympathy, sentimentality, and the rest of their tricks. The American Bar Association honored Anita Hill with the Margaret Bent Woman Lawyers Achievement Award, and Hillary remarked in her speech: "All women who care about equality of opportunity, about integrity and morality in the workplace, are in Professor Hill's debt."[1] Dozens of lawyers resigned from the American Bar Association to protest this award to Anita Hill.

Hillary and the Starr Report

Synchronicity was salacious the day the Starr Report, documenting William Jefferson Clinton's sex transgressions, was first put out, coincident with Hillary Rodham Clinton showing up to address an audience of the American people. On that the major *day,* Hillary was going to have much to *say.* She came to the people to speak and focus them on an insight and exploration into the colon. Hillary spoke about the dangers of colon cancer; surely this could help make the sexy Starr Report go away.

Hillary was surrounding herself with a colon aura. Those *longhairs* are hard weary workers. And, therefore, poop ruled? Off to congress went all the crap of a "right-wing conspiracy," but here in public the so-called first lady zoomed into an another area rife with corruption. Remarkable the nerve of conspiratorial intellect, to put on this face, to get this association with her presidential husband's disgrace. Law degrees sturdily support manipulators; she'd found it necessary to live in a nauseous spin world, what with the seemingly never-ending confrontations she and the pres husband had got themselves into with the legal system.

But power is everything; everything is in turmoil, and the postmodern psyche needs to get used to being off-balance. That is all that is left, it seems. Birth is everywhere, newness rules. Answers fly up then are submerged in a newborn puzzle, like your TV commercials: can't get a handle on much here today, and so the spin doctors can make most problems just go away.

The dirty work gets done by changing the subject, attacking the messenger, playing dress-up with Arafat-dolls for peace photo-ops and getting helpful billionaires who own media empires to paint suitable portraits to awe the frumped-out population. At bottom line it is liars under the noonday sun. Geraldo Rivera ate lunch knowing the pretenders are everywhere, and there would be no problem igniting the TV talk show frenzy he'd be serving for supper.

While Hillary is up to her elbows and sinking into her speech, Bill is setting up a super spin of his own. He is in the backyard garden of the White House getting standing ovations from Irish Americans! The public had been sold-told of Bill's bringing bountiful peace to the Irish homeland, a country torn by an imperialist-caused civil war for 300 years. Bill is starring in the role of the peacemaker. A month or so back he was handing out medals to his envoys that had helped him accomplish this great deed for Ireland.... Most unfortunate about the bombing in Ireland a few days later—the twenty-three dead, many children. It was the highest death toll yet in a single incident, but today peace reigns at the White House because these people are standing and clapping for

Bill, and television is telling everyone that it is just so. With people like Hillary and her vehicle *Bill*, all that is needed is an effort of *will?*

"Rationalization, could she be in denial?" asked Geraldo Rivera in a moment of surprising acuity. "Yes, he has weaknesses", had said Hillary Rodham Clinton, but her reasons came with the logic glue, she trying to stick words onto behavior and to justify certain actions—his affairs with other women—as a result of her husbands' being abused when a toddler.

It's this psychological glue that shows the alienation ambience these educated, rational-centered females inhabit. Focused on words, on definitions made in more words to understand other words, it yields these flashback puritanical feminists with minds suicidally squeezing away the hope of mankind. The earth connector goes mental—into the word glue—*democracy, equality, abuse, males as culpable, males as targets.* And how much longer until she's even forgotten her gender as gentle?

An uneducated medieval wife who instantly understood the crime, the implication and proper action, would not have spent life in this distraction. The modern woman takes courses and motormouths on radio talk shows asking: what is a woman, how can women know just how to act, to respond, to dress up and to let go?

Hillary as Victim

Hillary became a victim! A waif mistreated by pompous bluffing. Her sorry emotional jolt and churning, and this is really feminist have-your-cake-and-eat-it-too, allowed her to clamor for ruling power. Protect me while I undo your world, this could be Hillary's shadow song.

Many female selling tactics invoke the female *mercy-for-the-angel-baby-doll* vulnerability, and males go right along, as if caught in the hoax, in this monstrous float. As if the same person, day after day, can really motivate many men to marry for life, if the men didn't feel they were needed to protect the female, or at least had feelings of pity for the female, or had other feelings if she were pregnant. But as a victim, this Hillary's poll numbers become mouth-watering. It is said that New York state is running rampant and raw with these feminists, these male debasers, who think getting a male on a leash is possible, viable.

With Pres Bill on his knees to the female form and this

Monica's butt,
The Pres is being ridiculed by many in the nation as the big slut!
So has Pres Bill put the MEN on the run?
The gender feminists flop out their paws,
Threaten to make a fury and fuss and use all the laws,
If their hostage, this Bill Clinton, won't donate to their cause.

Who's the Boss? CNN asks, "Who's the boss, Hillary or Bill?" Swarms of women leap to defend the integrity, character, strength and wisdom of this Hillary. She is touted as perhaps the only survivor of her husband's sexual scandal, and it's said she should first run for office and then president—this would be her historic handle. This leap in imagination is very female perhaps. But it is antipodean to somehow figure Hillary is filled with Victorian female moral superiority (FMS). Is she a woman capable of the long suffering and the discipline necessary to attain this moral superiority, with what she must allow in her home?

It ain't gonna wash. Maybe Hillary has the feminist hallucination, of someone who thinks she can jump out of her vehicle victim role—and she's going to claim victimization by her upward-mobility vehicle, this Bill. Looking for support she claims a feminist life and an ability to stand on her own. But she has always followed Bill.

Looking up close there is male-bashing and blaming, plus paint and glow all over her show. And her husband's scandals are used as ammunition for the sex-as-a-weapon approach, disgracing the male, allowing women to claim territory high above the lowly cast men. She rises up, as Bill, and all other men with him, sink in shame, called as they are: inconsiderate, untrustworthy—liars who use and abuse women. This guy Clinton became the gender feminist propaganda poster-boy. He has been used to great extent to further drive a stake between the genders in America and around the globe too. In the world of information it's the anti-male scenario that is getting the attention and the detail. Hillary is the boss! Her side prevails.

The Super-spin Doses. When will we ever see her real wide body, stocky legs, whatever, Cable Ted (AOL Time Warner)? Hillary Rodham Clinton was nominated by *Time* magazine as

Man of the Year in 1998! Guess who also owns part of *Time?*

These folks gave Hill and Bill a lot of glow,
And perhaps without their media rah-rah this strange
couple would have had to go.

All this muck about Hill and Bill just disappears amidst the clapping, smiles and hoorays and the state bands' musical trilling, as a waving-smiling Bill and Hill were the everyday super-spin dose the plebs swallowed like a pill.

Feeding Mexican immigrants, who now are the number two in population count in the US, and the other newly moved-in cheap sources of labor and community disruption—feeding this helter-skelter melting pot of various culture-educated incompatibles on cable-scripted clips regarding "reality," well it is a cakewalk to consensus. Who could organize anything here? Many can't even speak the same language.

People do believe what they see. Sophistry on high, guiding light of obfuscation, the serfs claim it is education, the reading of newspapers and absorbing TV news, while they are being put right through, graduating in amnesia from the College of Laputa.

Slipping in the polls in her reach to be all she could be—and conspiring to *be* Senator of New York state, the first lady dame traipsed about in the country's White House and devised a plan to get more support and following. So as Linda Tripp is indicted by Clintonian courts for taping Monica L, some calculating minds see an opening to spread the blame. Tripp is made at fault for all this Clinton scandal or so many were to be made to think.

And regarding her Pres husband Bill, now Hillary in the media will bespeak: "He is not really malicious, he is simply weak"![2] Hillary's feminism is swollen with psychological explanation and excuse, and a country overrun by feminist ideology is ripe for the strike. With a husband who has been seen to cry, Hillary told the world the President is *weak.* Once she asked the press corps to please respect her zone of personal privacy, but now she is basically dosing up this dysfunctional Bill to the media—as a *victim* she asserts, of anger between his mother and grandmother, that is the scam! Hillary is appealing here mainly to those who had been co-opted and embrace a feminist science of psychology—the often neurotic, psychopathic and nebulous feeling-seduction used for the invisible or unaccountable justifications for crimes. Was Hill surprised to hear the latest New York polls had been showing her backing was down among women voters over thirty-five years of age?

Psychological Honey. Psychological honey for her busy bees, Pres Bill was abused she said, and the editor of *Redbook* came on the *air* figuring all this psychology is only *fair*. It shows, she said, that Hill and Bill are only real. *Talk* magazine pitches in too, by disseminating Hillary's psychological *he has weaknesses—was abused* interview, used by Hillary to get female support for her modern feminist rise to the senate. But in the interview some complain that she never even mentioned the US of A, only her self-interest and the problem—Bill.

"He was so young, barely four, when he was scarred by abuse," said Hillary, and "he didn't go deep enough" to remediate the illness.[3] Like a gambler, addicted and *fraught*, somehow in a clench, driven by unconscious gumption, subworldly forces, neurotically, pathologically attracted to sex—was this the husband she had *caught*? Hillary's poll numbers never were higher than when she was seen as a victim, and Bill's abuse was the excuse for both his behavior and for her being rewarded. She deserved to be senator because she had suffered the abuse of the abused.

> *And if Americans let Bill be Pres, then she would blackmail their doubt,*
> *And anyway getting power is what it's all about,*
> *It's the University of Victimology where all these fems have been taught,*
> *And listening to their psycho-babble is now the nation's lot,*
> *Hearing reasons for the abuses of Andrea Yates, Karla Fay, and Kurt Cobain,*
> *Susan Smith or Brother Cain,*
> *While the whole country suffers through the pain.*

The President is *like a baby boy*, and some of the feminists say therapy will be needed to erect a fuller, gentler, kinder and more noble man. Get the guy in some psychologist's sandbox and facilitate the creative excuses for all his abuses. Psyche excuses, like TV commercials. The *excuses* then like cosmetics, they give hermetic self-esteem. And Hill says Bill wasn't rejecting her by his sexual philandering with other females.

> *No, not the way these psycho-chicks prevail,*
> *Firing the new-found "invisible" reasons they hail,*
> *Painting Pres Bill mainly out of control, waylaid,*
> *By overpowering compulsion, this the reason why he strayed.*

No, Hillary is not to blame with this group. Compulsion is at fault they say, Bill's compulsion. (That's right.) But it is insulting, as these psycho-social fems certainly are aware, for a big man like President Clinton to be handled like a sick puppy dog. This psychology and it's rational *ride* into male-bashing, complete with intense imagination and the archetypes, the chief male in America it does *deride:* the sick, the lying, the brutal, the abused, the stunted, the uncaring, the perverted, the underdeveloped, the obsessive-compulsive President. *Just like a lot of the males around?* There were many analysts near this Mister President that were dumbing *down,* saying his *need for approval* was so great that sometimes he had responded like a goofy *clown.*

The Missing Link

The modern woman is the lawyer type. They are schooled in the rational, with the rational glue binding their personalities. And behavior. It starts early in life.

Infants learning adult noises made in words soon can formulate sounds to bring stuff to themselves, stuff they need. But when the young child begins to use and say the symbol *"I,"* he or she begins to *objectify*. And between the self, the "I," that appears in his or her speech and the self who is only partly represented there—the person with hands and feet and desires, the self with inherited ancient, primordial caveman-wise genes - between these two kinds of "I's" vast human continents and majestic seas are spanned. The whole self today of the modern earthling still deals from habit with existence on a life-and-death frugal plain and this self is deeply, deeply moved and *knows* signs and signals that aren't even acknowledged as in play today with his or her brain *...and includes the partial self that physically speaks!* There is still a pre-speech cave-person inside all people.

Power of the Unconscious. The *unconscious* it can be called, and it is not going to be nailed down by all this talk! The words are symbols to direct wants and needs, but language cannot formulate desires that remain unrecognized. Language does not have all the human senses on board. Thus the intuition that humans have is somewhere under the words, rationality and logic, and involves abstruse and ancient feelings. It's so profound, but this stuff—passed on in our blood, the genes—is underground.

Perhaps much of this *unconscious* was passed to our older relatives as *common sense*, perhaps largely non-verbal but clearly understood. How much of human essence has gone? Gone subterranean and not sensed, because people can become like refugees, alienated from themselves, when casting most of their energy into a wordy side-show, trapped in a verbose, swirling vortex void.

Words cannot grasp it all. Here is modern society with its scientific discourse raised up and worshiped. But here too is the separated individual, full of vanity, "facts" and mental snobbishness. Today the subjective stance is sought, and words are envisaged as weapons for liberation from personal worlds of pain, and used in hope for an objective future that is different, one that would be basically in conflict with the present world. But by putting all its hope here, society may be in for one big fall.

The Greeks Knew Too Much. The Greeks long ago knew too much and had too much to cope with—all the problems, all the solutions, all the different cultures living together, and all the various philosophies, religions and cults. They "knew" too much and it paralyzed them, drained their energy. And their culture feminized men, and so does our culture today. Women were on the rise in ancient Greece; similarly, men were depreciated and made insecure. Then the Greeks had two choices, either: disparagement or idealization of women.

When contradictory explanations are given to the modern woman, she must seek solution. Then the subject that does the thinking, the "she" that grasps the words to respond, words that suit her from her word-made ideology, this *she* is not all of herself because the pre-speech "unconscious" stands and floats. And, in fact, the "unconscious" demands results, not just wordy efforts, linguistic somersaults! No spin is settled for here.

Limitation of Words. Reactive rage emerges when words box in and define, making the subject of the words a victim. The unconscious wants solution, but it can be denied, over-ridden by aggressive fencing-in words. Often the real problem is ignored and paved over by rhetoric. Dysfunction results.

Words were made for use as *tools* to serve humanity. But humans are more than words. And as soon as the subject-persons use the symbol-words to define meaning in life, their selfish needs and wants are springing projected into the symbol-words, many needs and wants motivated from a presently unknown "unconscious" that existed before words even came into use—a memory held in the genes very real, very human, very deep.

The Hillary types, legally trained, can become distanced from deep understanding. Their reliance on the mind's *ambition* and *cunning* becomes their foremost internal motive and mode. No wonder so many lawyers are involved in politics! The mind's conflict is seduced under capitalism into the pursuit of *things* in hope of ending its anxiety. Now that Russia is "free" and under market economics, is it surprising that the Russian legal system has become highly developed since 1989? And the new president of the National Organization for Women is a lawyer.

Using mind—women may lose her center in the intuitive and travel to barren lands shopping for items to serve unorganic needs—and this will promote denial in woman. She could present herself as a stone. Or violent, judging, reactive to any slant, while in the mind she's told she has the right to demand subservience. But what the mind desperately seeks in thinking so much, so habitually, like an addict using a substance to escape, is what the mind itself can never really bring—security.

The wordy world of *today* has its citizen-subjects in constant *disarray*. Thought is reaction to memory, reaction to experience and reaction is conflict. Lawyers are all about memory, the recollection of the past. They are surrounded in conflict, and fear is ever-present because they may not have recollected all the facts or some judge may simply dump their word attacks. Their minds are bombarded and respond in kind, with war-like argument constructed out of words which only give part of the subject's insight.

When exercising "freedom" of speech in debate the person is constantly wording and processing and seeking solution. The person becomes the site of contradiction and attack and is constantly the site of much construction, thrown into crises by language and its social formations. Language is reactive, thought itself needs a target to work on, and thus much debate places the subject right in a victim role—reacting to argument.

Limitations of Language, Logic and Reason. Getting outfitted in religious dogma—some philosopher's system, some right-on ideology (the market?), numerology, astrology, new-age psychology, or scientology—gets an ego armed with *reasonability*. Then an unbalanced entity emerges, yearning for a future that is all thought-out in advance. Dogma and conviction can bring the subject person to the *confident and coherent sum* of her or his ideological misrepresentations! The subject, the person, is basically *seizing* answers because language-logic-reason does not have the answers to all things. The subject is abused by contradictory answers. Thought is, at heart, conflict.

The self is incessantly striving to do what he or she was told by their school—to figure it all out, to reason and be mature, to strain the brain, to calculate—the calisthenics of training to reach up.... How can those lost in this maze claim to be at the very height of civilization? This constant defending and battling to have it *right* serves up alienation.

> *Much to the psychologists' dismay,*
> *Talking about problems won't make them go away.*
> *First taught to think, rationalize, and with reason to debate,*
> *Thence ending up with most of the planet's heathen to hate.*

This system is the curse from the knowledge tree, and has sent most of mankind right out of vital allignment with even the pre-speech Garden of the Unconscious Eden.

With alienation is the table set, and the longhairs' agenda operates to keep the people in their rational network. The people are off-balance and constantly fighting to be right. They become self-abused in their system of affliction.

The kids are sent off to school, raised to live in everyday mental conflict, trapped in the wording-mind, becoming addicted to tension and contention. And getting used to beginning any discussion with their conclusions! They will grow into employees of the very governments and organizations that keep citizens *implicitly* maimed and drained—this today, the epidemic spread by educating based on the rational polemic.

Words of Jesus—Beyond Limitation. When Jesus came he helped spread the "good news" and preached forgiveness of enemies and brotherly love. Selfish money-changers met the rage of this table-turning messiah. And the laying up of treasures in this world was surely going to bring the evil *on,* for Jesus had *named* the prince of darkness and proved that guilt was stuck on those who rode *along.* In Jesus' name a creed of believers rose up, and they praised fraternal love. Fighting, war and personal competition came into contact with forgiveness, and Jesus' following grew with those overcome and distraught.

Now, today can we be saved from our divorce from living in human totality? Or will the ego-grasping words and logic lead to fatality? Love thy neighbor as thyself doesn't jibe with market economics (ME). But even Christ's sweeping invocation and plea for transcendental understanding (love) could be twisted into a good manipulative sermon for ME. In any Christian church today, a spinner minister could crunch the words to glue parishioner's market hopes and a murderous self-interest into an acceptable sermon replete with the love of Christ, the sacrifice of Christ and the standing alone of the unloved Christ.

Today some ministers are heard rallying their flocks to compete in the business world, to go head to head with the competition. Onward, the Christian soldiers are told to grab a piece of the saviour's doctrine, to believe and to be assured of triumph over the competition. But their focus on ideology and persecution builds resentment. And the vanity of believing they're God's darling and that *He* attends to particularly them, well, it suits separation. They dig in for lives of separation while imbibing gallons of phallocentric philosophy, competing, aiming for positions in the business hierarchy. Feminized calls are heard demanding civil rights, equality and democracy, the very things that are incompatible with corporate structure.

Equality—Democracy as Disguise. Does democracy mean myriads of mortals asserting separate personal power? Are all the dysfunctional results of the schools of rational victimology now also claiming to possess individual ruling power, so they can hopefully win in the war zone of the market? Schizophrenic.

The democracy-equality meme has everyone a winner, claiming ruling power, swimming equally with the sharks in the "free market." But this attitude is possible for maybe a few percent of the population and their buddies overseas, for those rich enough to do as they please. Another commercial spins somewhere in the back of the brain, repainting servitude and slavery into abstraction and hoped-for market gain....

Added to the sickening chemical pollution pumped into most of the public's daily life, the terribly murky media-created consensus debilitates people even further. Oppression brings alienation, then eventual passivity. Thus the yield is naturally to even more propaganda and false-consciousness.

But can the individual yield to love? The *subject* people are constantly challenged to defend. They must justify both ways of living—war and love—but as though they were not opposites and contrary actions or behaviors. It's nuts, this reality—go figure!

Millions of gnawing, abrasive, conflicting primate-descendants claim equality with all people in their democracy while each asserts a totally self-interested and individual independence! The market-run democracies claim to be the home of liberty, humanism, and rights for people.

Listen to many of the idiot paid actors, the heads of state, talk about letting certain nations into their global markets, but only if they become "democracies" and have elevated civil rights. Under the smoke screen of equality, democracy and "free" markets the International Monetary Fund (IMF) exploits an empire. Imperious, dictatorial, it dissimulates under the window dressing of free markets and democracy. The IMF is a covert arm of the US Treasury, yet beyond congressional control because it's formally an international organization—it is unaccountable!

By following the dictates of the "owners," the few elite in the IMF's colonies can become part of the exclusive economic army run by the bosses, the big power-elite capitalists. But the IMF makes client states cancel health services and social programs. And privatize a nation's natural resources.

The obsessive self-interest of the corporate world view filters down into the lives of each citizen. Market economics seperates, and only the "few" will benefit, while most fear being left behind. It caters to the ego and egocentrism. The ego then fights for itself, not for the communal benefit of the whole of society. What this has to do with democracy and the human rights of individuals is bewildering. It's corporate fascism. It's cruel, but to many nurtured on propaganda about democracy and market economics, who only know entrepreneurial exploitation, it's right on! Cruel, pragmatic, rational captivity.

Now gender feminists cannot conceive of themselves except as *individuals*. Many women now *dare not love,* for love may kill what is democratic and modern: the individual. Is it power that is her goal *today?* What of love, like that of Christ? Has that gone, vanished now into *decay?*

Mary Wollstonecraft—Feminist Icon (1759 - 1797)

Mary Wollstonecraft had a plan of education for both young boys and girls to establish equality "between the sexes as would shut out gallantry and coquetry, yet allow friendship and love to temper the heart for the discharge of higher duties."[4]

Mary desperately lobbied for women to improve their self-respect by becoming competent and earning their own way. "Only employed about the little incidents of the day, they necessarily grow up cunning. My very soul has often sickened at observing the sly tricks practiced by women to gain some foolish thing on which their silly hearts were set." An active mind, she said, would embrace its potential and not be led astray from its duties.

To Mary, "it is indolence and vanity—the love of pleasure and the love of sway, that will reign paramount in an empty mind." This has a familiar ring—sex as power, the spotlight garnered by the genetic celebrities (females), many cosmetically made up to obtain this "sway," and it is Mary who scolds those involved in the subterfuge.

Mary deduced that women may have to wait for times to change, for a society "enlightened by reason," and said " if then women do not resign the arbitrary power of beauty—they will prove that they have less mind than man." That's Mary talking, back hundreds of years ago.

But Mary, at age thirty-four, faced the liability of her rationalization. Her reasoning had joined self-esteem with a proper, married sexual love, in contrast with sexual promiscuity. Although she said that women were "subjected by ignorance to their sensations, and only taught to look for happiness in love," also she said that "even women of superior sense, having their attention turned to little employments, and private plans, rarely rise to heroism, unless when spurred on by love! And love as an heroic passion." She really believed that "true voluptuousness must proceed from the mind," and "that in all cases morals must be fixed on immutable principles; and, that the being cannot be termed rational or virtuous, who obeys any authority, but that of reason." The words sounded good.

But regarding Mary's feeling of emotion and its female foundation, poor Mary didn't do so well. Mary fell in love with a man! She had a baby girl by him. When he spurned her she was so off-put, devastated, that she attempted suicide. She jumped off Putney Bridge failing to kill herself. Interestingly, Mary did later marry. She referred to her future husband as "a convenient part of the furniture of the house."

So does the suicide response, to the lover she was infatuated over, reveal a side of women that should be out in the light? What was behind this attempt to destroy life? This is Mary Wollstonecraft, the spark, the source, the brains behind the feminist movement. Her coming undone, distraught and self-destructive under the weight of her thwarted will to power through "love," this may be the blind spot that society must watch out for. It may be an inclination of females, one with disastrous possibilities. Military provokers could use claimed bombing of children and the like to get society's permission for more wars. Females held hostage by their emotional sensations and ready to sacrifice life itself for the sake of their "love"—here the longhairs gain fertile ground in which to grow sentiments.

But in the challenge to bear another child two years later this feminist icon died while giving birth. Love and power may be two divine experiences in human life, but they must be somehow balanced, as one could envision in the symbol for the perfect husband and wife.

Now this Mary was heard to say she desperately wished to see the distinction of *sex* abolished altogether...save except where *love* is concerned!

> *Love is sexual, even to Mary,*
> *So scat dash away all who are contrary.*

Inequality of Sex

Exceptional culinaries these women in passion, their pride and feelings of *power* when in "love" reach the pinnacle, and a substance and capacity that, any male, she could probably *devour*.

Men sting in some sense of rational, reasoned, reflected shame, and they usually retreat into their doubt when held up to and compared to the sexuality unleashed and conducted about by the sexual symphony's "fuehreress." The lady-in-heat is submitted to as a goddess—*she* who with both hands on her hips brays below: *Who among you men, is here worthy of me, and can imagine such power!*—nasty even the attempt of any peccadillo. From this Mary's day and still unto *today*, sexual control has been the woman's way.

Cooking Males

The radical feminists of Hillary's generation squawked and squealed, saying males use and abuse, thrust, pick and suck at their bodies, like having a meal. Submitting to being a man's meal, would that be going on in a society that claims to give equality to all? Feminist paranoia is the reactive response of many of America's intelligentsia.

Radical Feminists—Recent History. The radical feminists in the 80's produced so much male-hate literature it was really a time of persecution. But while women were terrorizing the men, they were permitted to dress any way they wanted—ladies' nipples, shaved legs, breasts, buttocks et al. were dressed-up and sexually adorned and harassing, sucking the afflicted males' attention.

Well, for a man the 80's were like penal detention. A female support system was nourished in which females consoled one another by blaming men for their life's difficulties. It was the pleasure of group-hate, plus succor to mollify the group fear that one day there may be some dues to be paid up for the females' sadism.

Tons of books were written in the 80's encouraging women to just blame men for everything. Critical books promoted revolution, anger, distrust and established victims as—none other than the women themselves. Victims of automobile pollution, television, and war, then victims of menstrual cycles, and always victims of ignorant and abusive *males*—this the 1980's for feminists' *tales!*

In the 60's and 70's it is said women had focused on the *external* barriers to equality—jobs, elected official government positions. And so in the 80's it was claimed the *internal* work now needed to be done, so that women could *get over* their obsession with being in successful relationship. Divorce was the rage as

Shere Hite claimed 91 percent of women surveyed initiated divorce.[5]

Male Failings—the Women's View. Reactive literature cascaded onto bookstore shelves. The ladies and the younger girls plucked the maliciously worded packages and carried on—instructed in male sackage. There were titles like: *Men Who Can't Love*; some nasty and demeaning like *Successful Women, Angry Men*; weird and masochistic like *Men Who Hate Women and the Women Who Love Them*; basic hate in *No Good Men;* and commodity-like consumer-shopper types like *Women Men Love, Women Men Leave.*

It's mainly in the communication that these tracts seem to *avouch,* the guy is somewhat retarded and needs lying on the psychiatrist's *couch.* Women went and had affairs, and claimed it as a response to the male idiot's mumbling, stuttering emotive failure—failure to communicate like a woman!

The problem is that the equality idea became understood *as* reality, even if only word-manufactured in the head. And hostile women importantly began their own demise, when they taught men to replace women in their special deed—*the emotional pre-emptive empathetic strike*—that many an emotional and feelings-educated women has used to her delight, sort of like being the man's mother, manipulating a male subservient to her tender susceptibilities, finer feelings. In the 90's, after all the mistreatment, the humiliation, scorning and badgering, many men came through and made the effort to understand their feeling emotional aspects. But in the 80's it was mainly reactive rage and a dense dumbing *down,* of childish man as nerd and jerk to be run out of woman's *town.*

To think that all would be well if men could rise to the female level of manipulative, emotional power could possibly be suicidal for any traditional hope for marriage—of two sexes working and supporting each other. Shere Hite, in *Women and Love, a Cultural Revolution in Progress* (1987) concludes that women are fed up with the males of the species. She sees a large-scale cultural revolution going on, women disillusioned about their relationships with men. And (again) she says women are abused and oppressed by men, and that women are trapped by a longing for love and by their anger at men's attitudes. And that's what is causing the problem, she says.

Emotional and psychological harassment is universally experienced by women, according to Hite's scripted gem and its grind-down of male verve. But just what is a female longing for love and how does that trap a woman? A total of 70 percent of the women Hite interviewed stepped up to the plate and asserted extra-marital affairs, within five years of taking their marriage vows. They with others, seemingly guilt-free too, extra martially were swinging. Women have been socially conditioned to serve men and the brainwashing must end, says Hite.

To Hite, women aren't looking to marriage as a primary life objective like they used to. They were told they could have it all—husband, children and career, and many seemed to think that two out of these three would fly. From 1974 to the mid-80's the number of unmarried women between the ages of 25 to 34 doubled.[6] With women being the ones overwhelmingly suing for divorce, this empowered the adoption of Hite's new sexism, and its bashing, trashing of the male.

Learned Helplessness, Lies and Crummy Jobs

The truth it may be cruel to say, but females with jobs were still feeling powerless, because fifty bucks a day ain't gonna let you play at being a self-reliant entrepreneur by day and a self-actualized sex quarterback, leading the team of mesmerized buttheads, by night.

Soon a special law gets on the books for the victim-obsessed sex called *learned helplessness,* a cover-all cop-out meaning that women are taught helplessness and therefore some can't look after themselves. So they get special treatment. Awesome how demanded equality grunts out of the bowels, the air rapidly steaming with real meaning. Some of the gender will say anything, manipulate anything to get the support afforded to the animals, the children, the minorities and the disabled.

Many women soon line up to say *powerlessness* is actually a result of a previous loss and humiliation—even from the crib their fathers or other nasty males molested them in. Roaring hysterics grab on to a rape-*spin* to beat on the men; that it's untrue and made up is the real *sin.* Claiming childhood sexual abuse soars to the number one spot and sympathy-getting honor for females, justifying a failed-life excuse!

It's not their crummy jobs, no, or even their boyfriends that are bringing their stressing, harrowing their claimed nervous-breakdown situations. In the 80's it's sexual-abuse survivor syndrome, most of the abuse done by males in the childhood home!

The Psychology Industry depends for its survival and continued growth on its ability to create markets and manufacture victims. Once a person accepts a "victim" label, their whole life becomes centered on this new identity. Then their treatment and hoped-for cure is sought and bought from those "professionals" in the psychology business. The Psychology Industry creates problems, the "solutions" for which they sell. Society has bought in, and now anyone who is suffering is seen as a victim. And society seems to believe the bizarre idea that there must be some psychological fix-up for all of life's pain.

The Courage to Heal, a 1988 publication, claimed one-third of American women had been abused as children. Can this really be true? One-third, that is thirty-three per cent, one American woman out of every three! Gloria Steinem rallied around the growing *child sex-abuse* movement. Girls who were deemed to have "created" multiple personalities to survive this abuse were given great sympathy. And the media got more flames to fan, to raise up "true believers."

Next, a blistering attitude is served up against the younger college and high-school males. They raped dates. In 1985 Ms. magazine funded the Project on Campus Sexual Assault. The result is an absurd sexual hysteria and fear of dating young men.

"One in four college women will be sexually assaulted during college," stated the headlines on student newspapers across the nation. Those are Mary Koss's numbers, she did the research for *Ms. Mag.* Most of the statistics these date rape studies have used are *so* manipulated it is criminal for them to have been published as truth. But *Newsweek* will report in 1986 that acquaintance rape "is the single largest problem on college campuses today." The rape survey results are twisted to sell agitation and panic, to continue the persecution and maiming of men. They are examples of women's victim-consciousness looking for someone or something to blame.

To many women, personality relates to emotion. Emotional intimacy is what many women want. And if a man just wants her body there is no individual psychic respect, no appreciation of the unique feeling (psychological) human being.... *To think of men as incapable of achieving intimacy* without being forced into it, that is the gender feminists' spiel.

> *Many women can't count on having good sex with a*
> *man's body in their emotional state,*
> *So they are training the men to emotiveness (theatrics)*
> *on first date.*

Interestingly, some good news for women from the 80's: it seems sexual satisfaction for the female was on the upswing with one-third more ladies claiming satisfaction in the mid-80's than in the early 70's. Bitching and complaining get the male straining!

But Hite and most of her feminazis in kind were simply marching to the victimization tune that's still so popular today, accusing men of behaving badly.

> *Libbers lying through their teeth, but for the men*
> *can there be relief?*

Getting better sex is perhaps the greatest result for *some* females from this pervasive assault on males and the forcing of men towards females' melodramatic, affected bathos, nostalgia and romanticism.

Now, if males are struggling in our "evolving" economy, then to get relief through female loving, a male sometimes probably needs to get down and endure this sexual training. But it's a Lilith brain above, deceiving even herself that it is she who knows the way beyond sex. And making puppy-dog harmless men into exaggerated new-age males, sensitive but financially *broke,* well, it is another brazen *joke.* Keeping Lilith satisfied is going to get masochistic, and guys are deserving their coming punishment if settling for a measured mommy's praise, and she doing the tucking of their body into her *bed*—won't this eventually make them sick in the *head?* Because economics really rules over and above intimacy for most women.

In the mid-90's, X-rated video-movie rentals would rise to $665 million a year in the USA, according to *Playboy* magazine. Further, the number of Americans using phone sex would be a quarter of a million people per night, spending close to a *billion dollars* annually for their auditory launchings. In a year, the porno industry would actually take in about eight billion dollars from magazines, peep shows, adult-cable programming, videos and computer porn.[8] And that number is growing every day. By 2001, the chances that a movie released in the USA was pornographic: nine in ten.[9]

Lilith Fair

Each year, for the girls around twenty and the boomers led by Hillary—they were reminded of their gender at the Lilith Fair. Historically, the angel Lilith, said to have been the biblical Adam's first wife, had asserted independence and she claimed respect for an "individual" life. She returned as she pleased to Adam and he, possessed by her powers, had to bend to her. He was disposable. She was seen as at least the "equal" to Adam. She had a revengeful and demonic aspect to her assertiveness, as well as a creative and positive side. She carried a grudge, it goes, because God punished her for not returning to Eden.

Lilith represents the elitist woman and the winner over woman as mother-and-wife. She is often hailed as the creator of life and she wants sex. Although agent, enchanting actress and snake-corrupter goddess *extraordinare,* she's like a capitalist individual in her *despair,* as she chooses loneliness over subservience while still furbishing her character and brains, her perspective, with trapping technique.

Corrupting, devouring and attacking, this female Lilith does so much with such flare that moving up the corporate ladder now seems to her a natural aspiration. But the question is whether the image of girls kicking ass, being man-like, is another trip into fantasyland: the CEO at Avon is on high heels?

Some statistics don't encourage women to compete head-to-head with males—at your leisure check the politicians' and CEO's gender. And training the men to be emotionally acute and astute actually will only free them from the exclusive *reappointments* on the couch of "her" *anointments.*

Sex as a Weapon

Further aggressive modeling by women was featured throughout the 90's as the whole country sunk into subservience to the God Market and market economics. (GM & ME!)

The postmodern ethos of the *individual* and the belief in personal *power* as the cornerstone for the satisfaction of human desire now brought the ladies to believe that using sex as a weapon was just what they ought to do. Isn't flat-out sexual harassment of males permitted in our present overwhelmingly feminized society?

Many men are besieged—whistled way back into the recesses of their hot minds, loving to see the nakedness, but frustrated in the death days of the AIDS virus. As the saying goes—*the mind can hurt the male if he ain't getting any tail.* He's generally not like her, somehow not as free to experiment endlessly without an edge of shame, guilt or feelings of irresponsibility. And to him it's not *just* sex!

But look at the proud hard bodies and the revealing sex objects that strut and *preen*, pretending that they are not even *seen!* It is an awesome and freaky girl-thrill for many to walk the *block* knowing every male's eyes sway to the metronome of the *buttock*. And she thinking: *"die you bastards* dreaming that my special incarnation would brake to consider the needs of your brain snake." That's the torture masochists are used to. Masochists allow it and they feed off it. Hissing in contempt, the hard body of today may stare you straight in the *eye* and deliver her total *lie:* "Wearing revealing clothing is not an invitation to be stared at!" What? Wilt Chamberlain, the icon on the basketball court, gave his honest reply: *sex is life man.*

The 1990's crushed many males as women were told that men were really the weaker sex, because they were universally powerless over their desire for the female body. Furthermore, female sexuality was to be considered the greatest motivating force in the world. Take, covet sexual power.... Revolutions in revolutions....

The *numbed abstraction* that university lecturer Andrea Dworkin criticizes as the essence of the male gaze, aka the male *supremist capitalist pornographic exploiting* gaze, and homage to the female form, well, today young girls are being taught "to wear this outfit too." Yes, they are learning, encouraged through mainstream magazines, how to use this numbed abstraction to generate pleasure by watching *pornography.* It's surprising the objectifying mind took so long—must have been their conditioning, or purity consciousness holding them back, their Female Moral Superiority (FMS) still in drag, or something. Or the fact that an angel image, although still effective, isn't so needed anymore. The older image of woman, as morally superior, as an idealized goddess that needed protection—the mother and the source of life—this image had in the past got the men under women's control. But today, men become disposable and more redundant economically. Without men close by them, and because men have been demonized, trashed and marginalized, many women will try to imitate masculinity themselves. But sadly the genes aren't there, the testosterone levels are low and men's visual fetishistic sexual stimulation won't be assimilated. So a new animal is uncouthly being formed, assembled, a female mutant that thinks to appropriate opposite-sex characteristics as though she was on another shopping spree.

McBeal, Wurtzel and Company

Now is the female to offer up her soul and her emotive, feeling, vulnerable femaleness, onto the altar of individual self-sufficiency in this hardened, selfish and competitive market economy? Wasn't she the one who could come undone and break the lock of male mentality within her humid currents and help make her partner sagacious and suave, balanced-out and more at peace? Looks like a loser, as the emotive female is now a laughable frivolous neurosis who must snap out of her emotionality and get back to work. She's got a *job*, and there's no time to *sob*.

Always looking for her soul mate, her emotional needs twist the choice of candidates as they strut or fret their interview. But she's not lucking *out*; maybe she doesn't know anymore what the big score would really be *about*. So she fantasizes, complains and gets known as a silly bitch. Right out there and in a modern, very nervous vein, she endlessly searches for her one true love. There is such a nostomantic itch, a repressed need (and sex) to feed. But it's network soap-opera socialization (SOS) and *insane*, this McBeal-like *drain*.

Bitch. In the late 90's *Bitch: In Praise of Difficult Women* arrived, a book attempting to give females permission to proceed being emotional and unaccountable and to answer only to themselves. Go ahead, throw fits, say total nonsense, all this blends into a bitch – a totally self-interested consumer, hysterical perhaps, or un-reliable, but self-centered and thinking she's independent of what men think or want. As the author, Elizabeth Wurtzel, says: "It's about how nice it must be to just decide I will not be nice, I am never sorry, I have no regrets: what is before me belongs to me."[10] Wurtzel says this attitude is "second nature" to men...."It's as much in their atmosphere as snow is in the Eskimo's." All over the world men are "shouting orders and being impossible," says Wurtzel. And women are "hewing to these creatures' wills." The author of *Bitch* finds "the few women who manage to completely spit in the face of such an arrangement are naturally heroic." The "bitch philosophy" means "to do what I want."[11]

Although Wurtzel deserves credit for her courage to say it as she sees it, and for laying out her own personal details and confessions in the open, *Bitch* is too much a one-way street paved with reactive temper, and some blatantly false characterization. To Wurtzel, Mary Wollstonecraft "felt that there was no reason that only the men should be allowed to have all the fun. She wanted to live in sin and fuck around with all the other utopian philosophers...."[12] Wurtzel only sees Mary as a right-on, foot-stomping, self-actualized and very together woman, who viewed her husband and all other husbands, as only "a convenient part of the furniture of the house." Wurtzel claims that Wollstonecraft believed "that a woman is not defined by her relationship to a man,"[13] even though Wollstonecraft had tried to commit suicide over her relationship with a man.

Bitch promotes the bitch as a role model, as icon and as idea. "What we all want is to cop the cosmetic attitude," says its attractive author, Elizabeth Wurtzel.[14] Her face seductively adorns the book's front cover as she looks over her naked shoulder, painted lips open, framed eyes dressed and digging right into her audience. The bitch realizes that "it isn't the blondes who have more fun—it's the Sluts."[15]

Bitches are real Wurtzel says, because "at this point in time, it is no longer possible to fantasize a good girl who's not also a bad girl, it is impossible to think of Mary Magdalene and the Virgin Mary as anything other than one and the same...they are just different forms of intensity."[16] Life is intensity? Maybe for the emotionally high strung. A female rock star lately remarks that her life energy actually is drawn out of her nervousness. Has our society become so feminized that we *think* of all women equally, just because they are women - whether prostitutes or saints? Why Wurtzel ignores natural gender differences is a mystery. To her, are women supposed to be emotionally hardened, or perhaps underdeveloped, just like the accused men?

Bitchiness, Subjectivity and Unaccountability. *Bitch* represents the postmodern adulation of subjectivity, of nowness and of a person's creative *choice* in how one understands it all.

Everything is flying around in chaos—with the media lying, salespeople spinning, films fantasizing, politicians seducing. So trying for authenticity is beyond many people's capacity. The business of earning a living doesn't allow all the time needed to clear the smokescreens, get at the truth, and to hold the phoneys up to justice. Thus, in a form of self-defense, the female inclination to *subjectivity,* towards paying attention to the interior, personal and feelings-centered details in contrast to focus on the exterior details of society's management, control and direction has now become the worldview of the moderns. It's a form of escape from facing up to the reality that the 'enduring truths' about America are, in fact, fiction, propaganda. It leaves the search for objective truth behind.

Just as the nineteenth-century woman subordinated theology to sentimental literature, then debased rules and laws in favor of a feelings-approach to life, today a world has arisen, one that highly values *psychic relationships* between "individuals," relationships that occur in the present or within a short period of some part of a lifetime. History is dying—everything happens at or near the subjective *now.*

The monopolized TV networks ask the uninformed population to just phone in *their* opinion to them about major world problems. Then when they run their personalized war coverage, it comes from embedded reporters traveling in the military units. The subjective experience of the group the reporters are traveling with is all that is really being captured. Then TV allows soldiers' wives and girlfriends to be brought front and center. The "sweetheart" stories, of course, are all subjective. But this sentimentality brings women onside, and gives the feminine-subjective experience a big boost.

Sympathy abounds, but ironically many a cruelty or crime is shrugged off, because how would one be able to really understand what *subjective* torment caused the crime? Although this subjectivity is female-friendly and is feeling—and emotion—centered, it is also used to avoid responsibility. The moderns are constantly asked to see the world through someone else's eyes, whether it's Bill Clinton's, the boxing judge's who said the loser really won or the perpetrators of crimes that stand behind their slick legal troops.

Life then plays out as a live dramatic psychic event. The event is people and their dysfunctional relationships. It's the soap opera as all!

Painting on the Bitchiness. Wurtzel's *Bitch* gives the nod to the cosmetics industry for enabling women to paint on their bitchiness. Beginning in 1994 with Chanel's blood-black nail polish called Vamp, Wurtzel says the industry has brought to market additions, such as Very Vamp and Vamp-colored mascara "for that bloodshot, bloodless bad-girl look."[17]

The names used to sell the cosmetic products: *Wicked*, for Essie's nail polish, *Vixen*, for Revlon's lips and nail color, *Seduction*, for Maybelline's varnish, all invoke predatory agendas in the consumer. Subjectivity yearns for immediate power over others. Whether good or evil. Some shades are even named after ideas and concepts: Diva, Naughty, Racy, Fatale. Temptress, an inexpensive line of products, calls its dark shades by the names of legendary bad girls like Circe and Delilah.

Reading *Bitch* the thought arises: are the ladies, those out shopping the malls, checking out the items for sale, getting a message the cosmetic retailers seem to be sending: *Good Girls go to Heaven, but bad girls go everywhere?* Are women hard-working bitches, as Naomi Campbell called herself when she said "life is too short—you have to go for it"? Wurtzel says "to hell with dignity." She thinks Anita Hill is "a good girl if ever there was one," and that Princess Diana behaved with "perfect restraint and dignity for years."[18]

Staying the Bitch Course. Women are seen by Wurtzel as, "the repository of aeons of bad blood, beginning with Eve."[19] But even if they act decently, she says the world would still pick on them, find them bad. She wants to empower woman to stay the bitch course.

But isn't this just the victim-dictum again and a woman's excuse for unaccountability and low expectations? *Bitch* attempts to give women the lust to become self-made, and to stay totally independent and free. Too many women decide, Wurtzel says, after brief bitching and butt-kicking, to be nice. She wants the package, the whole enchilada and encourages women to see they shouldn't:

> "go along with the fiction that the world would
> have you believe and adhere to: that you ought

> to settle and be careful and accept the crumbs that are supposed to pass for a life, this minimized self you are supposed to put up with, that feminism and other political theories of woman cannot really begin to address because this is about something else entirely...Because, frankly, I have a tough time feeling that feminism has done a damn bit of good if I can't be the way I am and have the world accommodate it on some level."[120]

Sure, much of feminism can't address the main problem because fighting this gender war is a distraction from the main problem—the neo-con's corporate fascism that seeks to divide and rule by provoking the gender war.

Sex as a Weapon. Wurtzel admits, "Women have long held a near-monopoly on artistic villainy...we seem to be built for cattiness," and she almost admits to using sex as a weapon—but if she does admit it, would she be a double-crosser, a traitor? She thinks that men project "any idea, any neurotic impulse or erotic fantasy, onto her person, because she is the parallax view, the human Rashomon—because she [woman] is either that beguiling or that empty. Doesn't matter which is true."[21] Wow, is *that* womanpower? Then *Bitch's* author lets it all come off: "these days putting one's pretty power, one's pussy power, one's sexual energy out there for popular consumption no longer makes you a bimbo—it makes you smart."[22] And Elizabeth Wurtzel is sticking to the feminist lesson: *"no woman should ever lose her mind over a man, a woman needs a man like a fish needs a bicycle."* [23]

In the 90's women became in one sense equal to men at last, because both were obsessed with carrying out, and working for their living, working separately. And ever more apart the sexes could grow. Women's discontent and restlessness is in relating to a lack of emotional intimacy and is from letting the big picture—capitalism's social prison—slip from focus.

Women's sexual satisfaction didn't use to come in indiscriminate couplings. It wasn't just an orgasm, usually, for herself that she sought. Her nature has developed differently on this planet Earth. But with AIDS and male-bashing degradation compliments of those like Andrea Dworkin, and with popular culture increasingly anti-male, women are encouraged to pass on, go for a *career*. Later, a hubby she might get or what the heck, just incubate the little *dear*—her baby—that will bring some real emotion, and make her life *sincere*.

Uprising

So the thirteen-year olds around the mid-90's, these young girls intuited there mothers dirt-bag male bashing wasn't perhaps all that was happening. And the Spice Girls gave them more, more, more sex appeal—and then Backstreet Boys came in on their *knees,* pleading to the teenyboppers to let them *please*. The dynamic changed somewhat from the cold shoulder that the feminazis gave to the men, and it seemed headed toward a more realistic and natural, and less a mental focus than that of the femzies. And one more appreciative of heterosexual relationships.

The femzies tried to choke the new-wave girls on their flashback 50's retro-sex glue: victims, flowers, date rape, anti-pornography, office sex-harassment, women as needing protection, and women as morally superior, even as puritans. The 60's rev-women broke decorum and asked for an end to the double standard, asking for equal treatment. But by the 90's it's again the opposite as workplace categories of sexual harassment had begun to return women to the status of *hothouse plants*, the status of delicate flowers, who must be protected from the males.

Women in the 60's said they could handle male swearing, etc., that they were equals, weren't they? In the 90's the half-naked female slides into the workplace.

> *She's in denial,*
> *But inciting male attention,*
> *And aggressive male response, no matter how right-on and real,*
> *He's in the house of detention.*
> *So she's all dressed up, for that?*
> *Female sado-masochism all right, now projected unto the male hack,*
> *She's got police connections, they'll maybe come and break his back*
> *If she says he says anything about her sexy rack,*

A lot of moaning rises and twines to the lop-eared,
But this is from being alone, deluged and weird,
The scope is getting limited for a woman that can feel,
And the lack of dates is sometimes almost surreal.
Life more and more only as an isolated consumer
Is the future for the children of the female boomer

Spice Girls

The Spice Girls are so vulnerable high up on rubber heels, but still push stuff like sister-power—*sisters are doing it*—upon the public. And they taunt men—*if you wanna be my lover*—and—*I want a man, not a boy who thinks he can.* And their dancers, just like Madonna's, throw male dancers to the ground. But their message is also that women are "girls", no matter what their age might be. "Girl" should mean a young person, someone still growing up and learning, someone not fully accountable. As "girls" women remain much less accountable.

Brash, bratty, in seeming self-control, the Spice Girls have got tons of money from their talent. And they've brought sex back and modified it as less of a female-superiority thing. They don't dominate and insult men quite like Mad Donna did. It's pretty well the same act as Mad Donna (Madonna), just lighter, and this is some relief. And the Backstreet Boys sucking up makes it rather complete.

Spicers telling young girls in their global audiences that now it's *OK to do it,* is refreshing and gives hope that the genders will get together, have experiences loving and sexing, just like their natural-born ancestors. How real—actually living in one's body! But it's wiggle power all right, hips thrusting, boobs-as-bums flashbacks—as well as total heat, cosmetic supermarket splash.

But the insult still prevails to those who are male: *If ya can't dance, you can't do nutt'n for me baby*. And in a Spice video a woman physically assaults a man, repeatedly. *She knows exactly what to do with men like you*. Pushing the envelope, the Spicers' ask *what part of "no" don't you understand?* Mad Donna always pushed gays at the males, snickering and getting uplift, whereas the Spice aren't that mean, content to threaten in sweet tones and dissemble behind the image of a baby doe. To the Spicers, women are tender, well-dressed sex objects, needing protection and education. It's still about learning, being educated—the great opiate of the masses—as the Spicers' siren pleads saying: *I need to know the way to feel to keep me satisfied.*

But then it's *shake it to the right, shake it to the left* and *get down deeper and down.* Non-Spice Girls experience the pleasure of envy. Female esteem zooms as the multi-millionairesses exclaim to the teen fans and their aging moms: *You're a superstar, that's what you are. That is no lie.* Superstars with sex, with a bitching attitude towards men who must do as they want, or else, no poontang!

With Mad Donna the game was largely just a game of dress-up. Mad Donna had clothed the girls in anger, in an 80's economy of low expectations, and she outfitted them with attitude to torture the boys as somehow responsible. Sex wasn't good then, as Mad Donna cuddled with the homosexuals, encouraged masturbation and lesbianism and demanded basic contempt for males.

But with the Spice Girls at least the female enchantress was back, women obviously claiming power through heterosexual sex and demanding attitude in return. Can the Spicers be held guilty for obtaining "illicit sway"? Mary Wollstonecraft would say so. Do they debase themselves by their exertions to appropriate sway?

Spicers do ask the men for the truth, their truth, what women really want: *I'm giving you everything. All I want is the promise you will be there*—and probably in the protector-provider role. But it's the role that's disappearing. Women are brought up to be obsessed with careers and independence from men. Some say women have been psychologically neutered, encouraged as they are to go for careers and sex instead of families and marriage. And the guys are beginning to avoid the feminazis blitzes infesting every nook and cranny of social life. Men stay home, watch TV, and fly the websites.

> *He's on the internet—confused and off-balance*
> *Without his hero status, not in any most-excellent sexual dalliance.*

But the Quaker man of celibacy is unlikely to arise, there's too much *porn* the imagination will *adorn*. And pleasure is an antidote to the social insanity, and to our detachment from a natural inclination towards really getting the most out of life. Much of life is left in denial and deformation—the nation tuned into the official, politically correct version.

How can the males now be really who they are, deeply, with integrity and in a spirit inspired to create what the heart and soul desire when they are surrounded by all the selfish lobby groups, the longhair slippery agendas, the lies and disinformation on TV and in the media, and the gender feminists' reactive egalitarian rage? How can a real man still get free?

Spicers empower when they say to get it on and do it, but then there is something so important added to their message: ...*you've got to make it real, come freak out, lose control, it's time to free what's in your soul.* Now this giving up on control and the encouragement to go through the letting-go fear, knowing you're certain to emerge in a enigmatic psyche that's vaguely perceived as wild and insecure, one not very well-known today, but scary and *contraire* to early instruction, this is top drawer!

This is positive for males. And another feminist woman now sings of *sweet surrender* and of this surrender being *all she has to give*. A bit shocking, this expression, after grunge and Alannis-hyped rage, distrust, anger and frustration in relating to the males. Now this *sweet surrender* twitches the nerves a tad. Improvement? More female and more emotional, and more truthful?

The Spice Girls brought in a more needy female, a heterosexual man-loving type and this has helped to moderate the rigid consensus ideology of gender prevalent in the atmosphere—the political correctness, the stereotyping that has been keeping the boys and girls, men and women, away from each other. One small organic step, down from Western society's on-high female throne, and also down from the power pedestal of dominating lust, the sex-as-a-weapon not so in-your-face, as four-part harmony delicious tones begin to sweetly coo:

> "*I wanna make love to ya baby.*
> *Get your spirit free, it's the only way to be.*
> *I had a little love, now I'm back for more.*"

12
You've Gone a Long Way Baby

Until the nineteenth century, most European societies were structured hierarchically in the feudalistic model with royalty, land-owning nobles and church authorities ruling over small-scale artisans, merchants and peasants. (Just as it is today minus the spin.) With the French revolution, a social and political turn was believed to have occurred. Western democracy was said to have swept away feudal control of society. Mary Wollstonecraft lived in those times, and she became the first equity feminist.

Wollstonecraft
Mary Wollstonecraft (1759-1797), a champion of those oppressed, sat down and wrote out *A Vindication of the Rights of Women*. France was in the glow of the French Revolution and inflamed in the brilliance of its so-called enlightenment ideas—democracy, equality, fraternity, with *reason* allied with *humanism*. These ideas were publicized and cried up. In those times it was thought that *progress* would bring redemption. Then the release of mankind's potential would finally be accomplished. And together, humanism and reason would tackle man's social, political and economic problems. Then, with the benefit of social welfare, real progress could be made. Or so it was believed.

Mary's instant bestseller was to become the keystone of modern feminism. Certain that it was *domestic tyranny* denying the females their place in the *sun,* Mary said the laws had made prostitution legal simply through marriage itself, and they must be *undone!*

Women were jailed in their homes: "confined in cages, like the feathered race," Wollstonecraft said. And then: "It is true they are provided with food and raiment, for which they neither toil or spin; but health, liberty and virtue are given in exchange."[1] Mary called for universal co-education and a woman's right to work in the trades. Again: "How many women thus waste life away, who might have practiced as physician, regulated a farm, managed a shop, and stood erect supported by their own industry, instead of hanging their heads."[2]

Mary asserted that "every person may become virtuous by the exercise of its own reason." To Mary, education could "enable the individual to attain such habits of virtue as will render it independent. In fact, it is a farce to call any being virtuous whose virtues do not result from the exercise of its own reason."[3] This, of course, was before the anti-modern trashing of reason!

But what today is lamented over, the disappointment of the failed marriage of humanism and reason, was once a union held up as the future hope for mankind. People believed reason would lead to goodness.

Reason, Mary believed, would reform women. Near the end of the eighteenth century, Mary had said that the *way* women were treated, and "the regal homage which they receive is so intoxicating, that until the manners of the times are changed, and formed on more reasonable principles, it may be impossible to convince them that the illegitimate power which they obtain by degrading themselves is a curse."[4]

Mary observed that women "are notoriously fond of pleasure."[5] If they weren't given opportunity to develop their minds they would sink into the sensual—"it is not the enchantment of literary pursuits, or the steady investigation of scientific subjects, that leads women astray from duty." And let's remember Mary's analysis of women's downfall: "No, it is indolence and vanity—the love of pleasure and the love of sway, that will reign paramount in an empty mind."[6] She said: "For whilst wealth renders a man more respectable than virtue, wealth will be sought before virtue; and, whilst woman's persons are caressed, when a childish simper shows an absence of mind—the mind will lie fallow."[7]

Mary Wollstonecraft felt that women were "by ignorance rendered foolish or vicious" – this was "not to be disputed." She looked forward to "a *revolution* in female manners" to improve mankind. When Mary had called women slaves, she had meant it in only "a political and civil sense; for indirectly they obtain too much power, and are debased by their exertions to obtain illicit sway."[8]

Anthony and Cady Stanton

That the inspiration for the US women's rights movement for over the last 100 years came from Susan B. Anthony (1820-1906) and Elizabeth Cady Stanton (1815-1902) gives some insight into the kind of movement it is today—*She's got the kids, the house, the furniture, car, computer, dishes, even the tools, and her lawyer is after the rest, whatever is left, your wages, pictures, grampa's old war chest.* She's got the kids; he's got what? Money, she hopes.

The movement's legacy today is the legal system of the "owners" is now swimming with gender feminist sharks. The judiciary and political power has gone pro-feminist, suffering males to heel, to take the lumps as boomer women win big. Their troops are infiltrating all the bureaucracies, assuming positions of authority, and then dictating an agenda biased against the male. Stories of unbelievable devastation—to men—prove that marriage may not be heaven, and home may be in fact just where the heart dies.

The agenda of Anthony and Cady Stanton and the movement's basically upper-class membership brimmed with issues about racial abuse, inspired by the Negroes' predicament, and they campaigned effectively for the abolition of slavery. But male-bashing received an early boost, and soon it's *women* who began claiming to be the abused.

Cady Stanton drew up the *Seneca Falls Declaration of sentiments* in 1848. Here this mother of eight reveals the sperm-seed holders as the enemy: "The history of mankind is a history of repeated injuries and usurpation on the part of man toward women, having in direct object the establishment of an absolute tyranny over her."[9] And of course she believes men and women are created *equal*. Pro-activist campaigning from Liz and Suzie, yielded results. They demanded divorces, attacked violence, dumped on drunkenness, condemned wife-rape, and promoted the removal of domestic tyrant husbands.

But the burden of children, they thought, kept them all from being even more successful. Of the main activists, only Anthony was without children. But it's men, according to her campaign partner Cady Stanton, who have "endeavored in every way" that they could, "to destroy her [women's] confidence in her own powers, to lessen her self-respect, and to make her willing to lead a dependent and abject life."[10]

Although Anthony and Cady Stanton spoke for abolitionism and lived it—Cady Stanton married an abolitionist—*both opposed the 15th amendment to give black males the vote* after the Civil War! Why? Well, it didn't give the vote to women. And here their main meal—themselves! Deserting in self-interest, away they went, not supporting others and their need to know compassion. But wasn't this the female special talent to show, this emotion of nurturance, a life-support beam that's underneath so the heart can grow? The closed door left sisterhood more egocentric, lacking compassion for social injustices that occurred around them. The ladies would walk away again and again from partnerships, so often that it would even be seen as a survival skill to be so focused in corporeality.

But what's behind all the hue and cry about the oppression of women, their quest for equality—for the vote for instance? In the nineteenth century Victorian women had mobilized and successfully campaigned for reforms. They had brought in changes in the area of matrimonial law in the 1850's, and in educational opportunities in the 1860's and 1870's. By 1880 women could get a medical education and practice medicine in the UK. Female benefit and reform in property ownership, child custody rights and government regulation of sexual morality all took place from 1850 onwards. The vote for women was one of the last major campaigns. While it may seem surprising, many Victorian women opposed having the vote. Many argued that women's causes and interests were already being well represented by men. Other women wanted no part of something so degrading as politics.

But just when did men themselves get the vote? In our highly educated society, does anyone know the answer to this question? Very, very few, and that's because this knowledge would hurt the elites who want to bury their selfish, aggressive capitalism behind a smoke screen of feminism and prefer women at war with men. The information would explode a lot of hot air that's keeping the balloon of women's claimed mistreatment floating above our propaganda culture.

It wasn't until the end of World War I that the majority of European countries allowed all men to vote. That's in 1918! In most countries of the world women received the vote at the same time as men, or within a few decades of men. Often the vote had been given only to those who owned property. Other restrictions had been religion, age and the payment of taxes. In the United Kingdom men over 21 years of age and women over 30 were given the vote in 1918. But by 1928 all women had the vote in the United Kingdom. In the U.S.A. women were imparted suffrage by the federal government in 1920, although some of the country's states had given them the vote long before in the previous century. For example, the women of Wyoming and Utah had the vote in 1869 and 1870 respectively.

Nietzsche and Feminism

Around 1880, Friedrich Nietzsche (1844-1900) had warned of the *feminism* around Europe, "the borification of Europe" he called it, the nineteenth century attempt to make men out of women. He advised that women were going to start educating men, specifically instructing them as to just what was allowed and what was not. To Nietzsche: "Woman is indescribably more evil than man; also cleverer."[11]

Goethe, Wagner and Lawrence

Writers, poets, psychologists and spiritual leaders had been promoting a feminine value system long before World War I. Johann Goethe (1749-1832), had many female fans; he finished the famous *Faust* with the words: *The Eternal-Feminine*. The musical works of Richard Wagner (1813-1883), symphony and opera, aimed to emancipate woman. And Wagner thought of woman as the redeemer herself. *The Flying Dutchman* prescribed woman as the cure for the restless, unstable men; in Wagnerian terms *she* redeemed him. Are these artists and their thoughts somehow dangerous to women, examples of a Western misogynist culture?

In Europe woman became a solution to Wagner and Goethe and their kind. In America feminization proceeded throughout all of the nineteenth century, and it further characterizes the evolving

American culture into and through the whole of the twentieth century. Why in the new millennium is there such a hue and cry for women to get something like a vote? It's democracy propaganda blown to the sky. Men don't vote, women don't vote; many don't, sometimes over half don't. Men usually got the vote at the same time or not long before women. Mysteriously the twentieth century would bring a wave of reactive attacking and finger-pointing by females against their hyped and perceived oppressors, the patriarchy, said to be withholding women's equal rights and undermining proper democratic society.

D.H. Lawrence (1885-1930) made a big fuss in the early twentieth century, pointing out the aim of female gender-power. He also tried to reveal the importance men needed to place on their choice of emotional-sexual outlets. In the sexual revolution of the 60's the new generation missed the depth of Lawrence's warnings to men, many probably relating instead to his erotic passages to excite libidinous pursuit.

Throughout the twentieth century emotional therapy grew as women's needs came to the forefront. Featuring: women's rights, along with "oneness," nurturance, sensitivity training, multiple orgasms, relationship workshops, divorce procedure, pre-natal bonding, erotic-sensual sex education, women's protection, child custody and day care *and* mother-hen moralism from a puritan hangover—all combined while male action became vilified.

Democracy has become promoted as all about equal rights. This really attracts females. Sharing and caring are said to be at home in democracy. The *enduring truths* are recycled in the schools and in the media about America's mission in the world. The focus here is on democracy and its humanism. Feminist rhetoric that identifies the group as what matters is corrupted. Female characteristics—nurturance, feelings, inclusion—are then pasted onto the definitions of democracy. And "feminist" humanism is glorified as virtually godly.

A new-age *journey to the East* had quieted down many potential male "activists," as they went meditating inside their skulls, listening to sea sounds, whatever. Good skills indeed. But the owners (masters) had just pulled off another robbery while the men were out. The rich cats, having split the scene years ago, live offshore, don't pay taxes, hire politicians and eliminate annoyances.

Today the masses get the placebo *thought-tonic* of democracy. They are just the up-to-date version of the serfs and the rabble that used to annoy royalty. Today the masses *think* they have democracy, liberty and the rest. This class gets lip service and promises. The country's politicians may pretend to advocate civil rights, warming up the female appetite for humanism. It may sound like social progress but it is just all more bushwa ballyhoo. Always, it seems the debilitated, dependent underclass is bossed around by the land-owning aristocracy and their military hitmen.

Second-wave Feminism

In 1960, the *bought* corporate press reported that women of middle class America had been using *sex* as a means to *identity,* and that they were motivated to get more from life than what they saw as their mother's meaninglessness. Sex itself was said to be one of the few enjoyments in their otherwise bleak lives; thus the women hoped to "discover some genuine purpose in a new kind of personal-and- sexual relationship where they and their partners will be equals."

In 1966, the National Organization for Women (NOW) had been formed in Washington, DC. It lobbied President Johnson to include *women* in his Great Society program for the *underprivileged and excluded.* Underprivileged and excluded! Wow for NOW? NOW's president was a psychologist, and NOW gained growing support within the protest-conscious society of the early-adult boomer generation.

And in 1968 Miss America was zapped! The annual beauty contest was invaded by a guerrilla theater as women poured into New York from all over the eastern US and Canada. A *sheep* was crowned Miss America, and the Freedom Trash Can set up outside the contest hall was for the disposal of objects that made slaves out of women—false eyelashes, wired-cup bras, girdles, dishcloths. Here is where the bra-burning women's libbers emerged. And women who were seen actually *attacking* society caused minds to blow. The whole structure of society had coerced most women because it served so many of women's needs and agendas. But on the real right track, looking for humanistic social change, how could these female freedom fighters ever look back and begin again just blaming men? But by the late 60's they began female-only corporate hunkering down.

And they saw the male as the oppressor,
And wanted more the role of the aggressor.
The "speaking bitterness" meetings were anti-male;
The atmosphere of self-survival did prevail,
Somehow the meme so popular in that day,
Was of women's independence being the only way!

By 1973 there were over 2,000 islands of refuge for females in the women's liberation directory in the USA.

The 1970's fully inaugurated the market-method monster, as popular members of the intelligentsia heralded humanity's new savior, "the market," with a peculiar self-righteousness. For some, in a jungle-out-there-society, it is like a Dershowitzian wasteland: professional mouthpieces working their intellects into a blaming tizzy and wrestling with their self-righteous ego-solutions. Their rational exercise yard, their forum, is often the TV room. Here lawyers ply their trade, at home in the meme gymnasium. But some of these mental manipulators are racked, too, with their own personal suffering. *And distanced by anger and called sinners, they were told they were cast out of the promised land because of God's anger.* Because hate can be a pleasure, some let anger rule. It gave them focus.

At times any idea of order is felt a blessing. For many, "the market" would give organization to the persecution zone called *life*, and a solution to their fears and doubts surrounding human vulnerabilities. Survival of the fittest, that's what it boils down to. Competition, war, people alone in the "jungle". Regression, not evolution. It's the lifestyle permeating the 'descended grid' that the worship of science has brought. Alienated castaways could find great meaning in money and refuge in marketplace ideology, plus *justification* for their self-absorbed psychopathological projections. And many were provoked by the hostility of market economics (ME).

Used to being hurled around by the ruling elite, the persecuted boomers became trained to seek salvation from the God Market (GM). It was their grab for financial power, the big reach for satisfaction. The market methods gave them a right to be mean and cruel to others. The linear rationality of market economics meant business ran like a military operation. Winning became hyped as everything. Ethics was pushed to the margins. With a controlled media, people forgot history: the lessons of the past. It was the subjective *now*, and the profit in the "now" that mattered. Short term, abstract, preferably instant and commercialized answers were sought. In the war zone of earning a living! If economic rationality is believed to be the natural force that will bring order to society, then people's responsibility for their own actions is lessened. *They were on their hairless knees, and Bob Dylan in their minds swished the tune of the times—"you gotta serve somebody."*

Back in 1970, the women's liberation movement really took off in America. A strike to mark the fiftieth anniversary of the 19th amendment giving women the right to vote found the support for the women's strike to be enormous. Since the early 60's many revolutionary females in the vanguard had been fighting the tyranny of home and family, believing that it was here that their slave status was realized. Domestic tyranny was keeping women trapped behind doors, mothering and catering to men, it was said.

New Feminism

Feminism had become very powerful as a result of the social reformation riots of the late 60's, and in the 70's a new woman appeared. Full of envy, and whether radical, socialist or liberal this female wanted *more*—freedom, equality and power. She was mentally prepared for change thanks to the consciousness-raising victories of the counterculture in the 60's and the early greening of America. But back then, in the sixties, female students and young adults immersed in humanism had stood together. They protested against the rising tide of state capitalist autocracy, corporate power's hegemony gained through government control, that had been growing since the end of World War II, when *political leadership* had set out "to win the everlasting battle for the minds of men."

By the 80's, the women's libbers had jumped into the shark pool of shock, where progressive, liberal worker-based humanitarianism was being devoured, the fodder fattening the few bigwigs, the manductory vertebrates guarding and in control of this business world. Victims of the reasons of their times, these second-wave feminists tried to put into practice what the "experts" had uncovered, and they tried to be up to date and modern in their behavior. And the pied piper said looking out for "number one" was all there was, and thoughts of social responsibility were fraudulent and unpatriotic. Suckered to think that their own socialization had really been to blame and that it had made women servants to men, the feminists were then wet-nursed, suckled under the GM to believe in only ME. The women were re-programmed, *re-memed*, socialized anew, but likewise humanism got *reamed* too....

So second-wave feminism had jumped right into bondage, believing in submission underneath the omnipotent force of a market economy. All social organization, cultural creativity and public services were now thought to be given direction through interdependence with *unregulated* "free market" commerce. But does passivity before market economics, an abstraction, and a fear-related ideology, produce the evidence that the new entrepreneurial women were manifesting what Freud had called innate feminine masochism?

The temper of those times when Freud lived had resembled what was ridiculed and railed against back in the mid-nineteenth century by the working class press: "the New Spirit of the Age: Gain Wealth, forgetting all but Self"—this a critical appreciation of runaway greed by Adam Smith (1723-1790). It's the same today.

> *So is this the world the females wanted so much*
>   *to have a piece of;*
> *To be players of merit*
> *And the power to inherit*
> *Through energy expended*
> *And affirmations unended?*

Hadn't John Stuart Mill (1806-1873) said that *conditioning* was all that kept equality away, and thus "the nature of women is an entirely artificial *thing*"?

Now, today "You Can Do It" echoes from high-pitched young female voices around the western world.

> *But just following instructions from mad-moms dictum,*
> *Many readily will fall once again into the role of*
>   *the victim.*

This is the time of the SS—sexy suits;
The haberdashery corporate power demands of
its recruits.

New hairdo, makeover and threads. Get lean, flash flesh, dazzle at least, try to attract, attention—eyes, lips, cheeks, brows and bone, lids, nails and toes, legs, breasts, butt, all together now, or one part at a time, whatever! Is it manipulation as natural as fresh air, as real as breathing?

For the gender feminists, as long as the males were seen as the problem, or the main force standing in the way of the females' route to success, they were laughing. They already knew that many males had limited understanding of females, could be placated or re-socialized, and were more in need of emotional support than they were a threat to a woman's self-actualizing. But as long as women think it's mainly men that are the problem there will be men who blame their roadblocks on women. The gender feminists would likely feel *any* power over the opposite gender is valuable, and at some point their devilish tactics will probably flush them out. What's the verdict going to be, for inciting and misleading people, and distracting them from more meaningful pursuits?

Divide and Rule

Divide and rule serves the masters, those picking the scripts, forcing the public into abstraction and into distraction. The masters, they've got the music (trust) and film (emotion) to fool with. Why not hire a doctor of behavior (Ph.D.) for maybe fifty grand, or hire a hundred of them, and let them doctor around with the public's behavior? Because the *angry beast* must be kept an observer, confused and apathetic—unless shopping! Then the public must be instructed, when bodies are needed for purchasing power, for volunteerism, and for war. And for proclaiming western society's superiority. Skilled cooks feed all-day chocolate to masses moved by music, sports and movies, none of which most of them perform in.

Now what if these fifty-grand-a-year brain bouncers making the movies began writing the "stuff" broadcast as news too? Well, the masters could probably get their cake-eating citizens to groove on anything. Things grow in manure all right, but eating it is not healthy. In current films every important political event in the world is interpreted, given a biased slant. This *shit for the birds* is airborne, global, legal.

For example, there is a movie about an American president's dating behavior, and a TV documentary about a male mass murderer growing breasts and ruling a prison (with pounds of cocaine, and "tons" of money, too). These movies and documentary commercials serve to ease up focus on Bill Clinton's promiscuous mania, and they raise money for better (more) prisons that don't have prisoners (mass murderers) in charge and snorting cocaine while locked up in the slammer.

Richard Speck was the mass murderer who died two months after being in the TV commercial for increased state-police power. Top of the class, that longhair, the one who came up with using Speck to raise money. In the US the number of people in jail or under judicial supervision *tripled* between 1980 and 1995. And from then to 2003 the jail population went up a further *25 percent*.[13] But if citizens can't believe what they read in the bought press and can't trust what they see in the bought media, what can they rely on?

An army-recruiting officer was heard to say that he'd never seen a woman with nail polish who didn't want to be saved. But is nail polish what she can depend on to attract life's meaningful directions?

The agenda for successful survival in the world *must* encompass human feelings. One cannot run on willpower alone, or idea power, without the link to vast areas of sensitivity that rule moment-by-moment, day-by-day. Thus one cannot fully live in reality without allowing *doubt* in—vulnerability, uncertainty and insecurity. It's the source of need and the wellspring for action, this doubt—doomed be they that neglect this room in the house that must stand the storms of time and terror.

> *Trust under this tree, traveling pilgrims and be free,*
> *Facilitating, giving room to grow, this is what love*
>   *gifts to those who know,*
> *This "me"-empowerment selfish dog eat doggy show*
> *Is keeping short life's loving span caught in the undertow.*

The Psychology Industry has increasingly shifted from asking questions to supplying answers (removing doubt). It has allowed itself to be shaped, influenced and directed by other powerful forces in society in order to gain its own prominence. And about half of the US's population had sought psychological service by 1999.

Today, the weight of many government safety nets for women and children take away doubt for women and give a type of security, as women are familiar with being helped-out as "victims".

Emotional Intelligence and Power

Why would women forsake their gift of emotional intelligence? To join the army? Society increasingly seems to want both genders to be seen as literally equal. This has been thoroughly rationalized, and the concept has become a belief to many. So should the "girls" get weaponized and contribute to the military just like the "boys"? In the US to get equal in the army, women must reach one and a half million dead in combat. So, yes, there is a ways to go. And especially in combat attitude, examples: many women show up pregnant when their naval ship is to be deployed; women have gone on sick call four times as often as men; women were accused of screwing up in the field and needing males to cover for them in the first Gulf War. It is said that men in the military think women receive easier assignments and undeserved promotion, often by offering sexual favors. The men resent that these women receive equal pay.[14]

> *Smart, smarter and smartest, take your pick:*
> *These women ain't facing killing when some dick,*
> *Some teenage bone-brain who's hazed-out from*
>   *sensitivity (himself)*
> *Can be relied upon to place his body on the shelf.*
> *Rolling slabs slide into a vacuum at the coroner's hall,*
> *The fighters for freedom mainly men, that's all.*

Casper Weinberger, former US Secretary of Defense: "I think women are too valuable to be in combat."[15] Really, where does that leave the men?

Well, anyone having trouble getting the picture? Or big Al Gore, like a bedmate stooge of the female Affirmative Action *coup d'état:* "Women and men are equal or more so," in year 2000! He was a male in *power*, and an enabler of Bill Clinton, who some snidely call the real first *female president* of the US.

Clinton got the "chicks' " vote all right: just as in business, it's money that matters, and ladies are down the road in no time—government as husband. Emotional intelligence works on monitoring voter *appeal* in modern society. Form over substance. Not issues, it's charisma that matters.

But some women want a piece of the war hero action, too. So it's possible to hear someone speak as Hillary Clinton did at the First Ladies Conference in El Salvador in 1998: "Women have always been the primary victims of war. Women lose their husbands, their fathers, their sons, in combat." Wow. Primary victims? This sounds pathetic.

In the greater picture, the system of the *owners*, well, here the women aren't equipped to really tear and scratch, kick butt and bitch, because in the past it's something they *never* really were supposed to do. They have, in general, always worked for the status quo. The more chauvinistic the society, the more it protects women. And therefore the more it limits women? That's what Mary Wollstonecraft got at—men took responsibility for their women, their wives, and were legally responsible for them too, and this, Mary said, would keep females from really living enriched lives, having careers and standing on their own two feet. Today the government is taking responsibility. A domineering government gathers momentum, grows, absorbs gender feminists, single moms, and many everyday women who increasingly look to government for direction, support and protection.

Roles of Women and Men

In the past, men and women likely decided that males would do most (but not all) of the killing and protecting, and females would cultivate a humbleness and modesty in deference, gleaned to honor and applaud the risk males faced. Maybe women saw the men's joy when the women dissimulated in respect for the men.

But women, with back-up from their churches, did eventually claim a moral superiority. And they seemed able to provide the antidote to brutal wars and competitions. "She" became a higher being, and her operating headquarters, the home, was then established in the modern mind (19th and 20th century) as being close to heaven. Home was even said to be *where the heart is.* Here atop their nest, supported by the religious authority in her society, women adorned themselves in ethereal fashion.

Humanism is what fathers hope their children receive from their mothers. Because of women's typically more empathetic and emotional nature, young females learn appreciated humanistic behaviors and are treated so differently from young boys. The demands of testosterone are unique—the chemical rush of maleness obvious, like *carnivorousness*. So conditioning is not all; the physical basics are given and they shan't be ignored.

Having a menstrual cycle is rad: major mood swings on the ocean of emotion; travelers becoming adept at dealing with physical, emotional and mental fluctuations, as the experience makes women resilient, sturdy, able to withstand and cope with much that would trouble a male. A period each month is a woman's apprenticeship into humanism, because she must cope with being overpowered, must learn to submit to and *deal* with feelings, emotion and distress—she can't always be in control.

Self-understanding

Self-understanding cannot be achieved only by command, although there are many consumers who seem to think it can. Modern western culture claims all sorts of individualistic power and prizes can be won by using rationalism to justify living selfishly: to swim with the sharks in business without being eaten alive; to use voyeur sex power without the fear, the doubt, of a real encounter for pleasure; to marginalize males and expect them to receive less support than females in society.

Rational excuses are everywhere, in addition to those from church and state, justifying all sorts of evil. Meanwhile the prevailing ideology of GM drives guilt and shame into anyone who isn't getting lucky in the market. Wordy explanations can freeze feelings and bring extreme denial of basic human hurt and vulnerability.

Rationality unmodified by common sense, imagination, memory and ethics can become just more cold blaming, scapegoating, sadism, masochism. Reasons usefulness is to modify, to humanize. But rationality and reason without influence from our other human qualities will leave people in conflict— locked in the mind's neurotic demand to be correct and to have all the ideological answers. Then people start discussions with their conclusions.

Is it her "personal truth" that is instructing her internal thought-control campaign drumbeats? Her anxiety, it's a weary weight as 'Mother' churns in the washing machine whirlpool, daunting. She's unsure, untried, desperate for schooling, and so the Bitch becomes rad today, now that cruelty is King.

New affirmations make up her mind's personas,
As she is schooled to imitate the owners,
Today's heroines train their thoughts to compete –
Males set up like bowling pins to swat off her market street.

Rationality sets up the stage on which the moderns sit inhaling notions about what their final conclusions should be, watching live on TV—the cops pound teenagers. This gets many of the kids and their single moms grooving on other people's tragedies, getting a superiority complex because the cops aren't booting through their front door and filming their arrest for the fraud they're living in.

IV
Rebound from Victimization

13
Wrainbashed

"I used to get harassed by men and feel guilty that I was bringing it on. Now with the veil, the harassment has stopped. I don't feel guilty. When you respect yourself...."

Zombie-like, beady-eyed alcoholic feeding upon his allergy, betwixt and between, enduring the ride on a flight gone out of control, the beat so easily marches to the tune of sexual exploitation. Sipping Bacchus's juices in Hedonism Hall, many a guy drinks to get laid. That would solve all his problems! Sexy stuff, guys have been brainwashed. Anything now becomes possible, while possibility excludes itself in the reach for more alcohol, and more. Until before unconsciousness some deed is done, or maybe not this time. But a 40-ounce bottle of booze, a 40-ouncer with legs, is on her way; she's got his number, and it's just a matter of time. Truly lives of desperation awaken out of this self-abuse. The body abandoned, left on the migration flight.

Yes, "she" is coming into many a guys' life, and she might look like the angel he's been praying for. He'll think she's the answer, for now. And she is, if he's been lining up for drugged sacrifice and torture.

What he thought the answer to the problem of loneliness, boredom, that part of life he felt he should have, he could have with a fun-time relationship partner,... well, it's all become like a movie he's watching while he's on drugs. He's become a heavy loader dumping booze down gullets. Observing, but not really discerning. Ever since Einstein the notion of relationship, like, you know, the relativity feature, is rad. A relationship will not save him.

Well, at least not the ones he's finding out here, Bud.

Drugs

But why do you men even consider romantic relationships? Because you are restless, wanting more out of your life, disappointed in your failure to be at peace. Something tells you that there is something wrong somewhere. The legalization of drugs in our society enables a cover-up. Citizens reach for booze to blot out suffering. Then a relationship may be grabbed to blot out hangover angst.

It doesn't have to be this way. The underlying discomfort, anxiety and alienation—these fears can be tackled head-on without drugs. But drugs are glamorized; everyone's doing it. It's socially acceptable, and the government makes a fortune. The drug business...30 percent of Russian government revenue?

And once on drugs your world is changed. A cycle begins and it will never end...unless it is terminated. In a sub-world, you float gleefully at first, where desire is satisfied. But once thwarted, you again seek your elixir at the store or from the local dealer. Being on drugs creates a whole world of experience, where desire is satisfied but then it only begins again to build, and desire's object is then repeatedly sought as the answer to suffering. The whole process spirals around and around until the body dies, and you're off the hook.

The hook is addiction, and the idea that this is all there is in life: to just somehow get yourself through! Like something out there, outside yourself, will fix up the smashedness you've become. It's simple: when you're shaking in your hangover boots, emotionally dysfunctional and desperate for release, you'll find welcome-home banners in the party rooms in the bar below deck.

Rais'n 'em high, the skeleton's party below, as their wooden war-boat sails over a flat ocean and falls off the end of the earth. Ignorance would be bliss....

The pace of this drug life suits consumer capitalism. The western world's notion of evolution, of a continued progress and improvement, was for sure a major prop (crutch) and catch-all, summing up a desperate wish for a better future. People look to progress to fix their lives. Here, hungover, at least the mess can be counted on to show up, that mess they can try to evolve, improve—themselves. The ethos of the individual looms large, while all the drug addicts lurch and run amok like plucked electrocuted chickens. Intense, apocalyptic—life as we've grown to love it, like in the movies.

Progress, as it is "groked" by many, simply means envy is running the program. But any envy throws the person into fantasy, dreaming and projecting all sorts of pleasant scenarios. Then in kicks the consumer self, the seeker and shopper, believing heaven can be bought. Effort at personally improving oneself even may be dropped because here it can seem like money does it all. Although originating from a disquieted, agitated perspective, envy is seen as exciting, and today excitement is grasped as a benefit. This adulation of excitement over possibilities rather than realities is emotive and closer to a female than a male perspective.

Fun?

Booze-drug clubs are Red Mouth hangouts. S-E-X spells relief. On booze he observes, he doesn't reliably see. Sex is zeroed in on, and big boys walk the plank. Everything is corrupted. Then the repressed feminazis—usually the ones in the closet, some of whom don't know how much anger they really do harbor or why (but trained to focus hate on males)—they now show up. And they take these drug-frazzled emotionally uneducated big boys and begin the reconstruction—sort of like sleeping with the enemy.

What the finished product is like: a man with one close relationship in his life, with one person who he will be intimate with, who gives him hope for a future, perhaps with children. And just what is it that may stick about this wife? The one who now is perhaps his only source of emotional sustenance, the one person he can tell all to—all about his friends, or more likely former friends, because she might get rid of the "others". Well, she could serve him up for dinner, nail him in a social crucifixion.

His marriage to the mad hatter's choreographer, this soap-opera gamestress, will be at a great cost if things don't stay flush for her. Emotional control, that's where so many marriages originate. Many men on drugs can be victimized by dysfunctional women, some who are "knowing" parasites. Emotional and sexual terrorists of men.

Numerous guys are uneducated about "feelings," embarrassed and guilty. "She" is not and will hew this skill, and use him to move up her social ladder. Men can be the rungs of her ladder.

Your heart and soul (children) *and* your manhood please! She'll squeeze a kid or two out on the back lawn (applause), and she's finished. Hires the lawyer, takes her pets and whatever else she can get away with, and he's an "asshole." Sound familiar? Crippled men, ripped off. Bashed. Women organize and vote billions of dollars to themselves. Men don't seem to know what is going on....

On Guilt

Listening is absolutely everything to help sustain your life with dignity, energy. D'ya remember what that superstar baseball player Mickey Mantle (the Mick) said about booze? It ruined his life. Killed him. Does anybody hear modern baseball superstar Daryl Strawberry's explanation for his disgrace: addiction to woman, drinking and drugs.

To see the pitfalls and obstacles blocking the continued healthy flow of our energy demands meticulous alertness. Don't resist evil; don't try and make evil leave forever because it won't. It'll keep coming back. During televised big league baseball games there are often large ads for drugs painted right behind the batter at the plate. Painted right on the walls of the stadium! But don't let them take you over.

To be able to trust in your intuition and move towards safety means recognition of all the primitive things within yourself— whether greed, anger, lust, hate, fear, or selfishness—not a pretense of their absence. A presumptive ostentatiousness, a belief that you are not like others in these regards, will only bring those negative things right up close and smack-dab square into your life, because that's how it works. What you resist persists. Denial breeds continual dysfunction. Daily dues are paid from the terror raging within.

And forgiveness of those "nasty traits" in others is fine, but why go farther and sleep with all of them, those who live so closely focused in this stuff of panic. Because in their company you may only heighten your attachment to awful conflicts within yourself, and your energy could become snarled, blocked, and dissipated.

There are many ways of looking at things, and truly many who will comfort you in all types of morality. Still the ultimate judgement here should not belong to you dogmatically, in an ideological freezing of life. It is good to observe your thoughts. Let them race and wiggle around, watching how one thought stimulates another, and on and on it goes. Until the mind is quiet. Don't judge too much, don't buy into being so right—that is part of the problem. We're trained to see everything as black or white. This removes doubt. Back-up, let the mind run wild, observing it's constant reactive state. So two appropriate and useful rules are: 1) don't sleep with anyone who has more problems than you, and 2) there are no rules.

On Suffering

Allow yourself to suffer. Then it will pass. Allow all your feelings, and your suffering will flare into burning passion, and then transmute to love. Your energy will then increase, be sustained, and there will be more peace in your world. There can be a yielding when the desire to block out pain comes, and it should be a yielding into, not away from, the pain. To fight it only stimulates conflict and more pain.

Part of you would love the fight, your dysfunctional anger would find a victim to blame, to hate too. And soon you'd be at the brink screaming about life's injustice and desperate for relief and release. Red Mouth country!

Listen, allow yourself to suffer because your energy has area. It can expand—so yield and allow the pain of life to be in the world that is in you.

Foxy Lady

Ya gotta be hip to lotsa stuff, the manipulations Red Mouth is pulling off to get your soul in her hands. Sorry, no affective feelings allowed for watching today's baby dolls in high heels, unbalanced, wobbling across the street like helpless two-year olds. Heels raise up the buttocks seductively, and give the calf a more sensual curve. But a woman is handicapped up high in these shoes, and could not respond quickly to any physical danger.

Big, wide, phoney painted baby eyes too. Looking for sympathy? Or for control? And then the parts shooting at ya—the legs, butts, breasts—all consciously featured, each part in a show of its own. Believe it guys, you basically don't have much of a chance!

And if you—you who already are in dire straits here—are going to become alcoholic and come under the sexy power of drugs, then you are gambling with your life. You'll be out of your territory. When the drugs hit you'll have pressed the bullet into the chamber, and with wobbling hand the rising gun barrel bobs alone in a thick space, ever closer to "lock-on." You'll clean all that BS right out of your skull, a huge release. Foxy Lady you make me want to get up and scream!

So listen. Carefully scrutinize the motivations of Red Mouth. The road to hell is paved with good intentions. Would you: *Rather go on hearing her lies, than to go on living without her?*

The King

EAP. The King liked two broads. Would watch them lesbo-down on each other. Tribadism. Drugs galore, popping pills, digging sex objects. Then it's visual picnics with video. Alone, sitting in bed, away from fame, a frazzled man self-pleasures, turned on over flicks. The King, he's just trying to get chilled out, be cool, soothe out. The times they are a' stressing.

Elvis' pelvis. It's perturbing to grok why he chose to use porno to please his masculine hard-wired visual obsession. Guess it worked and cut down on messy personal involvement, divorces and protected against alimony payments and child rip-offs by aggravated mothers. And the variety must have been a plus factor too. Numerous visual sex partners. Drugs dug him into a hole he could not, would not, get out of.

Wallop Country Boy

Addictions,
Dysfunction at the junction
And away is taken a man's gumption.
Yup, mixing flicks
With doped up kicks,
This ever-launching of lust in rapacity
Did deflate EAP's general perspicacity,
As well as lambaste overall health.
No bright eyes, bushy tail.
Zombie pervert poops in his own bed,
While servants secrete evidence around,
Clean up, burn sheets,
King becomes kink,

It was the Army,
There he got hooked on amphetamines,
Gave him a false confidence,
Drugs smite,
Wallop country boy.

14
Mad Donna

*"I am a man in drag. Just kidding. I am a woman in drag.
I'm a man and a woman. I'm your worst nightmare."*[1]

Madonna

Social injustice in the late 1960's and early 1970's brought a generation out to protest, to actively identify themselves as bearers of hope and as riskers, to positively possess the courage to face status-quo authority and to demonstrate a desire for change. This social protest ran into the brick wall of conformist consumer capitalism. Then the protest was absorbed and marketed. Capitalism jumps on any trend, and is like a vacuum cleaner inhaling each and every commodity and idea, attaching a price to each and spitting all the stuff back out into the malls of the American Empire. Everything is for sale. Two popular trends emerged from the social activism of the 60's and 70's: pollution and feminism.

Fettered back into consumerism, the boomers gradually repented, became stockbrokers. The hegemony of the system was held aloft through brainwashing propaganda from the media and the terror of an ego-alone suffocation from the "free-market" economy.

The system had shown its muscle, its dissident garbage-collection, its recycling efficiency, and its general excellence at keeping the populace at odds, off-balance and lecturing one another via freedom to express individual opinions. Russian leader Gorbachev knew what he was doing all right, when he sold out his country. This system really works! Soon it's the revolution—in one's head!

In the media, feminism and pollution are allowed discussion and focus. Millions of acid trips later, in the war the World War II babies fought against the brutal self-interest of the ruling class, the fruits of a generation's struggle are heaved up as the social will to confront poison and to help women. Is this new? But thirty years further on down the line you can hardly see the sun through the smog, and women demean, bash and dump on their former protectors, the males.

Coca-Cola did re-establish itself as *the real thing*. In France, the country almost fell in the wake of the student demonstrations of 1968. Didn't hear about that? But then came the 1970's reality compensations, as pigs turned back into cops, as senators grew long hair, as the fashionable revolutionary co-opted attention and as imperialists must have left the country and gone to Russia, or something. But in America the revolution was usurped, became a commodity. Revolutionary hair, jeans, eye color, drug habits....

But the idea had been to change the system. Soon this meme had itself been changed to: change the system, but from within. *Teaching as a Subversive Activity* became college reading in professional preparation for fixing the system via school teaching, as the Moral Majority pointed its collective finger and coldly asserted in mature reasonableness: "If you're not part of the solution, you are part of the problem." Schemes to overthrow lying, manipulative oppressor bully-beasts became explained as the glaring rebukes and agendas of only dysfunctional "weirdos." Forget about those types.

Educated right out of their trees, dumbfounded citizens perpetually are exuding more poison and more hate. They are caught in a science-fiction tragedy based on fear and on a personal, neurotic, desperate anger directed at their inability to control anything much. The Boomers, sick puppies now around their sixties, they were nailed by the nifty-shifty, as the PR specialists vindicated even Nixon.

The Counterculture

But there was a time, a time when there had been an opening. The transformational moment existed in time and space in the revolutionary late 60's and into the 70's. Women were given prominence, another moment in history to redefine and realize themselves. But the system dodged the swelling revolt of the masses by using these very women. The ruling class recognized that putting up with feminism was better than extinction; feminism would serve to channel the discontent of the threatening social revolution while looking like the revolution itself.

Most of the American continent, indeed, and much of the western world did come close to changing. The counterculture had fused together millions in its hope for a kind of future that they themselves had been taught was truly worth fighting for. Why couldn't reality equal their hopes for the future? The resources were there, the desire for improvement ever-present, and the will to proceed grew steadily. The military-industrial alliances were in difficulty opposing such a unified, cohesive, popular social movement—one that never surrendered. The counterculture persistently demanded behavior in accordance with principles taught in elementary school. Individuals were becoming empowered, to take control of their lives, to participate in the creation of a better life for everyone.

The strength and focus of the counterculture was to *change the world not the channel*, to leave the comforts of entertainment distraction, to hit the streets, and to get one's body into demanding benefits for humanity. In the counterculture was a reservoir of potential energy—the boomer generation—to be mobilized, to swarm, to fill the cracks, to find the openings and vulnerabilities of the system. The streets teemed; the media was compelled to report the power. And the excitement reached every university. "Keep the faith," expressed counterculture hope. The revolutionary system was leading toward imminent freedom, liberty and dignity. The movement was so large that as it mutated vigorously the future was guaranteed.

It wasn't a gender problem that the counterculture was focused on. It was a propaganda problem. The system lied, burned, bombed, and then denied truth. And then it bullied and assumed unwarranted holiness. It resembled the bad guys. The counterculture movement fought: government propaganda, the persecution of minorities, the rejection of the disadvantaged, the greed and exploitation of political-business interests, imperialist murder in remote jungles and the cynical hypocrisy of only lip-serviced values grown too obvious to be ignored.

Protection from outside threats, to a country and its families, was necessary, but was everybody a threat to everyone else, as individualistic corporate capitalism so readily assumed? Yes, because capitalism has won? Materialism must be part of life, but then was envy and acquisition as a lifestyle to be followed? Sell a piece of crap? Wasn't empathy for one's fellow passengers on this life-train the major effort? Wasn't love all important, if the planet was to survive, if the values taught at home and in the schools were to be brought into reality?

Divide and Rule Again

Over the backs of the massing millions, a highway of hope seemed destined to lead the world away from Hiroshima, and into a new humanistic millennium. A new age of man would beget a society whose leadership was committed to principles of action for the benefit of all. This shared vision was the force, the driving energy of the revolutionaries. But somehow the dreams of a truly humane society became unrealistic, as Big Brother redirected attention by using media control.

To the delight of the status-quo corporate reapers and benefitters, the well-placed, imperialist-elitist monopoly-capital manipulators, those railed at as managers of the organized oppression—all along past the watchtowers of hope began the march of angry women. But they'd turned backwards, were going the other way and were routinely releasing gained space back into an expanding void, in a loss of momentum for the counterculture. They said they had reasons! Catastrophe, as many in a movement's membership deserts in a self-permeated panic, and wash up as a radical unit for one exclusive lobby group, one specific gang.

With an elitist gender focus, feminism and feminists forsook the counterculture in a classic opportunistic power grab that guaranteed that the big system would survive. Change and the hoped-for accountability—political, social and economic—would not come to pass at this time. Instead it's just self-interest, as the "feminists' " powerful lobby group was co-opted, as the feminists went to Big Brother and cried their inveigler tears. And so ended an attempt of western civilization to produce a real, pragmatic outcome out of its much touted democratic-humanistic ideology.

If you've spent most of your genetic past cozying up to power, it may be difficult to perceive that behavior. Ever since the counterculture protest, the government itself increasingly has been replacing the role of a husband.

And many a "she" just don't get it—the system is the problem:

Bash the male, make 'em wail.
It's dem dats gots us in this mess,
Full of hurt'n hate and the carnage,
Now everywhere a girl has gots to know,
Freedom comes where a man can't go.
Get yourself a good ole job,
That'll replace the brutal slob,
It's men that sin,
Caus'n nut'n but all these problems.

Then the long-haired boys had revved up. Doctors all of them, specialists not at medicine, no, but they are the Ph.D.'s, the doctors of behavior, and they could figure out how to get people to think and do. Think and Do. Making up phrases and phasing the serfs, these few freaks deliver the brain food for the "moral majority," like: being part of the solution; the Republican revolution; the war on drugs; the war on poverty; a kinder, gentler nation; liberating and bringing democracy to Iraq; humanitarian intervention; free markets; smart bombs; letting the private sector solve the problem; getting the government off people's backs. Like: the U.S. Patriot Act; the deficit problem; arming for peace; the war against terrorism; collateral damage; bombing to get back to the negotiating table, and endless other strings and strips of Newspeak backdoor brain changers. Worth their weight in uranium, these think-tankers are gonna save the country: keep it just as it is! Elementary essay: Divide and Rule Game Plan—The Secret Techniques of Maintaining Privilege in the Propaganda Culture.

Eventually Bob Dylan's almost sacred anthem of the boomer generation, "The Times They Are A' Changing," would be captured, sold, bought by a bank! Turned into a commercial where an old man looks out the window as the children parade by, involved as they are in the song's lyrics about a new world, and he is not to criticize what he doesn't understand. By now the old boomer is portrayed as toast, finished—a spectator.

What is this new world the kiddies are marching into? It's total bank money world (BMW). Full circle—the masses first encouraged into marching for social improvements are now hyped into marching for corporate imperialism.

It must have taken guts to sell that song, to dump the sacred trust built up between the poet of the people and his fans. Many had found refuge in Dylan's lyrical descriptions of a society troubled by conscience. But Dylan's selling of his tune must be his parody of the money-lusting going on today. And it is a stark reminder of just what is happening and exactly what is going on, Mr. Jones.

Mad Donna's Conditioning

Although Mad Donna grew up in BMW, it was actually patriarchy (from the Greek—the rule of the father) that typified Mad Donna's home life. Five older brothers, a strict disciplinarian father whom she said favored her and she could wrap around her finger, and the love of and for Jesus gave formulation to the growing young lady's world. She, the youngest, surrendered into the hands of fate, since her mom would die when she was six, and males splashed forth from all the rooms where she did live.

In the 60's, Betty Friedan's bestseller, *The Feminine Mystique*, had sold many females the meme that women are enslaved by marriage and domesticity.

Mad Donna was about ten-years old when the feminists broke away from the New Left in the late 1960's. Then, the women claimed they were being brainwashed and socially controlled by society (men). Differences between men and women were all invented they said, and sex roles were handed out arbitrarily to oppress women. Their radical feminism would be diffused and re-directed, accommodated in diluted form, absorbed by the system, then warmed until comfort itself became the priority.

Finally the females were directed to row away from the patriarchy to Fantasy Island—as heavenly collective nurturers of everything female and as clitoral goddesses of the holy orgasm, as sensual pirates of mood, but still the kingpins of shopping! This took a few decades but the system was up to the challenge.

Second-wave Feminism

Feminists were changing too, as Mad Donna endured the ravages of her adolescence. Into their mind's eye penetrated threats of hot vibrating victimization. Women wondered how to off-load the pile of garbage they had been taught about conformity and obedience, which they now believed they'd been conditioned to swallow under rigid male rationality and power.

Second-wave feminism sought to overturn the mythology of *a man's world with woman in her place*, and it claimed many social organizations subordinated women to men. Power at home, basically domestic control and emotional-sexual hegemony, was not enough. Public power, in the economic-business world, in the political world, in the intellectual world was viewed as the power withheld, the real stuff of the real movers and shakers. A woman's place in the home was viewed as a conspiracy to keep women out of the labor market and subordinate.

Separate individualistic power was becoming everything. Then a new, atrocious postmodern fancy began to barf up violent, ugly images in Hollywood movies and the media of the outside world. This took the edge off of the soul's need for approval. The psyche needed to be fed the raw meat of continual failure in long-term trust for anything in today's world, if it was to go along with the anti-humanism capitalism was serving up at home and in the Empire. The psyche has thus become used to being served a main course of inglorious defeat, and perversely nods, recognizing the undoing of mankind's very humanity as somehow deliciously savoring—because at least, in this chaotic world, failure is assured! Cynicism and selfishness therefore become easy to justify. And tuning out, ignoring the concerns of the world, suits people when all they hear is gross, ugly. Unfortunately, access to their souls may get blocked by these attitudes.

Western society physically and emotionally screwed around with nuclear explosions, labor control, imperialist mass murders, filthifying the environment, ransacking the colonies, but all the while maintaining a juvenile howdy-doody, all-American-apple-pie, flag-waving belief that somehow democracy and destiny were just about to fix everything up, any minute. Even if it was a jungle out there, a popular consensus meme had become socially ingrained that western civilization possessed the seed that could one day grow to save the planet. Or so some voice from deep down the well of rational liberalism had once assured the grown-up patriots when they were still elementary school children—bright eyes flashing, hearing about their special place in history. These special kids figured that they would tell everybody one day just what was up and what wasn't.

The American destiny was to set the record straight, right? And wasn't the American destiny to free the world from evil sadistic rulers who forced their own people to commit violent acts against humanity? The light of liberty emanating from the shores of America would be a beacon to the world. The guiding principles of democracy, freedom and equality between races and genders, would be shared, explained, taught to the rest of the world.

America imagines itself engaged in purifying and freeing the world, and this *imagination* actually can become *reality*. It is embedded deep down, as the future flower children were forced to hold their hands over their hearts and swear allegiance to a flag. Mental fantasy overrides reality, as the heat of a good idea replaces the facts and suppresses the truth. Rationalism rules— guts emotion, steals action.

Second-wave feminism had brought attitude. Germaine Greer, best known for the *The Female Eunuch*, and Gloria Steinem, declared guerilla war against men in the 70's. Women were told men hated them, that violence was the norm between men and women. Women were to chuck the vow of monogamy, the wedding ring and the husband's last name. They were to be promiscuous, adventurous.

The women sought to penetrate the power positions in politics and business. So through the 70's and into the 80's women put on a game-day face and entered the coliseum to do battle. The enemy—anything that stood in their way.

In public, it had been mainly male rule since ancient Rome, and it was still that way. But women were determined to be successful here. After all, their husbands and boyfriends weren't doing so well anyway. With inflation, earnings didn't go very far. So with almost no experience in Wall-Street fighting, these liberated female battlers began the war on Wall Street. They assimilated male character traits, talked more like jocks. And they began really disliking men, as the reality of the male competitive world began to strip them of cool. But they rallied, formed support groups, portrayed themselves as minorities in need of government assistance, and attacked the patriarchy as being responsible for all the anal-retentive idiots around. Porno then spread across America, like a refuge for males.

Mad Donna and Truth-telling

Mad Donna and truth-telling collided with bleached roots bearing witness to a material girl's need for illusion. Once an embarrassment, bleached roots reveal a woman under construction. In the collage that's pasted daily (hourly) onto their faces and their body parts, streaked wannabe Madonnas are looking for a foundation on which to underpin their goal-oriented portfolio dreams and greedy faith.

Early Mad Donna took on a campy, funky, pre-grunge style: rags (idea of scarcity), nets, bulky socks (no money-no footwear), hair tied with kerchiefs, a million bracelets (cheap), safety-pin earrings (shocking) and crucifixes dangling around belly-button level (sexual torture)—a frazzled, make-do-with-what-we've-got look. The fans grew up dancing to Mad Donna's machine music and wondered how they'd get away with the felonious cosmetic-duping their heroine had made into lifestyle éclat: cheek paint, highlighter, eyebrow-lying lines, blinker-lash makeovers, gobs of black blinker-goo. First the foundation...and on and on. (Guess the number of modifications the madam applies over her body?)

Smoochy-lipped Mad Donna gives credence to the usefulness of make-up—for actors! Is that what these females fans think they are? Actors in dramas, made meaningful by the males sacrificed upon their cosmetic altars of boredom and alienation? Mad Donna, our lucky star, slides a finger into the glistening red gleam of—her open mouth. Her racoon eyes pan the scene and beg come-on from the camera. For the camera she can be, indeed, a cosmetic slut. Does she ever take her face off? Must she always be making up her mind?

> *At the gym each morning she froths, the aerobic*
>   *fit to make,*
> *The rest, all the dress-up, well, it's just fake –*
> *Gunk, color, base and hue, put on like glue,*
> *Trapping attention an actor must do*
> *Much painting and brushing and framing anew,*
> *Intent to pretend, to the starlet extend,*
> *Public permission and privilege for the rules to bend,*
> *Open-eyed and innocent allowance to enact a role,*
> *A happening—professional acting does set sail to soul!*

Bountiful dreams and hopes and choices,
Juxtaposed to devil-do treachery and human deceit,
The social body needs healing, and the plays are its
   conceit,
Only a play with characters sublime,
Rendered to help raise empathy divine,
Pretending and painting here, why it is all
   judiciously fine.

Power and Machisma

In "modern" postmodern thought, it is, of course, power that matters. Finally everyone figures that the good guys and the bad guys all want the same thing—power to control their lives. The Germans and the Japanese wanted power and fought for it in World War II. TV commercials are all interested in one thing—getting power over consumer spending habits. And on the personal level human beings are healthier when experiencing success in determining their own lifestyle. So in this way, everything becomes relative to what each person, corporation or nation wants and needs from each unique situation.

The honest response is to assert one's desire for power, and fight for it, or else succumb to others' desire for it. He wants the kids—she wants the kids; he wants sex—she wants attention. Whose power will dominate? Success is everything, winning is everything. Today even down to the cellular level, the teaching goes, each living entity strictly fights for its separate survival.

Power is seen as a centrepiece of life. Everywhere everyone is addicted to this power—in love with it. Nobody thinks they're going to fall into the trap of believing and fighting and dying for communism or nationalism, because now that's just like putting up your life to be used for the power purposes of politicians and corporations and little mustachioed neurotic dictators. Right? No, the public says, it won't get fooled again. So now people cultivate their own personal power. Today everybody thinks they should be self-interested and doing their own PR work, on the lookout for profit, benefit, more power. Goals are demanded; few moments are allowed to exist on their own.

Having power demands commitment, discipline, organization, positive thinking. So off to see the wizards—the instructors, book writers, counselors, shrinks, whomever—went the burgeoning schools of females, caught in the current of learning how to be effective in an individualistic, competitive marketplace. She wanted in and was more than determined to get in. Growing testicles was no problem: "It's all a state of mind," said Mad Donna, "My dick is in my brain."[2]

Machisma had spread as Dodson's *Liberating Masturbation* (1974) empowered ladies to go it alone, without men.[3] Glorified as a freeway to freedom, masturbation seemed to remove males from power. Dumping traditional gender roles, trying to remove any dependence on men, the aim was independence and freedom from a perceived woman-oppressing society. Now unfettered, guilt-free auto-eroticism incited more hype for woman's separate power. Females could now cull an exalted cosmic goddessness through achievement of orgasmic oneness with spirit. Here some of their egos could assume the neurotic stance of the victor, and put asunder the alleged corset-prison of women's inferiority complexes.

The deified belief in female-superior orgasmic capability would bring many females into physically active encounters with their newly conceived, and highly rated, unconscious selfhood. That idea, in itself, was powerfully exciting! Having freedom to use sex, seemingly without constraint, soon gave women a means with which to confront the older generation—perhaps some saw it as a way to bring cultural change, and a humanizing liberation from society's alienating technocracy. A case could be made that repressed sexuality could lead to fascism, *so lets do it* at least once *in the road.*

Downunder in Australia, on stage with two attractive female back-up singers, Mad Donna eyes them both seductively then screams to a packed stadium crowd:

"We Fuck GIRLS! Ya! We FUCK GIRLS! Don't we?"[4]

She's just scaring the shit out of everyone, especially the guys. Just as she likes it. Getting attention at home living with her six men took a lot of button pushing. Her sister act is close to being her whole act.

Men as the Enemies to Overcome. The whole technological apparatus in America had been seen as male-structured, phallus-oriented and oppressive to women. Men were the enemies, the problem, but not their male creations, the corporations. Female power was thought to be needed to connect to the vision of a matriarchal society. Training men towards female pleasure-needs brought the feminine into prominence. The bedroom became center stage; the personal would become the political. And a route to clasp power was through sex.

Mad Donna doesn't like giving oral sex 'cause:

> *"Who wants to choke? That's the bottom line. I contend that's part of the whole humiliation thing of men with women. Women cannot choke a guy...."* [5]

So that's out! She creates distance between the sexes. Very competitive....

First-wave feminists had worked to promote equality, worked on welfare reform, and worked with a vision of shared, egalitarian community. Sex and power were not the main meal, not visibly, not yet. As the feminist movement was overrun by the media the movement became part of its own problem—it was absorbed into the system, given placebo-token amounts of money, respect, jobs and task-force commissions.

But the rational buy-off approach did have its limits, and soon disillusionment sparked a new idea.

Must women rationally learn everything because their intuition is overdeveloped? To compensate or something? They elevate rational-word learning as such a promising activity, as though answers can and will always be found.... But the Pavlovian education pursued in public buildings has laid hold and punctured some of their power. Less and less in nature do we see that is theirs.

These women's new idea was participation. Get into the business and political system, fight, study, take courses, produce! And it really worked in many ways for many women. Male combative challenges were side- stepped. Smiling, nurturing responsiveness was very popular. Flesh-flashing derailed a lot of guys, while kindness and consideration enlisted fan clubs.

Male Reaction. But the sixteen-hour Starbucks' daze-days began to overload all the Mary Tyler Moore software running inside the new business women. Datebooks bulged with promises, and life was lived on the run in a system that had seemed ripe for the picking.

Women had begun to think that she was having it her way. But there was a cost. By the 1990's there would be a 600 per cent increase in lung cancer in women. The price was also screwy sweetheart relationships, as women prioritized each hour of the day and found serious interests outside intimate relationships. And the guys had begun shaking their heads and saying stereotypical stuff about "women," but they still believed that it was other guys who were the victims (losers) with women, not themselves.

Trained to compete, trained to smash faces, trained into insensitivity and forced into alienation from so much meaningful human experience, many western guys can't figure dick. Told to respect these women, to look up to their moral superiority, to work, support, live and die for them—he's now being told it's just his ego that is the problem?

Yes, he wants control of just how he will do all of this for her anyway. But then she thinks he is bullying. Then a confused objectification brings her at least two self-interpretations: she's being victimized, overpowered by male aggression into subjugation; his power is dominant. Or, her other interpretation is that it's only words—"How do I feel?" But whatever she feels won't overpower the decision of today: it's "freedom" or bust! Her power is being threatened... and soon she may take *the house and kids or the car and computer and run to mommy and daddy, or the government. And they will console her because they've been conditioned to do so, and she is a real pro at the crying game.*

The problem is she's sort of a rookie at this killing game. She's used to being unaccountable, but now may suffer the responsibility for pushing distraught decisions down upon society. Because women today think they are "free", can she change her mind? Freedom is changing your mind? It sounds TV-driven, commercials interrupting a life. Her consumer-spending and voting power is what the corporations and the government respect, and their courthouse judges give her all the benefit of some doubt. There's a legal wasteland full of her lackeys right now, but sooner or later real survival skills will have to emerge. Some forms of feminism promote only female community. It becomes all about her reproductive freedom, her children and her home with them. But soon the route back to the safety of her nest may not be there. The males in the future could bond in defense of their fatherhood, and malaise could overpower the reasoned exertions of the hesitant.

Female Response. In the 70's and 80's, however, the females had been getting on pretty well. They had the appeal of the underdog, the excitement of rebellion. They could garner bleeding-heart support power at the snap of a finger, and it was legal to use their sexuality as a weapon—awesome combination, hard to mess with. By 1985, half of university enrollment was female. As well, a tremendous increase in new professional positions were being filled by women, and soon university figures would reveal that even more women than men are registered in post-secondary education. Female- privileged lifestyle-shaping exists on campus, where it's warm—trees, ponds, bands, dates, busy work, etc.

The original women's movement wanted to improve, evolve society. But the corporate stranglehold is too great, so they retreated. And instead they just attack men. Going after violence on TV threatens big investment commercial dollars so the market monster bares its teeth—the goons show up on the women's doorstep. The result is commissions, task forces, enquiries, promised-reforms, but it's all hogwash. Pass the popcorn—change the channel.

Pornography and Victimization

Soon the rad-feminists are in bed with the ultra-right religious Moral Majority, like it's schizophrenia time, as opposites confront a common perception of an enemy—pornography. No base sexual objectification permitted here, these females want their garden parties run with exuberance! Subtlety surrounds the silent directing thread of social action—the sex-of-life focus that the females have managed to get control of. Men are out of their control, and females aren't in demand if the VCR's of the nation facilitate pervert-dirt and male self-satisfaction. It's males the Moral Majority and the rad-feminists are after—to humiliate men's natural addiction to sex.

As in the past, men are ridiculed—a brain in a penis, dirty old men—cheapened, debased and demeaned. Men's addiction to sex is made to look sick. This suits the female control purpose and is a route to power forged over the souls of males. Guilt keeps men nice and quiet. But these right-wing religious Christian ladies, even though told in the Bible by Paul to keep quiet and follow male spiritual guidance, are raging, making a racket. And they're teamed up with the rads, the Dworkinite Gender Fems of Sick Sex, the ones who see intercourse as a cutting into female genitalia.

In 1970, Kate Millet's *Sexual Politics* trashed marriage as an institution dominated by male pornography.[6] Soon male-female relationships became all politics to many females.

But it's the rape of male pleasure that is jealously jumped all over by these raving, hysterical rooster-women. Every act of sex not initiated by the woman is being called rape!

Power, power everywhere, even tell you where to stare.

Pornography hasn't been found to cause violence against women. In fact, even further male addiction, and subjugation, to the power of the female body must come from obsessive porno watching. But society only gave a small window to women to attack something; the corporations are too big. The radical feminists hate porno because they hate the *patriarchal exploiting capitalist gaze* that they say uses and abuses anything. And they get stuck on the gaze part, the male's instinctive disposition they know intuitively is a sort of weakness. And they use the males visual natures against them, especially so in the shark pools of gender scrimmage where any weakness is scored upon in righteousness. But almost naked sales-lady realtors door-knock the neighborhoods looking for listings, business—parts and pieces ripening on doorsteps. So should male realtors ask to carry guns to help them close deals, to equal out what they feel is unfair?...

Apart from all the reactive male bashing, and the growing response from some of the men, today men and women are still blanketed by passiveness. This resignation is brought on by their innate knowledge of a great messing-up of human dignity, and they sense that horrific lies and grave injustice have been done to humanity. The media strive to keep them in fear to make their governments look necessary for protection. Many escape into sensual pleasure or into entertainment, where they don't have to do anything. There is fear to face the blackness surrounding the soul. The soul is strangled, flung asunder on the frozen field of compassion's failure, where private tyranny is now seen as a route to freedom. Pushed into stalemate, standing alone, perturbed, wanting to blame but also self-loathing, people are reactive rather than revolutionary. And most are keeping too quiet and are too self-conscious. With nerves racked and wasted, they contemplate some gender feminist koans like "the biological family is an inherently unequal power distribution."

Meanwhile, paranoid radical feminists scream hysterically that pornography endorses violence toward women. Feeling swindled, but scapegoating males, many in the women's movement have got the essence but not the cause of the contemporary smothering sludge covering the soul. It's bewildering: the rads joined up with the women of the ultra right-wing Christian Moral Majority, the group who they had called "the most patriarchal, repressive, anti-female forces in the country"? It's cuckoo-brains, forming this coalition just to create an enemy. Was this evidence of the "projects of creativity and transcendence" women coveted but felt denied?

Then another koan, this oldie from Mona, in 1894, is recycled: "Motherhood in our present social state, is the sign and seal, the means and method of a woman's bondage. It forges chains of her own flesh and blood; it weaves chords of her own love and instinct." [7] And this is dished up, more recently: "Not only sexual violence but penetrative sexual intercourse is the key moment in women's oppression. All men are rapists, all women are their victims!" [8]

Bashing boys is easy! In the past prostitutes were forbidden by law to taunt passing males or to physically grab at them. Because males would respond! Once involved, they became easy prey for the spell-casters, and soon the smiling hope for love's massages raised cash. But today the males are passive, many now with low self-esteem, and without much gender support. In general, they've been done-in.

There is a cry whistling high above the clouds of all this women's victim-claiming woundedness. They want relief from impossible suffering. They want relief from the impossible truth that comes slowly and is one day certain to take away everything—even life's breath that's taken for granted. One's approaching death may feel similar to a picture of prey surrounded by savages, and everyone knows it's only a matter of time before lights out. So should a woman get a man to do the dirty work and then blame him for everything annoying and thereby get the ever-life bitching right out of her system? Then he becomes the sacrifice, the offering up into the ethers? Just as animals, children or slaves were once sacrificed to exorcize badness, rottenness and to clear the human air of dysfunction, isn't he, too, abandoned?

> *The victim-dictum says soon boys be underdogs*
> *claiming (real) abuse*
> *from present snapping low women on the totem pole*

Attacking, getting attention, sympathy and then screwing around, playing mind-games with the sex in the hope of securing control, power, isn't that the point? But sex is also an outlet. Portraying women as victims of porno, and asking for protection from men wasn't what the feminists originally wanted. Because this only featured an old view of women—as weak, in need of support—not the liberated, independent scenario so much was being made of.

Like a moving apparition, pale ticker-tape words slowly slide along huge concrete and steel buildings in smog-infested metropolis. The neon word-flow through the mist reads: *Is late capitalism the seven-headed beast, the whore ingesting the world, excreting from its entrails the remains of human hope?*

Mad Donna's Mad Damage

Living at home in a microcosm of a patriarchal fraternity, Mad Donna learned to use feminine charm to manipulate men and achieve her purposes. Now she wants to know how to challenge the system without living in hate. She wants to know what she has to learn in order to know what's right for her. But who, she asks, has the right to tell anybody what to do? Then she asks what she will do with all her anger. Sex is spread all over the place as a suggestion of what to do:

A smorgasbord of fashionable excess sparkles and booms across the stage, light and show-biz theatrics booming into a black night: Australian orgies on stage: naked dancers, crotch caresses, simulated orgasms, spiked-nipple breasts. Her show is similar to the lightning bursts from an old army's artillery barrages.

But isn't this war over? Sex is dead! The AIDS virus now a mortal threat, and Mad Donna, maybe she's gonna be the last one out, as microscopic life-forms virus their way on through, killing the mortals. Some may even believe that homo sapiens are triumphantly eaten today, devoured in a Hieronymus Bosch purging of libidinous impurity.

She taunts; she threatens. No lady can keep up with her, or very, very few. She's a blessed starlet and a workaholic too. And she wants men, needs men, dedicates her work to her father, gives him credit for her discipline, etc. Needs the force! All this sex stuff is nostalgia—a means to power. She snatches some sperm from the gym guy, incubates the stuff in her internal microwave oven, and becomes a full-blown momma. Relationships are messy, so it's the self-actualizing, pseudo-pretending world of me alone, go alone, don't need no drone clone leech'n offa' me no more. But her kid may become a hostage to her unmet needs. And then her hasty late marriage to another man, who knows? But in no time she's back posing for the cameras in a kick-male-butt ride'm cowgirl attitude.

Multidimensional Mad Donna. Portraying a sex-maniac variety addict during the Black Plague II (AIDS) gave the public a kick-butt, in-your-face man-acting woman with fantasies all about. Mad Donna thinks Revelation, just because someone printed Revelation in a Bible—well, she believes you know, that this raving surrealism is the God-given approval to invoke a total hedonism. Her first love, her first coach, the one that gave her the courage to step out and really go for it—well, he died of AIDS. And she's caught by her emotion here. He was her role model, her ballet teacher—fabulous, demonstrative, extravagant. And she wanted to be like him.

Often, she says, she's fallen in love with a gay man. That's OK, right? Revered by many in the gay community as the broad who cares, she cozies close to the forces that overturn the sacred heterosexual reign.

A sex diva who hangs in with homosexuals? It's a non-mystery, life was always that way. It's the irony, the zen-ness of living, this helter-skelter shakedown of the kid who had to succeed, had to have center stage, who gleaned the means by coping and competing, by immersion in her all-male family. And she's the youngest, the sibling position that learns how to get its way. It's she who the fickle finger of fate pushed out center stage in the time of woman's anticipation of "more, more, more." And she's running the campaign for chick supremacy from gay bars? A phoney lesbian, a divorcée individual with a nymphomaniac stage presence surrounded by her gay babies: "Effeminate men intrigue me more than anything in the world. I see them as my alteregos. I feel very drawn to them. I think like a guy, but I'm feminine. So I relate to feminine men...." [9]

She's in a multidimensional personality profile, so ultra-contemporary, so up-to-date, it's sickening. She's a television with numerous channels, a brain overloaded with thoughts, a zoom lens pulled into fantasy dress-ups, and a lifestyle commercial for Marshall-Plan capitalism. Ambition rules; her career is a glory, capturing the world's attention, earnings astronomical. Driven personality, dressed for success, Mad Donna gets the spotlight—the attention of the globe.

She's a material girl, and diamonds could be her best friend. She's a woman capable of successfully competing with men. Liberated, she claims she wants to be both sexes. She can function within the oligarchy, and her messages concern women's new attitudes and possibilities. She's aggressive, daring, foul-mouthed—just like some men. She's mean sometimes and will turn her back on men, dump them. Machisma marches on to the next watering station, the next man. There's so many hungry ones. Just look'em in the eye, and it's instant burn, instant meltdown—out there in Monroe Land, blonde barracudas shark around. She's got the edge, the fashionable man-bashing act and the beautiful frame. Thus towering above libidinous losers (men), her sexual-supremacy characteristics allow membership in a symbolic winner's circle for those genetic celebrities possessing a desirable female chassis.

Second-wave Role Model. A second-wave role model for the growing baby "chicks" of the late twentieth century, Mad Donna was the women who groked male power, then used her talents to dare, to challenge the socially conditioned behavior and conformist expectations of a society nervous for change. Funk, grunge, experimentation in style, she took the young post-hippie flappers through external feminine style changes. They were suffering an arbitrary angst, trapped as bored spectators in an entertainment culture. She was aggressive, man-challenging. *And she made "material girls" out of the pubescent wannabes, those told by their pissed-off moms to trade slavery to homophobic men for careers of their own.* The wannabes were to challenge the patriarchal system with their bag of female tricks, to absorb male character traits, to learn how to think "marketplace" and to compete.

Women's world was getting closer day by day;
Supplanting males, taking and getting
   Affirmative Action (AA)
Would clear the way.

Wonder Woman and Hedonism. She had "balls" they say, but what's come of it all? Making fifty or a hundred million a year doesn't benefit women, just Mad Donna. She's a megastar and is accorded a stature once reserved for nobility, for a queen. This mover and shaker inspires young ladies to play dress-up, consider lesbian encounters, dump men and to psychopathically incarnate into whatever mood is happening. She leads forward into a past of fickle womanhood and has added a deliberate, modern emotional shockingness, threatening to tear society's traditional morality to pieces. And she does not know, really know, what works here, but sovereign hedonism is all she's really into. It's a strip act, and she's a hard worker plying her trade.

Hints of a new type of woman emerge and then warp into Marilyn Monroe and Marlene Dietrich. It all becomes random, scattered skits with her sexy Highness incarnating into so many forms that present minds don't know how to figure this female. And that is what makes some feminists so pleased. In a daze guys gasp, surrounded by a post-neoteric conundrum of her multiple personality, all action being relative to every stimulus. To Mad Donna, S&M isn't about sex; it's about power and who is dominating. It seems Henry Kissinger's asseveration that power is the ultimate aphrodisiac got attention from some of the high school students of the 70's.

This wonder woman, in the beginning, brought great hope—a new vision of adventure and freedom for women. She dared to transgress sexual boundaries in her posture of a rebellious youth, confronting an unrepressed female creativity. Well, at bottom-line, the radical social changes frothing in her wake were no more meaningful than the "Revlon Revolution" commercial aimed bulls-eye at female inadequacy. This lipstick feminism, it's greasy oil-spill wafting over the waters of female abuse, humping the waves and endlessly trickling through as a new freedom, is retrograde and part of the problem. But as second-wave feminists entered the business world and took on roles as career professionals, Mad Donna and blonde ambition imbued the daring-do.

Women now wanted what men wanted and did what men did—only better. Or so the gender feminist recruiters liked to claim. This attitude amounted to becoming like the enemy, and bedding down with males could be sleeping with the competition. Big-screen motion pictures began portraying women as the bad guys, Venus's fly traps, as men were eaten up and spit out in a series of female low-life flicks.

The films helped illustrate the moral reversals that had to take place for women to compete in the typical modern business world. Hurrying to get corrupt, double-dealing, manipulating facts (and as usual their figures), learning to snow job, negotiating, winning at all costs (loss of integrity, health, marriage), women were portrayed in a piranha pool competing with men, not just with women as in the past. The films featured women jettisoning "caring" when stalking prey—the sacrifice demanded for cash-register goal-scoring finesse and power. These "bitches-of-diamonds" marched to the "pussy-power" anthems that Mad Donna laid across America. They had about as much depth as the hits of Mad Donna's male entertainment hero—Michael Jackson.

Plastic Attracts. One day Mad Donna had rode the curl of her determination and landed in Los Angeles and charismatized DeMann, Jackson's manager, into becoming her front man too. Plastic attracts. Her career then took off. So into the palace of purgatory she joins Michael and Elvis, those managed and marketed with surgical precision. Here sheer hype brings fame, and the fame itself is the drawing card to bring dollars to the dealers, where The Event becomes spectacular firework displays, music, and, of course, the star! Hollowness spectacles. Mad Donna's dance and march music lacks depth, and can be empty-headed, but has got enough verve to help support a female take-chargeness, independence and competence. Girls need to take a "Holiday," dance to the music, and everything will be all right.

Australia and the "Girlie Show." Mad Donna and American imperialism had hit Australia with The Girlie Show, a study in sexual snobbery, female capacity, and punishment to those who can't or won't justify their "love." Under a gigantic American flag and with her troupe militarily dressed and saluting her as "Yes Sir, Misses Sir!" she sings, "We can turn the world around," then states: "You can't have a good time until you have law and order. Is that understood?" Law and Order! Over and over, she bullies her screaming audience to respond with "Yes... yes... yes," – time after sadistic time and then, after their masochistic compliance she answers back with a..."Fucking Awesome"....[10]

Their reward for obedience is another song, and it's about nobody standing in her way. She is going to "beat my drum, ring my bell, and I don't give a damn ("fuck" the second time) if I go to hell." This little ditty is repeatedly banged out with group gusto, dancers fly and the drums do beat as light control on high vaporizes resistance, the rendition's repetition bringing the audience on to the sadistic side, the side she is best at. Over and over the repetition continues, leaving little room for anything but immersion into an ego-cruising barbarism, with urges for self-aggrandizing narcissistic projections of every sort.

Following this uprise, Mad Donna gives another shot in the arm to the old familiar power she knows the *sheilas* are sitting on. With a snake-murmuring, deep-throated sensuality, she asks (pleads) for you to *justify* her love. Dressed in a man's tall top hat, with a pervert patch over the left eye, she's dripping with covetous open heat. A ton of males and females fawn and slave around her, she asking to be kissed, to be wanted: "I just want to be a lover." She's got pragmatic power here, but demands that her love be justified. A taunt, a challenge, a dare, but most of all elitist, totalitarian and full of insinuation.

A packed stadium of excited Generation X'ers seem to believe in this as a rad happening, arms waving in the sea of their own Woodstock. The cameras swoop over the hordes showing up to witness a *celebrity*, and that's the real bottom line—but she's insulting, daring, bullying, deceiving and selling. As the tune ends, Mad Donna freezes, ever so tardily turns, and then hedges toward the back of the stage, veering into an ever-dimming light that shrinks slowly into a surrounding blackness.

Effect of Superstardom. Liberated women reborn as Las Vegas show girls? A result of the pajama parties becoming such big draws with five older brothers and their buddies around? When fame itself can now become power, who is to pass judgement upon a means to an end? Mad Donna procures more cash than heads of state, corporate chiefs or revered triple-bypass engineers. Facts about the coinage heights of superstardom bring anxiety; it's weird, unbelievable, unreasonable, this celebrity world of wampum.

These stars take attention away from the men and women at the controls of the economy who have the real power connections, and away from their front-person politicians. Swindlers, with hidden agendas, the politicians glad-hand too much, emulate the smiling stars and are accorded too much respect. Meanwhile the celebrities, from recording industry to movie market to sports cartel, keep the public playing goofy head games—distracted, entertained into fuzzy stupefaction. Thus the crooked hands of the power-elite ransack the cookie jars left unattended in the warm rooms, in heated public buildings, protected by publicly paid personnel.

The stars recite all kinds of recipes—on morals, values, personal beliefs and on the codes and principles of proper living—so many that the bewildered and overloaded audience, in the chaos of freedom of choice, goes plunging into disorientation. There is too much choice, too many personal solutions. Anything can happen. No one way is correct. Everyone is an island. So most give up, become spectators. Many stars take the public's focus and channel it up into useless interests and thoughts. Envy and hate recycle over the idiot issues that distract the goofy-idea people, while boys and men salivate over jocks that may have what they don't—talent.

Gay Men as Male Role Models. Mad Donna heralded in the new queerdom—an interesting choice of men to identify with. The boys that would be girls jumped out of the closets and onto her stage. The matriarchal society had a foundation as Mad Donna and momism looked empathy over the queer flock and gave refuge. Publicly seen as a benefactor towards the gay community, Mad Donna cuts deep into the male psyche. Allowing sympathy to those she can't control outright through innate heterosexual power, she gives the message that it's all right to be a queer man. That will get attention. The straight men are disdained, rebuked, taunted, made guilty, disposable under the reign of her kind of female power. But her greatest power is male-seductive, and one must wonder where she would be if a real backlash to male-bashing brought male revolt and an actual mass flight into The Queerdom?

But looking more closely on the scene, she sees some gays as in need of help. Many aren't a threat; they want to be like her, like a woman and a lover of men. Gay-friendly, she's pushing buttons again, this female icon wants to rumble in the jungle. She's shit-disturbing again at the dinner table! It was a way to make a presence in the men's locker room she grew up in. The culture of America was ripe for terrorism, and little Lulu was the focused detonator for the job.

Straight men are tested; gay men are embraced. Then pubescent boys are weirdly brought forth as possible commodities to play with. Sexual abuse burns boys, as Mad Donna video-rides off into the night with a kid who hangs out at the ticket wicket in front of an adult private-booth strip joint. In her music video, Mad Donna is the disrober for dough, spurning the packed stalls of voyeurs to start sexing with the youngster. She plants a big kiss, wiggle-wiggles and leaves hand-in-hand skipping up a hill with the four-foot something pre-teen. The vagina dentia of Greek mythology, with rows of dangerous teeth for man-eating, may incarnate these days and feed upon young males budding in metropolis?

Our Miss Mad Donna begins to explode any claims the leaders of women might have made about being the guardians and perpetrators of a moral code in society. Female moral superiority (FMS) is out the window. Change the youngster to a girl and have a male perform Mad Donna's role, and it's the slammer for sure. Mad Donna gets away only because FMS used to be "reality." And the thought is still around, usurped by many and used to boss society around. It brings power and that's what matters.

What's this sympathy for the socially abused about really? Sensitive men are only gay men? And what is it that gay men are so sensitive about anyway? The newspapers and the national propaganda networks will serve up more answers amongst the stews publicly stirred. It's all served as fun food anyway: inflation, the budget, bull markets, mass murders, sex with children, boy-friend lying, whatever. Ever wondered why so much of the bought press and owned media are pro-gay?

So there is a power benefit for women to give gay men the OK. The gays keep straight men off-balance and justifying when the gays are showered with female love. Gay men challenge the heteros to immerse themselves in *feelings* to get attention. And this sideswipes many straights, standing silently, refusing to budge when certain females terrorize-taunt-insult them, trying to break them down to where they can be controlled emotionally.

Using the Male. One agenda is: woman testing man to see if he can be broken. Just what does it take to move him, trip him, slay him psychologically? Homophobia perhaps. His sexual and emotional center is her target. Can she find an advantage?

Another agenda is feminizing all the men, training them to please with an overt emotional focus that is full of her need for sensitivity, empathy and consolation.

Further toying—if the breasts can be pushed together and held there, they make rounded cheeks and a crack down the middle recalling a derriere. Here the pied piper leads the buttheads into her further service, into servitude, as rebuked males who may receive grace only if she chooses to give her heterosexual reward to them. Yes, it can work magic, that *image*, that fabulously followed and mesmerizing rounded butt that has been of such help promoting and producing male volunteers for her programs....

Public consumption of abuse is running at record limits. Why shouldn't a girl be her own star, jump right into her own Harlequin romance—somehow she'll find a way to create her own explosion of the dysfunction that's like what is decorating the television hills, Harlequin halls and cinema malls of her middle America. Then she can grab society's trained female sympathy and a settlement, meaning money. Boot a dummy dude out of his home into some low-rent cockroach camp. Slaughter a male, bust his back on the edge of gender feminist dysfunction, create one of the cripples lining up for social-service cheques and seeing the kids every second Saturday, if lucky. *Even allowing children to be near men is worrisome....* And the zest of all this real life drama brings the "victimized" real "live" tears.

And here is the point: many women need to feel and to somehow connect with the tragedy of life, but are enduring a politically correct cold-storage freezing of their sensibility. The business model demands cold, bottom-line attitude. It suits a merchant in search of profits, not an emotionally alive and sensitively alert woman. Woman's anger at capitalist economics is transferred to men. They are her scapegoats.

The "business" of relationships and the need to purge the grief-sorrow-anger of this life sets up the diabolical collusions and machinations witnessed in contemporary relationships. Sacrifices were legal once and appeased the compulsion to witness suffering, to make atonement, and to give to the beast in the hope of receiving grace or forgiveness – or today, maybe it's in the hope of simply getting "market" savvy.

The generations before cried too, and their tears were real. It's horror now, because she's setting it all up, manipulating the pieces while knowing better, and because her grandmother's Cro-Magnon vinculum reaches into her genes. Her grandmother needed, really needed, a man-helper to survive, perhaps to thrive, and therefore any loss was catastrophic, especially if the feelings, emotion and dedication between the mates was filled freely with affection.

> *She's saying today she needs no man,*
> *Why embrace dependency, there is a better plan,*
> *Boys are toys, with whom she can play (gambles),*
> *Ride the emotional roller coaster, leave him in shambles,*
> *Close-up and personal, in her own TV soap drama,*
> *It's the double shuffle of her lamb, bah! gamba.*

Madonna's phallus girls and their phallus mom were obviously not going to make much of a dent in the patriarchy. They were integral to its working. Their aspirations were to be equal or better than the males in the game; this was how they had been trained. They had bought into the divide-and-rule propaganda pabulum served up in an elementary education, paid for with public monies. They wanted only power, for many reasons, some noble-sounding like freedom of self-expression, Emersonian self-reliance and personal responsibility. But their new competitiveness served state-run corporate machinery established years ago.

> *Independent consumers, undermining mainstay men,*
> *Their windfall chaos keeps corporate systems*
>   *winning again.*

Yes, the goals of the girls and the boys became almost the same, as all became self-persecuted, masochistic in their strive for "excellence." Separate individual power points hungry for energy, more energy, laboring to store energy. Like ants carrying loads (products) back to the nest, these insect cowboys (girls) ride roughshod over asphalt on the lookout for deals—a deal, a steal, a bargain, a market killing, so they can make big bucks and "fuck off." Getting out is seen as the reward for basically everyone. Except the clinically ill or psychopathic workaholic executives caught somehow loving the S&M life and its devilish perks.

Dressing Up Disco—in-step with the Power Elite. The disco music of the 70's is thought of as lax, vacant, simple machine music that has only a beat and is therefore danceable. This was Mad Donna's teen-time, and she copied it and pushed it on the public. The women's movement of the 70's derailed many positive, evolutionary radical-reformist voices while disco dished up audio-Valium. Popular entertainment culture became rude, dumb-headed and vacant. The power elite pilfer as the dazed consumers disco. Double platinum *Vogue*, Mad Donna's biggest hit, continued the drag of disco into the 90's.

Two decades of dumbness-numbness. Nerd mouthpieces are rearranged as TV anchor-people everywhere, giving almost no news and info that can't be bought. Mad Donna's *Vogue* encourages letting your body go with the flow while imitating dead stars and being fashionable. As if dressing up could give a character that could be counted on for any meaningful length of time. Going bra-less, topless, was a gutsy statement of bodily reality, but are any women doing it today without being paid? Why not? Mad Donna's dress-ups show how an actress could use different costumes in various roles, for various effects and purposes. But thanks in part to her, fashion is now personality achieved without effort.

Mad Donna Co-opted

The Reagan revolution took the world forward into the past, as old money reconsolidated its grip. Women bashed men, indulged in hating, blaming and bitching at the bastards they were taught to view as the enemy.

Flaunting sexuality and sexual capacity, Mad Donna dresses-up to bash, berate, terrorize and demean. Five older brothers gave the squealing female Ciccone chick the smarts. A victim of the female cop-out of the 60's, Mad Donna thinks a level playing field means career and personal power, and stacking the decks with sexual hegemony, with female affirmative-action government support and protections and with acceptance of an "inherited" female moral superiority. And she's done marvelously – icon status, millions of dollars – an ambitious person who's made it in the jungle-out-there.

What has she done for her sisters? In general, they've come a long way—from original unity, feminist concern and serious responsibility and commitment toward improving the whole social world. Sure, they've made gains in feminine supports and privileges, but that has been the general trend in American society for the past 200 years! So, it's plainly more of the same.

Apart from the revolutionary females of the 60's and the few socialist types lurking about nervously—attacked as idiots in the 90's and into the new century—there is general blindness to organizing all of society into healthy community. Women became rational believers in their oppression by men. Their emotional and intuitive power was overpowered by the state-served rationalist education they had to endure. It isn't being shared enough with men, in the pursuit of social improvement for all.

Women are dropping their identification with the whole social body. In the scrapping and clawing for an individual fulfillment that the postmodern person believes can be found, a victimizing, manipulative strategy is in. For power some ride on the backs of lingering sentiment towards women, connected to the believed female moral and social superiority of the past. Today, however, lying has been accepted as but another strategy. And men are still targeted as a means to financial freedom.

Mad Donna obliterates all the female competition. In the shark pool of corporate, state-maintained cartel capitalism, it's popular to think that it's *power* that matters. The cult of competition serves corporate bosses, and it's therefore promoted. But in spectator society hundreds of millions of people aren't even in the competition. Self-critical and introverted, hiding failures, on booze, etc., they shy away...another day....

That Mad Donna thinks of herself as a revolutionary is a huge wake-up call. Are these really the revolutionaries, those who clamp attitude and dictate the behavior that perpetuates a familiar class society and rule by the abundantly wealthy few over the numbered and herded minions? This is really a revolt where common sense is overturned, replaced by a rational freezing of the emotional force necessary to make change. To see the resultant apathy, from sea to shining sea—where sometimes over fifty million eligible women refuse to show up at the voting booths come election day USA, this assures the survival of this system. No matter, Mad Donna says she's not happy anyway, and says she doesn't know anybody else who is either.

> *"From when I was very young I just knew that being a girl and being charming in a feminine sort of way could get me a lot of things, and I milked it for everything I could."*[11]
>
> —*Madonna*

15
Mistaken Identity

Princess Monroe sold sexy charm and personality; Princess Diana sold what? Even silk bedclothes, ready servants, gala and gay caviar carnivals, tons of horny suitors with huge bank accounts and regal control power didn't allow her to prevail. Mother Teresa wouldn't let her off the hook. Mother Superior didn't jump the gun, and she died right after the Princess, thus giving a needed contrast between herself and the fond illusion many seem to be living in, concerning Princess Diana. An upwardly mobile sharkess sank her teeth into the loins of the Wale Prince and rode the male-baiting surf of the times for personal glory, stardom, celebrity.

Mother Teresa crawled in the dirt with the barrio-dwellers, the distressed, the wretched of the earth, the diseased and dying. But the Princess didn't feel no pinch, no down-to-bedrock, out-at-the-heels communion with misfortune. Mother Teresa's hands of compassion reached out and comforted, but the diamond-clad Princess worked with her agents as a cover-girl promoting her shoulders as a new centerpiece of style to trap male attention. Meantime, a tabloid magazine boldly declares: *Di Can't Get Enough Sex*.

Her celebrity, it's fun food for men-haters, feminazis, and it gave women an uppity bully power knowing that Diana pulled off the insult, scourged the future king. She frolicked in dream melodrama supreme, the seemingly in-control female complete with an ounce of maternal care for a world forced into poverty by her relatives and the power elite they hang with.

A new type of role model for young ladies? Well, if marrying for money is new, or using men as vehicles to build personal careers is that uncommon, then she might be the one to get the shower of envy come awards night. Shapely legs she showed, breasts beckoned and she was thin enough. Special hairdressing, tons of eye gook and lip paint, and thousands of British pounds worth of threads upgraded her performances.

Using males, even a Prince of Wales, in the reach for personal glory! It's all ok now and makes good sense, with bottom-line separate profit the order of the day. But the real Mother T encouraged letting go, giving up resistance, accepting fragmentation and receiving salvation through forgiveness.

Feminists and Di

The people mourn themselves: beaten with media clubs, lied to each and every hour, their ancestors dead on some castaway foreign battlefield where they fought for truth (General Electric, Boeing) or someone's definition of freedom, or the Queen or some God. There are times today when average Joe and Jill seem to have gone psycho, know not what they do and can be trained to even idolize the enemy. Then their brains could perhaps use a giant enema.

The media is so compassionate over this Diana because the gender feminists have infiltrated, and it's clear that with any female fault—away from here they shall steer. Charles may have picked a suicidal adulteress complete with eating disorders and an inferiority complex, but she is portrayed, as usual, as a victim—of him! Creating a media angel, a conspiracy exists, and for Charles it's into the pits. He has to be the devil in counterpoint to her angel. And the male bodyguard crippled by the car crash, who gives a damn about this victim? The gender feminists seem to equate *men* with something like *sin*. Clearing up even half the delusions brought on by the feminist-friendly spins broadcast everywhere would begin to restore some respect for men.

Mass Manipulation

Stuck, heads dazed with spin, after watching TV—then the educated "morons" believe what they see, give up on doubt and much that they feel? Surrounded by corruption and festering ideologies of scarcity, educated citizen "jackasses" are just asking to be busted? Upside-down logic smogs through the air. Some kids believe nothing matters, because they know somehow that a huge cruelty lives and is at work in their society. They are in fear, but *the fear itself is exciting.* Understand? Their psycho-excitement can scatter, deny a certain focus, maybe bring a death-wish, maybe help bring support for wars. (Now the pin-point particular stipulates is the time to beware!)

Today everything can seem made up. All that matters can seem to be self-interest, promotion and selling. Constantly commercials are aimed at manipulation. So trusting nothing, but used to surrendering to movies and TV and thus keeping the gates of the mind open, the new generations are ripe for annexation and appropriation by the pros, the longhairs earning a living by producing and giving special "meaning" to citizen's experience.

The negativity and monotony of schooling, the robot-like memorization and the enormity of facts whistled through the mind's eye can deny compassion. Compassion is replaced by a rationally trained linguistic prisonerhood.

A false consciousness develops from living in a propaganda culture. Rational over-education is alienating. All this distancing then turns over one's natural and personal understanding of what-is going-on-out-there-in-here to the long- haired vampires, who are forced, induced by a paycheck, to ride on board and feed with the bully elite. Beyond freedom and dignity, these ghouls of social control make beds and get results, as many people are seduced, lie down hypnotized, and buy in. Ultimately seeing is believing: the President smiles, holding the hands of Israeli and PLO leaders: Peacemaker leader-image burns into the TV watchers' brain.

For Princess Diana's TV interview, the one that garnered such a good feeling for her from the public, they bring in big-screen cinematographer Sir Richard Attenborough. His previous biographical interview had been Mother Teresa.

> *Get the paint, arrange the picture,*
> *The hired gunslingers now do dicker;*
> *For the dollar—they adeptly attach the collar*
> *Big Brother demands, secretly to neuter,*
> *But publicly to inform and educate, build a proprietor.*

The Public Misled

Squashed under the heel-boot of public education, the rationally educated may become redundant. Some can't fit their souls (bodies) into any great appreciation for the gigantic experience of life. Endlessly gnawing with burning frustration, like insects unstoppably forking in the dry dirt, their minds dig further into cerebral hemispheres.... But the rational fabrication structures are not producing comprehensive understanding. For society there doesn't seem to be any grand understanding, and no popular mythologies circulating today are fully and adequately interpreting to the masses the spectacular, awesome existence featured here on planet Earth. So the desire and need to know answers grows and grows, but the solutions the educated people are given are so varied, so complex and so contradictory that bafflement sets in.

Many have gone mental, but in a cynical way, using their rational answers only for the "new," the temporary, not for long-term solutions.

Everybody uses their "spiel" only to sell their point of view in the present moment. Words are used to dress up and persuade. They are accessories for use in the mundane world, the world that won't last, the world that is of desire.

Popular Christianity and Buddhism and the market may explain a lot regarding victims, but can they bring mankind into organic health? Mental involvement may let offenders off the hook. Rational over-use lessens the emotional, intuitive tug towards understanding. Everyone discusses an issue of contention, like Bill Clinton's oral sex with young interns, George W. Bush's tilt toward attacking Iraq or Texas death-row pick-axe murderer Karla Faye Tucker's reborn religious convictions and plea for commutation. After all the talk, after all the highways of free opinion proffered up to the demigod of reason, well, the public is exhausted.

Rational structures can't deliver justice unfailingly, and the longhairs must know it. Witness the deluge of TV discussion focused on the President's mistress crises. By over-talking, the emotional force is undermined, and eventually, after endless jet streams of script spoken by many talking heads, the issue flattens out, gets even less clear. Now the mop-up boys roll in and tell the public whatever they can get away with. The public have been disarmed, so to speak, by all the fudging information.

Forebrain, endbrain, temporal lobe, hypothalamus,
medulla oblongata too,
All this grey matter just won't do,
For to give life its aura and majesty and even fearful ado,
Heartfelt and gut connection needs positive sensation,
  to ignite the clue,
While modern mush-heads flake out, TV couch-potato on
  through.

Di's Tragedy as Sideshow

Trying to squeeze Princess Diana's tragedy into their idle lives—the public is using the tragedy to get some tears flowing and some real non-rational emotion going. It's insulting—using Diana, yes, using her death to elevate themselves as survivors. Here the emotional necrophiliacs do feed. Twisting a rich neurotic playgirl into Mother Teresa may seem hard to handle. But a public, beaten and abused, needs a beacon, a focus, a burning candle of acknowledged sympathy.

So little organic wholeness is dished up nowadays by the brutal bunch of business lieutenants and their media minions—those who point the finger in the scramble for a believed scarcity of commodities, land, medicine, air and time. Underneath somewhere, the need to cry bursts all over Princess Diana's misfortune. But it is necessary to identify the compelling origin for its expression. The lying words of state leaders and the flunkeys they dine with, and the spin put on these words by the PR persons and the bought media have led some reporters and newspeople to aggressive tactics. They are trying to expose the negatives about those who control a country's money and munitions.

But the counter-fleecing is expert, the results are in,
The power elite and their media always win,
Newspapers, radios and networks galore –
The news they relay can't hurt them no more,
So good at even telling bad news
About themselves, the Masters amuse,
Laughing at the elimination of doubt,
And anyway, being number one is what it's about!

Royalty is to big business like candy is to children. It quiets consumers, distracts, gives momentary solace, trust in a future and keeps people in their place (below). A celebrity train weaves the nations as little citizens stand in their stations, waving and leaning to steal a glance at the royals and their most fortunate circumstance. The nightly news serves to blitz nincompoops with alarms of struggle and flight: fifty to one hundred living species evaporate each *day*, and in Russia 100 suitcase-size nuclear bombs have just been stolen *away*. So brighten up the moment and wave at the royals, note down the event in your own diary-editorial, a *highlight*, a privilege to be included in their story all *right*.

Some of the press chased Diana because she was part of the process that controls nations. Trying to catch rich bloody liars is tremendously difficult because their professional staffs find the leaks, plug the cracks and maintain illusions. So when a fault appears and the ground begins to move, the press race to watch.

Diana dumped the royals but wanted to be one. She mixed with the elite, slept with them, and used the press to promote herself. Diana had a history before her marriage of emotional and psychological problems. Her affairs with her lovers began before Charles returned to his liaison with the older woman, Camilla. And Diana called Charles a terrible father, something which does not seem true. As a star celebrity she tried to lose what her brother called her "deep feelings of inadequacy."

Being allied with the bullies and herself one of dozens of stars that the average person is seduced to live their lives through, her every move was watched both by the bullies and by the "dirty beast" public.

> *Forsaking marriage and venturing out from her nest,*
> *The common thought was that she's only trying her*
>   *very best.*
> *Male bashing and crashing, it's now so popular to vent,*
> *All women's troubles over patriarchal cement*
> *Gone so rigidly numb,*
> *A woman gots to kick butt to get rid of the scum.*

A Princess through marriage but like uncounted commoners, millions upon millions, she drops the man she once wed for better things.

She's got Royal income, had bred herself out,
Now it's time to find what her private destiny is
really about....
There must be a reason, a reason for one's life, right?
A marital transaction that couldn't withstand the
rigors of time,
This princess knows with her look and loot everything
will be just fine.
Men are held in contempt in most of the western world,
And with support from her head-banded sisters,
the fist is curled,
In the fantasy lands of all the democracies, it is their fight!
Many sisters don't care that she's living high off the hog,
Only that she step all over the Wale Prince dog!
Bristling with anger, reacting to their rage,
They want this dysfunctional Prince locked in his cage.

Prince Charles raised concern over social issues in the mid-1980's. He even allowed his royal armor to be somewhat removed and for his vulnerability to be evident. The Prince's Trust was set up to work for social needs. Woman-power loves a dullard to feast upon, but Charlie has a heavy role to play, and royal silence is part of it. So Diana jumped into the social advocate role.

A woman, a mother, who could refuse?
Not happy with fame and wifely cool,
This Princess played Charlie for one great big fool,
Cake and eat it,
The kids to be Kings, you just can't beat it.
Around and around the world she did fly,
Anything of interest she probably could buy,
But glory, the crowds that raced to greet her,
Massive hoopla—it all did sweep her
Into a very understandable modern megalomania.

Fans fawn helplessly, looking to take personal meaning out of the celebrities' lives, because effective mythology has left their own. Except for the Legends of Hockey, Legends of Football, Harlequin romance, Cinderella, etc.

Fame by Association

Many citizens have no popular role models that can give substantive meaning to their present lives. Their heroes usually come second-hand, produced and directed by the professional media and big screen corporations. And star athletes can become only ten- or twenty-second sound bites. Not really what is needed to uplift and focus, give substance or truth to the people of any country. Instead, citizens get the media information and its electric-hot consciousness of present-day breakdown, disheveledness – the news flash just around the corner. It's about fear, and the royals provide distraction.

The myth of the individual torridly churns around Diana. The individual, the center, and no longer a renter or wife, now as a "shooter" she could start a new life, and began this royally blessed starlet to sweep the currents to align with her mythomania (reasons).

Wallis Simpson was another starlet who dabbled in royals. Indeed she became notable only because of her control over the King of England, Edward VIII. Their marriage in 1937 precipitated his abdication from the English throne, for marrying this twice- divorced commoner and an American to boot. Wallis became a luminary because of her proximity to power, a most famous celebrity. Here is evidence of the *rise of the emotional man*, and of the power this transfers to women once his virtue is compromised. She and Edward were top spot in invitations to attend spectacles of the rich and famous. Like conversation pieces incarnate in human form, they traveled the world as sought-after dignitaries and blue-bookers, paid homage to by the big shots in the modern urge to get close to power.

For fame has become power. No matter that the fame comes from adultery, axe murders or embezzlement of millions of dollars, it qualifies as an interest point for societies and as opportunity for vicarious indulgence. Citizens look for meaning, lessons and stimulation for their own lives. But there's no mythology to build a life on here with these flash-in-the-pan personages. The newly rich and a rising class of business and performing stars want to be seen rubbing shoulders with a Wallis and an Edward, as if a royal legitimacy might now by association color their public auras. Useless but for notoriety and the royal connection, these two, Edward and Wallis, freeloaded and cavorted. But their power was deception, for they were but an entertainment and ego predilection.

The Entertainment Elite

> *Celebrity rules. Actor, scammer, harlot or tennis duo,*
> *It has taken this goofy life right into the big name glue,*
> *Elevated to heights once reserved only for royals,*
> *These rich con artists and rich jocks*
> *Only distract and reforming plans do foil,*
> *As the masses are caught mesmerized by the*
> *   entertainment-culture locks,*
> *Pretending to be the Top Gun, finding the hoop,*
> *   shooting a puck*
> *Pretending to kiss, banging a baseball, pretending to fuck,*
> *Crushing a quarterback, pretending to care –*
> *   these clowns are today right in the luck,*
> *Getting adulation and the big buck.*

The entertainment elite don't care about much; things are going well for them, and they feed on the general public's conditioned hollowness. In one hour they can earn more than the majority of people living in their country do in a year! They are so famous that politicians hide behind them, cater to them and like to be seen with them. They offer nothing to anyone, maybe a pittance here and there: a concert for blown-up peasants, a concert for starving children, a PR trip through a hospital. Diana actually touched a person with AIDS; the royal-via-marriage body could go so far!

These riff-raff worth thousands of millions get guru status, but many are unstable theater types that buffalo through numerous roles, switching personalities like politicians. Or they are persons limited to physically excelling at some movement and looking for glory (endorsements). Kept in an elite world of giant syndicate-controlled conformity, they see the masses as fickle. But they coddle the fans to keep their egos and the paychecks flowing and filling the airy mansions they inhabit.

Why let the stars, the celebrities, provide stimulation and an aura around daily living? Living vicariously through these actors, hoop-shooters and singers blunts and traps, and it demands subservience. No meanings of depth are obliged to come from the identification. Superficial details swamp insight, and distraction and escape are the true consummation.

Princess Diana launched her career as a star, first by marriage to Charles and then stepped on to an ultra-modern stage by breaking the marriage contract. Then the *People* magazine cover of March 1996, headlined: DI-VORCE HER FUTURE BEGINS. Di stands in a white-striped business suit, the one hand on hip intones the demand for space, the deep V-neck revealing naked princess skin. It's like some of the newborn business chicks, dressed for success and flaunting the flesh—from above and *below* these power trippers are in it for *dough*.

Wallis Simpson, in 1987, had Sotheby's auction some of her jewels. An ad about the auction read: "For the woman who knows what she wants and gets it. Wallis Simpson, the woman who stole the heart of the King of England and refused to give it back." Millions of dollars came in for Wallis' trinkets. Many who cherish a connection to the famed are after a piece of the action. So the circus train continues, as the carnivores seek solace in taking possession of another's quarried reward. Why would someone want to wear a dress that has been used by Diana? Is it to be number one, to be the one and only person in the universe in possession of the material? In the end, is it a personal triumph of possession? Like imperialism's control of colonies? Sadness somehow indicates that this modern vision may be one for observers, not doers. It's likely the audience mentality—with one's life lived through others.

Stealing hearts, Diana thought she was in charge, and hers' was the modern woman's world to scan. But it came to be, and this is the gist of it all—that the choice to follow one's imagined reasons for a separate course may have startling results. Leaving her home and marriage environment, striking out with much ado and *fanfare*, invited the ghosts of righteousness to judge the actions as foul or *fair*.

Diana challenged many and did climb upon the chariot of celebrity. And after having won the many masses as a Princess of the People, fault lines appear. A chasm opens as wealth and privilege, diamonds and the regal gowns bloomed into jet-setting romances. Her image became deeply clouded and her high-struck image began to crumble, then got blown down. The earth shifts and nature must fall into *place*, as choices bring results—it is not always a storybook matter of *grace*.

Public Feeds on Celebrity

And the public feeds on Diana's melodrama. Of course, Diana was used, and her raking relieved some projected frustrations for her former captivated subjects. To the one-upmanship beat, ghouls celebrate in the slippery slime of the disease of conceit, having bettered the one who dared trump the King. The proof of success is that they are the ones still living.

Celebrities take so much and offer so little that their private life is demanded in return. The public uses the celebrities' lives to help endure their own. That is what it has come to. The public has given up on doing much marvelous with their own lives. They've got the stars to place their hopes on, to take the shots for them and even to bleed to death for them. Unfortunately these quasars turn out to be mostly black holes as far as giving anything useful or expedient back to anybody, except maybe their agents. The public aim their lives for safety, but there is not much room for the mediocre at the top. Thus a quiet desperation rules their lives.

Mediocre man adulates ingenues and mimics—those unstable ones capable of being almost anything. Didn't Gene Wilder say that all actors are insecure, and hadn't Woody Allen remarked that actors are the most screwed up of people? That actors adept at the variegation necessary to pretend to various personalities should get 20 million dollars for a movie role is absurd. And then to be given hero status because they are now rich is more than absurd. And the athletes, many still mentally in adolescence, good since their early youths at making balls or pucks roll, slide, drop or shoot through openings—why should they make more money than a chief of state, top CEO in business, or those in health care and social work? The actors and sport stars—neither benefit society much, both are self-interested opportunists. And as long as the average Jill and Joe worship at their feet, well, the rich and famous and their comrade politicians, they are discretely snickering.

The politicians and their bosses are able to hide behind the stars. This keeps *you*, the dirty public beast, feeling good and inferior, a sub-par star. And you're soon to be even more out to lunch when it comes to the know-how of the science specialists dealing with any *crunch*.

The specter of a giant rip-off is growing. The public sometimes thinks the wrong hands are in control. But the public is weary; they drive resignedly through the poison, back to the walls of their houses, turn on the telly. And they start pleasing the belly, get lost in the colors, the pictures and the sex appeal of an invader machine that's bent to peg out any passionate non-profit reform—the distraction comes at a price, carries a toll.

Working Girl

Diana's death moved many a working girl. Educated to be self-interested, the woman working today wants some hope of a future in which her own imagined success story could come true. To get a prince and his wealth bountiful can be a fabulously fortunate windfall.

> *Off-chucking the males,*
> *It's popular game, and in legal warfare the female derails*
> *The so-called dense dudes not hip to the trick,*
> *Then matriarchal punch*
> *Gets rid of the dunce,*
> *She's got the kids and his bank account at once,*
> *Although it's not chic to speculate in men,*
> *This is a way for those who desperately think to win.*

Gender Warfare and Androgyny

It is getting frigid in this western society. Gender warfare made relationships really a drag. Who wants to live with nothing, as androgyny compacts everyone into the same package: women pretending they are the spiritual equal of men, and men pretending they are the emotional equal of women, just as though the poles *had* reversed.

Wasn't androgyny just an aberration brought on by a society of disinformation, where assertions of all sorts of equality spring up randomly from many self-interested factions? No matter the lies, deception and lack of truth to many of these claims, they are legal and even taught at school. The absurd number of "truths" that are circulating without any solid base in reality may cause paranoia and suspicion and cause people to suspend consideration of much today. But it's mediocrity that emerges, when confusion and distrust is implanted in people's rational structures.

Sexuality is an individual thing, but its neglect can produce infatuation and an overwhelming isolation. Social purpose has little pull to the islands unto themselves that fill the streets today.

Is it capitalism that brings on their big headaches and introversion? While people are being competitive and cold outside and rationally trapped within—a lot of work for personal and collective abundance and health just cannot get done. And those whose supraliminal being is too obsessed with the consummation of sex, are they filling their lives with so much despair that they cannot see any public purpose above their selfish, but very typically human, pursuit of pleasure?

But the ticket to riches, security, kids and even perhaps fame, for women today Prince Charming is now disposable and marriage doesn't mean a damn? The female kids of second-wave feminists possess images of Diana as a victor, a winner, a female on the move, on the go, creating her own life, herself, capable of wheeling and dealing, breaking convention, beyond the limited scope of males. She was some sort of an indicator to them of the matriarchal society to come. Now that she is gone they are forced back unto themselves and perhaps to modified images of talents they possess.

And poor Charlie, he's made the loser list—along with Trudeau, Canada's dashing Prime Minister, whose wife gave herself up to rock stars for momentary pleasure. Adultery. And Paul McCartney, too. He knows a thing or two about modern women, eh? His second marriage to the handicapped woman has fast-tracked Sir Paul to hell. It's no mystery, these betrayals are real, and are evidence of our society's direction. Most men are gonna be done in.

16
21st Century Foxed

A woman can make of herself a gift to a man. And this woman can be an empowered, independent, even antagonistic one, hostile to many male notions, memes or preconceptions about what a female ought to or should be like. This woman, perhaps a self-actualized accountable human success, when she makes a gift of herself to a man, in complete abandon, this gift of her surrender increases his power and love. This surrender is not a mere weakening of her forces, but a total affirmative gift of herself, in carnality. Experienced women know what this gift means. Some men do, too.

On Empowering Women

This was Friedrich Nietzsche's position from over one hundred years ago. You haven't heard about him much? Nietzsche was the man who knew how to dare the most, the most excellent writer-philosopher of the nineteenth century, who *deeply and profoundly* influenced so many of our present century's brilliant minds. Nietzsche was the kick-off into postmodernism: will to power was the message, action the result.

To Nietzsche a proud woman goes beyond mere surrender and docility. She is complete, and her ego knows that there is also an increase in *her* power in "*the drunkenness called love.*" In their sexual passion women acquire "*their pride and their feelings of power,*" he said.[1] They are closely tied to the sexual-emotional nerve connections. Their personal knowledge of the "act" is wide-ranging, because they understand what it demands of them, in their psyche and in their feeling soul. Their comprehension can make them resilient and wise, and their capacity surpasses any for most men.

A woman's situation today is a conundrum, with the postmodern worship of separate power unto each separate person. To give the ego in abandon may now be thought of as surrender to male brainwashing and to socialization as a sex object of lowly status. This is popularly considered suitable for a slave of male desire, and therefore for a woman's self-esteem could today be believed to be a loss of power.

Today the social system turns out insisting, snapping advocates of independence, the female who thinks she must now be free to act rationally like a man, to seek wealth and power. She believes the modern world is going to turn into her stage, for her to have her hour; she is taught the radical feminist manifesto must continue. She entwines currents complete with claims of abuse, and then stretches them to spread above all and create the roof over the *female shelter* of *society*. Her power demands services: protection, childcare, female-favored policy and all the other social safety nets.

> *She's interested in her gain, simple and plain,*
> *Consideration of men's needs are flushed down the drain.*

The sexy sex masters couldn't give a heck about the abuse of males, although many are ever ready for help from men, or from government agencies, to ease their female "plight." Even the aristocratic women seem to yearn for support, in all forms, including taxpayer's money. Are women just naturally insecure? Why is so much help needed? This may reveal a bona fide disadvantage for females and promotes a question: is it naturally *harder* being a female than being a male?

But if this *femaleness borne with difficulty* is then to be subjected to the feminazis' instruction to distrust males and go it alone, it's soon apparent that *crazy McBeal* is going to be a popular female circumstance. Is a whole new world going to jump out in order for these many nervous, rational, individuated females to take over and save themselves? Or is all this talk of patriarchal hate promoted in the media to keep society divided, and to keep the masters in power—with the serfs all tuned in on the status-quo consensus channel? With both sexes working there are more harried consumers scrambling to make ends meet and needing products related to being employed.

> *No one can organize but for the distrust,*
> *Opposition to long-haired agendas inevitably goes bust.*

Families at the Crossroads

So we don't know if this twenty-first century fox has a future in maternity wards, or if she is heterosexual, or if her offspring will slowly slide into becoming *wards* of the state. Are males to be rebuffed as merely carriers of chemicals to be fast frozen and used when called upon? Are the bucks they once produced now unnecessary, as mothers cut open social service checks from state and are also hired before males in the workplace?

Once the two-sex union was a benefit for physical survival. Each sex unit helped to provide food, shelter and safety, as well as emotional-sexual health. Now life carries on without marriage between the sexes; the rent is paid. But are sexual-emotional marriage contracts now only evidence of immature and outdated need? Has the female surrender and gift of herself to a man become only another consumer item? And does a person only gain power at another's expense?

Unknown Woman—Fourth-wave Feminism:

> *Off into the wild blue yonder,*
> *Fourth-wave feminism is bringing home much to ponder.*

It's called *unknown woman*, this fourth wave. Because there is no one that a grown-up female can refer her progeny to, to emulate. Name one female heroine? The new *real* female is claimed as the one not socialized by the patriarchy into roles others find useful—into victim roles that the consensus has grown to love so much. So the *real* female, she must now exist in the subconscious they say, or in the unconscious. "She" is in the process of evolving into this fourth-wave woman, they say. But all that really means is she doesn't exist yet. We're all just waiting for her to pop out in bodily form. And she will emerge perhaps in the next hour or so, or in the near future or maybe in ten or twelve millennia. It's in the works they *say*, the real woman who is going to save the *day*. We don't know what this star of the women's movement is going to be like.

> *There hasn't been anyone constructed of this stuff, as yet in this crusade,*
> *So just move aside while the fourth-wave female earth-creature is made.*

Has unaccountability gone so far out now that even lack of self-understanding is being justified and glorified? *Unknown woman* gives a lot of free space for all sorts of behavior. Unaccountability and the psychological feelings approach to life allow the fourth wave, this—new, radical liberated-type woman—fantasy.

Of course, moral reason and a stand on rational principle needs the added modification and *balance* of a feelings approach. But most present-day use of this necessary *feelings* approach is only aimed critically at male shortcomings. Men are accused of insensitivity. And many who partake herein gouge modern men—those males who take women seriously, who strive to harmonize this female creature with their attention, those who make an effort at understanding as well as protecting her.

Is today's woman becoming all illusion, head to toe, and pulling legions of males into her lot with a *pretended* submissive sexuality? And believe it, that can be *her* thought, that it's pretended!

Now her female icon role-model rolls out at the beginning of the millennium as *unknown woman.* Is she to be guided by anarchistic nihilism? *She is postmodern, resentful and open to great fear. The clouds darken within all her mental construction as her enemy often becomes hidden in nebulous psychological, perhaps fantasy, lands.* Meanwhile, the paint streams from her cosmetic wounds, applied to punish and remove stunted males through trapping their gaze and attention and forcing them into another fantasy—her seductive, sexy dissimulation. But these men, many who are attempting in their manner to construct lives of meaning, are stumbling, holding dreams now unrealizable as their "soul mates" have gone voodoo. And is he to her a cruelty incarnate, the living devil—these educated, reasonable, *jackass* men attempting to construct meaningful, reasonable lives?

Men—Be All You Can Be

Listen men, how about a consumer approach? With action the chains are broken, then you can take some steps forward. The goal is to live the words: *Be all you can be.* Live, in-color lives that emphasize a man's natural-born life capacities, those characteristics and abilities that uplift and give the positive sex the right to carry on for the good of all society. The task is more than noble, and it could be the only way to save the world and humanity.

There's so much confusion, the greedy bleeding hearts and the hating feminists muddling any carpe diem to actually get things right, get things straight. Men, you could begin to shop for suitable lifestyles, and choose one large in *male empowerment.*

The elitist establishment, the system, it's quite content to have gender *war,* immigrants moving in next *door,* talk shows on TV—it is keeping everyone off balance and non-threatening. The government just takes polls, then their words say what the polls tell them the public wants to hear. The government money goes to where corporate bosses want it to go—just like always in *these* democracies.

But let's just say the system is set up, and let's try to work with it. You know, guys, you could organize and lobby, threaten to cut *throat* with your *vote.* Your lives are in disgrace. You may be too depressed to make many moves, so much heckling, criticism and bashing have been downloaded unto your frame. From youth through adolescence and into adulthood your male shoulders have been weighted down by the insults to your gender, so much so that the distraction occurring from this negative mode of life has you afraid to spit in "maternal" woman's face. That's how you've been forced to see them, women, as the vessel of birth; women as the sacred and sanctified one, the mother of all beings.

> *Men it's you they are out to victimize, but can you*
>   *call the winner in, realize,*
> *And see the truth of your demise, stop seeing the*
>   *world through women's eyes?*

It's not something new; women have been marching to their xenophobic lobby-tune for hundreds of years—this, the selfish women's tune, the exclusive gender bias. Today she's successfully taking over and unseating men from some of their noble places. In Victorian times and until after World War I, when a divorce occurred it was usual for the man to automatically get custody of the children. How much does that disturb you today, guys, and what has really changed here?

Why is it thought that feminism is new, when the modern women's lib forces began at least 200 years ago? Feminism strengthened at the time of the French Revolution (1789) during the screaming fist-raised killings and under fervent memes—ideas of equality, liberty and fraternity. These memes were shown early to be perhaps only unworthy matronly dreams, as Napoleon—dictator, male, absolute power—and his marching military machine were soon given the power to set the country right. He was worshiped and promoted as the savior from all the *feminism, equality and equal rights*, all the "vulgar bourgeois mediocrity" and "spin" that had been promoted by the French Revolution. What say, you've gone deaf, you didn't know the joke of official-version created consensus? You didn't know that the egalitarian hope of equality and democracy failed right at the beginning, and an aristocratic seizure of power was the result?

> *Presently George W. Bush mouths the democratic jingle,*
> *But among the aristocracy of today, purposely hidden,*
>   *in a tangle,*
> *The rich find their own with whom to mingle.*

Men—Why Marry Out of Pity?

So why marry women out of pity? Putting the female on the pedestal of sympathy is just another form of control, and it is evidence of men's will to power, to control her this way, in Rousseauian sympathy. She is idealized like some heavenly bird down from the heavens, suffering in the winds of earthly struggle and flight. You want to live in brainwashed ignorance? Some women need a religion that glorifies being weak, or makes the weak strong. So popular but humbled and diluted forms of Christianity and Buddhism fit her bill. There are women who want to make you men like women too, and if you live with one, she may do it and win, and your life as a man could be cast away. So many men marry in sympathy, pity for the poor thing, for her tears, her emotional cave-ins and susceptibilities.

Another bunch could give away their years like a military-male sacrifice—to protect the wounded girl, the one that's bloating, growing the baby she's just told you is yours and is for real! It has been estimated that forty percent of births are unplanned today. The hush-up around this topic must cease. A university *study* says that in England, between 1650 and 1900, extramarital *first conception* pregnancies were likely between 40 and 60 percent of total births.[2] And at the beginning of the twentieth century it was estimated that between 30 and 50 percent of marriages occurred during a pregnancy.[3] There it is, how many marriages are forged.

> *Pity, and duty to protect, and there goes another*
> *guy's life into neglect.*

Once she's got him nestled in, under emotional-sexual control, in her environmental territory, chances are he won't even know she's taken over the show. Off many men go into the pathetic, dreary couch-potato white-noise fuzz of the TV radiation glow, while society continually barrages him with feminized agendas.

Everywhere, and on the radio or TV, he suffers the lies of gender feminist organizations and their operatives in their biased power positions. School boards and other public institutions are now in their control. He just cannot get free. The gender feminists have brainwashed the sisterhood into contempt for males. From anger swells the *victim-feminist* perception of a criminal man. But seeing males without innate goodness, as degraded, will obviously lead to crises. Thus the institution of marriage may be just about to totally explode.

Brought Up by Mom

Ironically, the *socialization* the gender feminists have been blaming for restricting their access to power turns out instead to actually be full of feminist agendas. It's mainly women who teach in elementary schools. *Males are mainly under female control in their formative years. At home, with their mothers.* Early in life its males who are paralyzed, the ones brainwashed, forced to believe in feminism, its—idealism, reactivity, political correctness, *resentiment* and egalitarianism. That isn't going to give a guy the stimulus to *be all that he can be.*

Today young males proudly leap to mouth the words their

deluded female school teachers and brainwashed moms give to them, even if the answers castrate men. And then the ladies smile, for the teenage little dear has actually voiced an opinion, despite the television wasteland spread between the *dear's ears*. The husband, if one is still *around,* his face and eyes turn to the *ground.* He's so lost, worn down, and knows in argument he can never really win without his wife's emotional power being swung to his side. So the sickness grows, and spreads and the lives of men pale, thin.

There are no leaders anymore, politicians talk out of the sides of their mouths, keeping the story going. They say they work on *equality*, meanwhile those at the very top are the elite rich. But for the everyday working masses the "women" have moved right in, taken control. They manage welfare offices and school boards; they hire their "sisters" for government jobs and for university management positions. They are recruitment officers, screening out undesirables, keeping the "feminists" with all the clout. And they manage day care, so single-moms can get income and get it on their own. Politicians find it hard to pull off another victory without milking this feminist lobby group.

Many moms preach murky and ever-so-subtle anti-male sermons, trying to catapult themselves away from men and into some hoped-for matriarchal wonderland. But this land of where women rule has never existed. That is, in the history of the world there has never been a society with women at the physical controls, no matter what the "spin" may say.

Today women have set things up so that they have choice— work, marry or both. She can have kids, husband and job or just a job and kids, or combinations of lifestyles. In the US, in the mid-90's, women earned 7.6 percent more than they did in 1979, while the men earned 14 percent *less*.[4] The international global market has done as expected, driven wages lower and lower, created all the part time insecure employments and now two incomes are needed to run many marriages in this "time of unprecedented prosperity."

> *Today many men in marriage are simply unaware,*
> *He'll be lucky not to get thrown overboard, drowned*
>   *in despair,*
> *The kids and mother afloat, and he without a prayer.*

It could be cruelty incarnate for those men caught in this snare. She may rule marriage as a taskmaster, with details endless to *guide* the man-child now working off her *side*. Punishment is as for three-year olds—withdrawal of attention. She's got corporate allies and motherly sexual-emotional glue to keep her esteemed and protected. And underneath her a court-supported dominance—so what use is he? The women's claimed desire for equality may be transformed—into female despotism!

"Men are much more trouble than they're worth. Sisters are doing it for themselves." This is Germaine Greer's opening statement, what she calls the "truth", in *The Guardian* in November, 2002. She declares "men have always been redundant and, second, women and children have always had to make do without them [men] while pretending they were indispensable."

This is Germaine Greer, one of the feminist leaders of the twentieth century. She's the author of *The Female Eunuch,* published in 1970, which would join Betty Friedan's *The Feminist Mystique* as two of the bibles of the boomer women's movement. Releasing repressive sexual morality, Greer had thought, would free up female sexuality and identity. And Friedan had blamed economic and political inequality for holding women back.

By 2002 Greer is moving on and talks about the unique *male* chromosome as being the most decayed, redundant and parasitic of all. She then characterizes the Eastern world, presumably Muslim, as about to destroy feminism's success at fixing up the devastation from all the world wars caused by the male elites. "A tide of male supremacism has risen in the east and is streaming across the world, promising the restoration of virility and virtue, a pure and manly way of life exemplified in holy warfare."

In 2002 Greer is stumping on the fact that "the human race could continue on earth if 99.9 % of the human males were wiped out...." You see, it only takes a small number of men to create all the sperm necessary to continue populating the planet. Greer then roars around tossing vile deprecations upon men. She writes about "terrestrial species where the male is often jettisoned as too costly and too useless to be allowed to survive once he has contributed his sperm." Australian marsupial mice catch her eye. She then lectures on about the male mice of the species, who immediately die after rigorous intercourse. Although many small mammal species are becoming extinct, these mice, says Greer, are the most successful of their species, even without the males who have died. The females raise the children on their own.

Greer trashes male sexuality and suggests the sex men supply is inadequate for female purposes and in need of "pharmacological enhancement." She next talks about the mating of hedge sparrows, where the female "mates" with one male who helps her to feed the fledglings, while she actually conceives with another male. Then Greer asserts: "Human females like sire and father to be the same person, if possible. They do not get this - they can get by without it - but they want it. Most of the time, they don't get it. By and large, men are not interested in fathering; they are not very interested in siring, for the most part, but they are even less interested in fathering."

As far as Greer is concerned women have always been able to survive without men. She says the "authorities" knew women would get by without men and so they sent the men off to the wars. *The authorities!* Greer also seems to be suggesting women mate with "superior males" to get superior children. And it seems Greer suggests to do so some women may become one of many wives to a superior male. She talks about how Mormon wives are satisfied with their communal husbands, and with their companionship with the other co-wives. In our present day society Greer says, "women insist on a male of their own." But that's old fashioned, she implies, and now that women are self-achieving and their sexuality has been loosened up, she is implicitly asking, do women really need just one man?

Next, in 2003, this godmother of 1970's feminism is on the bandwagon promoting her new book, *The Boy*. It's reportedly full of pictures of "ravishing" pre-adult boys with hairless chests, wide-apart legs and slim waists. Greer won't say how old the boys are, but says she expects to be called a pedophile. When Greer was asked on Canadian television what attracted her to "boys" rather than to men, she said, "Sperm that runs like tap water will do."

Childbirth and motherhood exist, however, in a women's world for Greer. But it's plain that Greer also intends to stimulate women to have children outside marriage, to mate with married men and to devise all sorts of strategies to obtain superior babies as well as domestic security for themselves and their offspring. It may help to remember that to Greer men are "freaks of nature, fragile, bizarre". And, as well, she says men are "nuisances."

She's postmodern, very cruel. And thrilled, no doubt, that by April, 2004 scientists in genetics have created mice by using two females—and no dad. That's right, a mammal born with no father and two mothers! It shows, in theory, that someday two lesbian women could have a baby.

Blast Off

Now it's time for males to have choice too. Why buy into a nightmare—today's type of marriage and its turmoil, male defeat? Poorly chosen mates could breed hostages—the children. Most men are regularly held hostage to some sort of sex. There is no easy get-away for them. The wheels of justice seem to give almost everything to women, and "he" has virtually no supporters in feminized society.

Marriage for *many* western men is Russian roulette, and thus many of the older, mature males will confess: it was the one they married that was their worst mistake in *life,* catastrophe was brought on by being with this *wife!*

Men, your mommies and school teachers, even movies and paperback novels, have set you up for all this female-sympathy glue, and so you might be thinking weird, deranged things regarding love and marriage. For some men the *"dressed-up lie"* that they *"conquered"* and married is going to turn, and with a vengeance she will demand just what they should do in, as Nietzsche put it, the *"long stupidity of marriage."*

Foreign Rules

You guys have three wheels on your wagon,
Maybe deserving rebuke and scorn from a female dragon.
You've lost initiative, it was robbed as you blanked out,
  blew a fuse,
Watching network TV and the NEWS,
The school system hacked your testes back
And your rational logic head became your sack:
Let the oval plums sink back into place
And take what you need, act in a manly pace –
Which means fun! Perhaps sixteen wives and each
  one especial too,
Living and giving (money), each one their due.

*They'll be happy, it's protection and security, then
   it's your "love" they want,
Stop being a soap-opera's black magic doll,
Taking the blame, responsible for whatever she's
   wasting away today about,
Taking the fall,
Get up boy, a man's got to have clout,
And see what your need is really about –*

*Consider a future for the "I," not for us or thee.
A man's freedom is envied by a woman, she's so
   attached to her body,
To relationships, to high tempo passion and fear,
   and she strains
For male support, offering momentary relief, libido gains,
But your acceptance could then bring a life of
   grieving emotion, disdain,
While she's claiming all she is doing is fixing your pain!*

*Maybe at a distance or in heat is where her charms
   most delight,
But it's a crash landing that's being set up for men's
   obsessive male flight,
As hate propaganda rockets through her sensuous mists,
Where he's crucified, humiliated, his mind chased
   into fits,
But bewitched by fancy, thinking to draw near,
And to marry to cast off his fear,
With his love held close he pictures a life sublime
   where all is right
And can envision his idealized better side now able
   to stand in the light,
And with initial sex and its emotional therapy upon the gut,
The male will think he is now surely in luck,
Move right in, let my noble life begin!*

*But if she is really a hiding autocrat,
marriage will provide a throne; he emotionally-
   sexually instructed,
She plays the dissatisfied monarch, and he now the*

> *sad sack directed*
> *Towards the fixing of matters that do not address*
> *The heavenly fortress,*
> *There where she works out the rules for her needing sympathies.*

Female as Slave Myth

> *...Look at it guys: do you want to draw so close to this female that your heart is in her hands?*

These the ones who are always victims, and you today not even her hero, just a mark.

Today females believe, as they've been wrongfully told by reactive raging feminazis "cows," that women throughout most of world history have been kept uneducated. They say they have been restricted in even getting sexual knowledge, even kept non-sexual, devoid of even knowing they could have orgasms! This the story, the tale told for idiots.

Just listen to the mean-spirited, manipulative and insulting words of Paula Kamen in her 2002 book, *Her Way*. It's men and the patriarchy that's keeping women from having sex *their* way, says Kamen. Men are too often indifferent to a woman's pleasure, she says, and men are ignorant and dense about how to satisfy their women. Kamen says American culture "has hidden and suppressed knowledge of their bodies" from women.[6] In her mind, American culture has denied women the information about their true sexuality and forced them into choices that suit a "traditional male framework."

Kamen claims education helps women to evolve into lesbians and good masturbators. It surely doesn't take grand insight to realize these are activities *without* men. But under a section entitled "Targeting Men for a Change," it's men, she writes, "who need the most consciousness-raising about women's sexual realities."[7] Kamen wants a woman to live up to sexual standards "derived from within herself" instead of "living up to standards set by men."[8] She believes that women today *are living in a man's world*. The "superrats" are an example to Kamen of the evolution of women—they think and act like men, are sexually aggressive and have more partners and premarital sex.

In American society it's male norms, however, that prevail,

claims Kamen, and "if women feel the basic and rational need of wanting an emotional connection to sex...then they feel they must be weak."[9] So Kamen wants it all—casual sex and emotional commitment. If that's not available, then it's the patriarchy's fault.

To Kamen there is an orgasm gap and a masturbation gap, and both occur because of certain knowledge being withheld from women on purpose. In her studies, the higher the education level the more a woman knows how to satisfy herself, engages in lesbianism as well as in anal and oral sex. Women need to *learn* how to have orgasms, says Kamen. They also need to learn "information about the clitoris."[10] Often women only found out about the prominence of the clitoris "accidentally and later in their sexual lives, usually through friends and women's magazines."[11]

Kamen conjures up images of men as "indifferent" to women's sexual pleasure, many described as being selfish and ignorant in this area. But more are being trained to please women today, says Kamen, and the "increased number of women receiving oral sex has been particularly dramatic."[12] In the future, Kamen states: "Anal sex represents women's next sexual frontier for practice and public discussion."[13]

Kamen believes women are evolving by "demystifying sex, separating it from love."[14] She says women have *learned* how to do this, to separate sex and love. She introduces a university campus survey about *women's* sexual practices that reveals "about a quarter had engaged in spanking or bondage...10 percent has experienced a threesome, online sex, or a 'golden shower.'"[15] Kamen's sources also show her that "28.6 percent of women with a master's degree had had anal sex, compared with 16.6 percent of high school graduates."[16] But women's pleasure, Kamen says, is secondary to men's because society goes by male rules. Thus she thinks knowledge of women's sexual capacity would logically be suppressed in a male-dominated culture. She says society needs to "validate a whole new realm of female-centered choices."[17] To Paula Kamen, "we have only begun to understand female sexuality, to define sexual freedom in women's terms...to organize on behalf of the reproductive rights of the least fortunate...."[18]

So although it's the men, Kamen says, that most need consciousness-raising about women's sexual reality, to her it's women's lack of *education* and *instruction* that has kept them victims of a society run by men. But to comprehend Kamen's picture of the victimhood of women means accepting women being so alien to their bodies that they need explicit instruction about how to live in them. Is it possible that a woman could live a whole life span and not "know" about the clitoris? Aren't these people living in their bodies? The rational approach, the mentalization of knowledge, obviously may have driven many out of their bodies, and into their wordy heads. A denial of a woman's emotional needs has to result from this.

The huge gap between the mental understanding of reality and a woman's true emotional needs in everyday life causes the war to rage on, where the disgruntled rage on, reactively seeking an enemy to blame for their unfulfilled lives. It's men and their system of control over women that is blamed for the alienation of women from themselves and their true needs.

But where will women's emotional energy find what it needs? In uninhibited pursuit of pleasure? Unlikely. The body can experience lots of variation in sexual practices. And maybe orgasm will be more easily achieved if someone works hard at the task. Is it only erotic pleasure that the soul seeks? Or every sexual variation that can lead to orgasm? The female soul wants more than this, has priorities and desires the sexual below the family in importance.

That's the real insight here. And doesn't it seem insulting for women, or for any human being, to be characterized as stupidly and ignorantly failing to live in their own bodies?

Freud says the superego in females is weaker than in males. To him, the absence of a strong superego equals the absence of a strong sense of justice, which is necessary for moral behavior. The predominance of envy in women's mental life is, to Freud, evidence of a weakened sense of justice. Women run more on their feelings, said Freud, than on a sense of justice (superego), and are therefore less moral than men. It's been said that a person with a lesser internalized superego (conscience) would tend to disown her guilt and shame and blame external authority figures instead (Hall, 1964).

Paula Kamen's instruction will keep women alienated, complaining about their mistreatment, blaming the patriarchy for any dysfunction. And her books will be displayed by the mainstream bookstores, and business is good in the business of women's complaint. Unfortunately, many women may now be kept out of a heterosexual relationship that intrinsically grounds them, because there is a balance that proceeds from gender co-operation.

There are societies who, in the past, consciously attempted to control women's sexuality. Today there are cultures that have laws regarding female behavior, particularly a female's relationship with her sexuality. One must ask if there is an advantage for all of society in curbing women's sexuality? And also ask what results could be expected from *unlimited* sexual expression by the female? Stay tuned.

Contract a Woman to Carry Your Child

> *Consider: incubate your future children in most excellent circumstance—plan who, and when, to hell with fateful happenstance,*
> *Contract the one-and-only to carry—your child, your life,*
> *Get away from the children of this wife, the one who holds too much of your hope,*
> *Who controls the waters of your emotion and decides if you will drown or just float.*

Guys, out of your personal victories in life and your success in overcoming the smoke screens spread by the spin and lies in your society, and from your *seeing* things as they really are—from the freedom gained herein, you are worthy and entitled to wish for a child. The warrior, victorious over even his senses, a master of his virtues, he the self-conqueror, this man may create a child, a monument to his liberation. But first he must build himself, upright and strong in body and soul.

What need he of this folly, this humbug of marriage so many have given over unto? For most it is a bad joke—for the release of sex? These lifelong contracts are entered into without knowledge of even how to love. She may love infatuation, submission, service, safety and money. He may just love good food, good sunsets, order, challenge and women that do what he wants. What is this love that is held so high? Isn't it basically about false security, money and personal pleasure, today's idealized human love? Isn't it the children begot from marriages that are really loved? So you could take Madonna's challenge, all you Western Feminized Men (WFM), and *rent a breeder*, just like she did to get *her* baby child.

So there are eggs for sale on-line on the internet: models, athletes and those with high IQ, waiting for your decision. You can pull through and create life dazzling, blessed and true to a man's work—service and protection.

> *Now you can select a child and the mother too,*
> *And the challenge is again right-on, something a warrior man can do.*

Get the kid you want, stop letting *her* get pregnant and thereby becoming the conductor of the symphony that *used to* be called your life. Now your life need not be burdened with anger, revenge and hatred over the causes of marital strife.

Scrambling for money, that's the problem, you *say,* and if only there were a lot of money the problems would go *away.* Notice how when men get rich they get out, divorce, have numerous lovers. Get a handle on it you forlorn males, from Bruce Willis to Andre Agassi to Nelson Mandela, money always allows the plums to rightly brew and run with the waves of male accountability. Seven by Four! That's Mick Jagger's recent formula—seven children from four females. With financial freedom many men can choose. But even without financial freedom men can commit to a personal drive for excellence that is worthy...he the successful descendant of a chest-thumping happy gorilla.

Masochists can have trouble being in contact with their own needs and wants. Masochists can have a problem expressing anger. And masochists think to win by quietly outlasting their opponents' cruelty. Men must learn it's alright for them to complain. That is how to start to get things right.

It's time to *choose*—even though this choice, guys, would be so new to *you,* while you're working things out, working them *through.* She could be a treasure when viewed correctly. Virtually all the guys agree, nod immediately, about the fact she's from another planet—that's right on bro! And at times effort must be found and used to keep her, *up there and at a distance*, and as a *treat, a treat in heat*, not welcomed in like a brother onto your street. That is not where she belongs, and just because someone told you that everyone is the same or equal doesn't mean it is always true.

Her emotional glue, it can be like baggage, but *use* her understanding, you straight-back males. It will help build you strong and more powerful when your hands are full. And it will entitle you to knowledge, yours for *you,* to help you work in your freedom with her emotional *glue.* One life, one day at a time.

> *"And I am sure that the ultimate greatest desire in men is this desire for purposive activity. When a man loses his deep sense of purposive, creative activity, he feels lost, and is lost. When he makes the sexual consummation the supreme consummation, even in his secret soul, he falls into the beginnings of despair. When he makes woman, or woman and child, the great center of life and of life-significance, he falls into the beginnings of despair."*
>
> D.H. Lawrence[19]

V

The Feminization of Society Revisited

17
The Male Click Experience

> *After twenty-five years of marriage, years of dedication,*
> *work, sacrifice,*
> *Building a functioning and life-sustaining environment—*
> *for the kids, for the wife –*
> *Now it becomes time to start beating this wife,*
> *The partner that slept beside you through all the strife?*
> *Or, now that there is no mortgage left, the bills all*
> *shuffled away,*
> *Paid up for each day, the kids in college or working for*
> *pay,*
> *Now the wife is gonna lose it and frying-pan collision*
> *Is gonna make hubby's skull crack just like clay?*

Women murder their husbands a lot. In one study it was found that that forty-one percent—41 percent—of spousal murderers are women friendly. Here the female leads the assault into extermination in roughly four out of ten executions.[1]

Failure to get the gist of this, guys, you cocky sports fans overfilled with a male presumptuousness *when* physical action is conceived—your life could be rubbed out by this failure to *believe*. Women kill a lot. Husbands. So after a quarter century, the seemingly successful married couple—like wooden carvings standing painted, side by side—may now confront each other anew. But are they aware of homicide as possibly their next matrimonial experience?

With the swirling propaganda, low expectations and gender-hate infesting a neurotic and divided society, what could be expected but more low-life bestiality? She ain't listening, and he sees his mortality, the short living span left, and he blames her for his entrapment. She may have gone mental—wording—and failure to properly digest word concepts like *equality, freedom, gender, slavery* and *patriarchy* can bring intense corruption into the bowels of any radical-feminist discrimination.

Warrior women act today, or have enough self-esteem(?) and take-chargeness to hire a *thug,* someone to off the husband, if they see him as simply another *mug.* This marriage can be for idiots. Like a packaged deal, the scorpion *mate* could in the end have the other to *hate.* What must be so *wrong* in these unions painted once as *strong?*

With the marriage, cheering and waving and rice-raining in the hail of an ideal love; the garter lifted and thrown—the scramble reveals scratching need as other future candidates lurch, trip and clutch, focused on personal gain. Are they hoping next to be blessed by this type of luck?

Off into an oblivion—modern marriage—the couples are useful, to the GM as a big-ticket item consumer *group.* Their needs now feed into the market *loop.*

He gets regular sex; she gets a helping financial hand. Is that it? And twenty-five years later it's a toss-up; maybe a slight edge must be conceded to him as the murderer, it's a close call. But domestic violence is where equality actually exists! A woman, studies show, batters more than her postmodern man, but it's close to equality here. So just because an erection is muscle contracting into *hard,* doesn't mean it's the man who is guilty of the assaulting *charge.*

Women hire specialists, hit men just like furnace men, plumbing men, electrical men, all working to keep her needs in *tune,* even when it's the removal of her *"goon."* But to be searching for his penis *thrown out in the road...* this a possible punishment for males not educated about the amount of female murder and assault—this comes from ignorance! Getting hitched is the entrance fee into this *mode.*

Eight-inch carving knife and the unsatisfied Bobbit merge. Slashed while sleeping! He has been tortured indeed, but while he is in stitches, our courts the female have here acquitted.

The 41 percent of spousal murders females are here found guilty of—well, they don't include: a successful poisoning that's been classified as a stroke or something else (and poisoning is the female's preferred murder method); nor does it count third-party hired killers or boyfriends persuaded to murder. (This type isn't *documented* as a woman killing an intimate, but is instead classified as a third-party killing.) Thus the number—41 percent—could be a lie. It's probably higher. Go figure, but get a grip!

Sleep on man, at your own peril.

18
Lash

This Information Age is full of newspeak— tacts—
Tactical lies spread as facts.
These lies grow and spread,
Affect social interaction and what is said,
They deny much satisfaction that could exist,
If only the spin doctors, propaganda would desist,
The males take a great thumping –
From all the gender feminist dumping,
Hitler's provocative propaganda was read:
Its lies brought sorrow by those who were led,
Did believing ears
Wipe away fears
To be politically correct, thought right,
Carrying out vile persecutions, as though sleepwalking
  at night?

What's really in the present economy, the one the media often exults as magnificent, robust? This economy and its teeming stock prices is leading what is called the Information Age. While the average Joe and Jill make less in real dollars in 2007 than they did in 1973, the "facts" blink otherwise in the "free" press and much of the media.

But like Homer and Bart in *The Simpsons*—who can get a handle on all the destructive spins ripping in the wind? Homer is lazy, incompetent, and Bart, his son, is doomed to failure at school. They are modern, dysfunctional dumb-assed males, and devoid of high-level creativity or intellectual pursuits. In *The*

Simpsons, it's mother and daughter that get special treatment, and it's the daughter, Lisa, alone, who surely has hope for a sunny future. And Homer? He is a borderline drug addict, which means he is handicapped from the start. Aren't this father and son just like the modern men vilified in the mainstream media in America every day? It's everywhere.

Any man who stood up to the spin about the economic numbers presented as truth would be politically incorrect. Political correctness is in part the result of "female paranoia" about the truth being told rather than feelings being protected. Now females serve under market capitalism and its capitalist governments, many buying right into the phoney numbers and lies the government issues about the economy—after all, they've had little experience running the show. They support government and corporations *instinctively,* because that's where they think the power is. And they are buying into ideology about equality and into information that paints men as self-destructive goofs and annoying boneheads—men who they learn to call *acute brutalizers* and *bullies*.

Attack of the gender feminists

So much has been written and produced on the American campaign trail by anti-male gender feminists that the growing-up Lisas of America are so *rad brainwashed* about men, so coerced into the sisterhood that they support anything female. With much nodding approval of any feminist *stance*, young women could be today's somnambulists, programmed to OK any feminist *rant*. A psycho-socio pathology is thus to be expected. Sickness in both sexes often equates these days to a *sexless sickness*. It pervades, and the boys are being set up. Will they have to cop out, deny their testosterone-based leadership and then admit to corruption?

> *As the hard drives purr he's sinking through the guilt*
> *Like a cat stretching on a quilt,*
> *And the nation, he thinks, will benefit in mysterious ways,*
> *Meanwhile Ms. America is scheming*
> *As the males are flick-dreaming.*

On the internet sexual images reap the highest business profit. And half the revenue for hotel pay-per-view movies in the United States is earned from "adult entertainment."[1]

The bottom is fast approaching for this soap opera as boys consider going into denial in order to be seen as worthy of a girl's love. The picture solutions almost work but can't replace a real female, and if guilt arises from addiction to quick fixes, then bad attitude will only serve to bring on neurotic *insurance*, cynicism. The pictures become prisons for the alienated and the angry.

The ubiquitous indulgence of the male gaze without organic contact and reassurances from humans in the flesh puts a zone resembling sleep around so many, and allows the agendas of those that are more alert to persevere. And trapping any beauty, habitually using beauty to blot the pain, the ugly and mundane parts of life, will in time make the mind insensitive. Social programs and social responsibility aren't foremost in souls always showered in sexual images, satisfied to some degree but lacking human touch. There is frustration, anger and confusion all around the guys. They are hostages all right, to their sexual addictions and their desire for beauty, but also to the gender feminists.

The gender feminists have risen in the ranks, and politicians feed funds to help these "oppressed" gender whiners in exchange for their scheduled delivery of votes. Well, these man-haters now control universities, school boards and city councils. They have taken control it seems, almost everywhere. It's obnoxious and it's repugnant, and most of the older men are missing in action. Are they sleeping? Their sons are rebuked, whereas he himself is vilified. And now many a husband has become afraid to confront his wife. She has got hold of him, and he's been driving her to new and various destinations (malls) for as long as he can remember. He's got to keep the waves smooth; she's the boss and hostility means his sexual and emotional life could be turned into horror, it could be lost. He thinks he could lose.

Today the boys are getting weird views of *themselves,* and with just a few more decades of female deprecation, the little boys will dance for the male-bashing misandrists in circles, like cute Harry Potter *elves.*

Because we were told that we are in this Information Age, we believed the polls and studies that got our attention through the media pimps and dealers. There is now a substantial history of false information, particularly studies and polls from feminist-affiliated bodies. The information promotes lies as truth, "tacts"—here *information* disguises a biased study, poll or research method. Many research studies have the names of universities or established media behind them. But they are better called what they are—*advocacy research*—that is, facts gathered to make slanted or partisan conclusions believable.

Women *live six years longer than men,* but that isn't enough,

> *For gender fems without fail,*
> *Are out to get the male!*
> *And with spin and lies*
> *They data-rape the guys.*

It's the big rebuff! God damn lies are spread to further elevate these gender feminists and to promote them with all the other females as goodness incarnate. It's so common, the womanly propaganda, that it's become accepted as *true,* and our sons are being captured by its *guilt glue.* The creative tissues of their male brains are now virtually in jail.

Thus, a counter-attack must needs commence:

Truth about Single Motherhood

The facts do not support any idea that women raise children better than men. Stuart Miller and Rich Zubaty in the December 19, 1995, *Washington Times* stated:

> "Eighty-five percent of prisoners, 78 percent of high school dropouts, 82 percent of teenage girls who become pregnant, the majority of drug and alcohol abusers—all come from single mother-headed households. Less than 19 percent of any of these categories come from single father-headed households."[2]

Worthy food for thought, but the court systems in the US and Canada line up to support women, the gender that is supposed to be so good at nurturing, or at least used to be. Today women have become the "oppressed" ones, as women claim to be hindered and discriminated against like the handicapped, disabled, racial minorities and homosexuals. They are bailing out to the woe-and-blue-tune of the oppressed, while the eyes of the court reify validation to the spoof, supporting the women's *sin*, making reality fit the *spin*.

Getting market *savvy*, moms need to review the "inner mother" *badly*. Is their natural frustration now acute, and motherhood a curse? According to the US National Center for Health Statistics, a child living with his or her divorced mother, as compared with a child living with both parents, is:

> *"Three hundred and seventy-five percent more likely to need professional treatment for emotional or behavioral problems and is almost twice as likely to repeat a grade of school, is more likely to suffer [from] chronic asthma, frequent headaches, and/or bedwetting, develop a stammer or speech defect, suffer from anxiety or depression, and be diagnosed as hyperactive."*[3]

But these afflictions were surprisingly uncommon in the 15 percent of single-parent households headed by men. Miller and Zubaty, using data from the Children's Rights Coalition, also state that biological mothers are found to physically abuse their children at twice the rate of biological fathers.[4]

Up to approximately the end of World War I, men used to be given the children when divorce occurred. Was this the right course of action? Today women can earn their own living. But with up-to-date data showing that placing children with single-parent mothers is likely to be detrimental to both the children and society, the tradition of placing children with their fathers is exonerated.

Today a feminized society that knows not what it does, or rather, a politically run society that is in basic denial, follows the trend of catering to females because of their votes, and approves transfers of money to them. And with the propaganda emitting from their perfumed cloud of *female protection and privilege,* plus the smoke and mirrors of their innate dissimulation technique, they hypnotize and hijack both the male desire for procreation and the male urge to save and protect.

As long as the gender feminists are winning the *spin thing*, then a frenzied, frantic and awful rendezvous is being set up through collective guilt and its neurosis. Women as a group may relish men suffering. Many see female gain coming only at male expense. There's security in a group, any group. But winning against an enemy that doesn't exist is impossible. Most of the feminist propaganda assaults may only show the men how unprincipled many women have become. And then hatred will grow. In the US, 38 percent of men that the court has ordered to pay child support may not have either visitation or custodial rights.[5]

Children are often abused because of their single-mother's poor choices in men that she brings into her life. Some of them will see the children as competitors for the woman's attention. And the level of crisis escalates if the boyfriend-lover deliberately seeks to undermine the children. The physical danger to children living with stepfathers has been documented. Martin Daly and Margo Wilson of McMaster University studied how stepchildren are abused by their surrogate fathers: "Such children are sixty to one hundred times more likely to be beaten and eleven times more likely to be killed than children living with their natural parents."[6] But Miller and Zubaty say that, "incidences of abuse were almost non-existent in single-father- headed households."[7]

Backlash against the Women's Movement

In 1991, Susan Faludi's *Backlash: the Undeclared War against American Women* solidified impressions around the subject of men's and women's power.[8] That it coincided with Anita Hill's sexual harassment allegations against a man nominated to be a judge on the Supreme Court is relevant. Because here was a high-ranking member of the "patriarchy." Clarence Thomas fit Faludi and her follower's picture of a male out to restrict women's participation in society. Thomas was eventually appointed to the Supreme Court. But sexual harassment charges then exploded across the country. In 1992, at the Equal Employment Opportunity Commission (EEOC), 45 percent more allegations were received, compared with the one-year period before Hill's accusations.[9] Clarence Thomas had been previously the Chairman of the EEOC!

Soon thereafter Bill Clinton began making the news, first as a presidential contender, then as a sexual disaster area. But even before his election, beginning even before Gennifer Flowers, the "bimbo eruptions" tracked this Bill Clinton's trail. Clinton's problems only helped Faludi's case against the shortcomings of a society she saw as supporting male privilege.

Clinton, the Big Kahuna, Mr. Large, was a Federal Reserve Bank connection for his favorite free-loading feminist-flunkey sponges. Faludi and rage-feminism lucked out with Bill Clinton. Here was a guy obsessed with women, a slave to his attraction, with sex scandals flushing out all about. Here the gender feminists had a male to ridicule. So in general, the reactive female camp did well with this Bill. Without their support he would lose his job. They had him in a testosterone basket. So the elitist feminazis types, the grudge-bearing bunch, began to try to take over America! And up front and center, soon they are going to produce the next president of the United States, they think. Why it's going to be none other than Bill Clinton's cuckolded wife, Hillary, the super-victim!

Patriarchal Conspiracy. Faludi talks about war against women. She says that the media lies and misrepresents women, as well as brainwashes them into traditional marriage-oriented lifestyles. The media desire to take back what women had gained in society, she says. Her book pretends to be scholarly, although it is thinly veiled propaganda. It promotes a widespread conspiracy against women.

Similarly, in *The Beauty Myth* (1992), Naomi Wolf alerts women that they are pawns of a widespread brainwashing conspiracy. This time the conspiracy is to keep them neurologically obsessed with beauty. Women are the victims, this time from society's expectation for women to be beautiful. This expectation forces females into "a secret 'underlife' poisoning our freedom; infused with notions of beauty, it is a dark vein of self-hatred, physical obsession, terror of aging, and dread of lost control."[10] This *beauty myth* is used by the evil patriarchal society to wear down and weaken women and also to remove the gains they had made, says Wolf.

The patriarchy is also out to pressure women to diet, buy clothes, use cosmetics and hit the gyms in ways that are "destroying women physically and depleting us psychologically."[11] Wolf sounds alarm bells, incites fear and promotes anger: "We are in the midst of a civil war over gender.... It is also a war against men."[12]

Faludi claims the formula of the beauty industry is to aggravate women's low self-esteem and high anxiety about a "feminine" appearance. Naomi Wolf claims it was the success of the women's movement that brought out deliberate male antagonism and the conspiracy of the *beauty myth* to checkmate power at all levels in women's lives.

Faludi's focus is on the slant of news coverage in the media as being distinctly anti-female. But Faludi skews data, according to *Time* magazine. *Forbes* magazine judged Faludi's book "a labyrinth of nonsense followed by eight pages of footnotes." Ironically, Faludi is guilty of exactly what she accuses the American media of—slanted and deceptive reports to warp, coax and influence the understanding of society's present gender conflict.

Faludi rails on about women being severely *punished* economically for the social gains that they made in civil politics prior to the 80's. Both Faludi and Wolf agree that it is an economic backlash that is keeping females from getting more power. But they both misuse facts to incite rage, cynicism, hatred and conspiratorial paranoia within the women's community. This misuse of facts could backfire if their victims realize the spin " tacts" aren't really the true facts. And then, sooner or later, there may be a real backlash. Both Wolf and Faludi must recognize the potential for a whipsaw to their intentions, because recently they have taken more supportive, motherly positions towards men. Can they sense the destruction they have wrought? Or is it more cunning and wiles, dressed as sympathy for men, an act to deflect responsibility for their outrageous intention to render men as women's enemies?

Consequences of gender feminist Fabrication. The influence of Faludi and Wolf is real; their books are best-sellers. They've been assimilated, and it's too late. There is no get-out-of-jail-free card here. The price society is paying for Wolf's, Faludi's and many other gender feminists' fabrications will last for generations. Today these generations have had their guts ripped out of them and live in stunned ignorance. All the while our educational institutions functioning in this Information Age misrepresent the stupefaction that has inundated mass culture.

Political correctness (PC) is stupidness, and "stupid is as stupid does." Society in general is becoming stupider by allowing superficial manners to protect feelings rather than promoting truth. It is also becoming more elitist, more separated and more divided into cliques. Specialization in occupations and fields of study has meant exclusion and separation for most. Increased immigration is a further catalyst for social distancing. Then with gender warfare, male and female are further apart. All these causes of isolation aid in the dumbing-down of the nation through spin and political correctness.

On Absorbing Patriarchal Rules. When Wolf and Faludi assume that women must defend themselves from an enemy who is waging an undeclared war against them, they mean patriarchal society. But because this conspiracy against women's progress clearly could not be witnessed on the streets, they've got an internal, cerebral solution. The women, they say, are being persecuted from *within,* by internalizing rules and discipline taught by modern bureaucratic institutions such as the schools, military, workplace and hospitals.

In contemporary society, Faludi and Wolf claim that patriarchal direction of the media brings an all-pervasive domination over citizens. They say this control of society becomes omnipresent. So the modern citizen in front of the television continues to internalize patriarchal disciplines and becomes self-policing. Thus indoctrinated, subjects keep themselves in check.

The self-surveillance of the beauty myth, and the heat behind Faludi's *Backlash* derive from woman's sense of victimhood. Wolf and Faludi believe that the women's movement is undermined when woman's internal self (psyche) is being socialized and conditioned by a patriarchal society's propaganda and guilt. Thus they complain that the system is aiming at turning women into docile and compliant escorts of men, in an oppressive position of subordination. The gender feminists fear that controlling the internal dynamics of the individual is the speculative plan to get the woman carrying out the wishes of the patriarchy.

Feminist Advocacy "Research"

Mainstream heavyweight support for the gender feminist victim-spin came from the Ford Foundation, a supporter of much feminist advocacy *(sell cars).* For example the Ford Foundation picked up expenses for the 1992 Radcliffe College conference: *In the Eye of the Storm: Feminist Research and Action in the 90's.* Here it is stated that the "backlash" against the women's movement, against women's research and against women's studies is to be explored by the sponsor, the National Council for Research on Women. This organization represents over seventy women's groups, including Wellesley College Center for Research on Women and the 140,000 strong American Association of University Women (AAUW). Here the gender feminists would set ablaze the *meme*—an *idea* that wants to knock out the competition—that an undeclared war was being waged against women and is spreading all over the nation and the world!

Well, the gender feminists are right about a conspiracy to cripple a gender, but their perception is self-deceptive. Maybe their labeling of a gender war against themselves as unjustified and immoral results from neurotic guilt, the guilt of those who have falsely, but knowingly, portrayed a merciless campaign as being *against* women. Because what is going on is a lambasting of men by those who seek female-gender power and privilege. World War II brought the *oppressed* into public consciousness *as the good guys*, the bad guys being the oppressors. So to portray men as oppressing women automatically garners sympathetic response, if believed. And the media promotes support for women to rise up from this "oppression." Much of the media "educate" and support the *lesson–addiction* of today's females around civil rights and democracy. Editors and producers feed robust propaganda into the mainstream mind.

But many in the media may be victims of the people they publish. It seems the lies and spin of many feminist wagers of the gender war are the *only* "reasoning of the facts" that most editors have understood. But on a higher, more-powerful level:

> *This gender bias and gender war is used to keep*
>   *serfs toiling in distraction,*
> *Not capable of any concerted major action.*

Gender antagonism is promoted in mainstream media; here it's so sublime. Innocents of the Information Age are incited into rage, as these consumers, thinking to kick back and unwind, huddle around their television sets, but get instead the anchor-parrot quarterback's instruction—an incision—in prime time!

Christina Hoff Sommers of Washington, D.C., has seen the enemy and writes:

> *"Activist organizations like the National Organization of Women, the Ms. Foundation for Women, and the American Association of University Women, strive constantly to persuade the wider public that women are urgently in need of the protections they will help to provide. These organizations rely on a pool of academic feminists to faithfully produce books, data, and studies that demonstrate alarming amounts of sexism, discrimination, and gender bias."[13]*

History of Thought on Female Instincts

The cunning of the gender feminist is nothing new. Male philosophers and thinkers throughout history have commented on this instinct in women. Arthur Schopenhauer and Immanuel Kant, top thinkers of their times, cautioned about the deceptive nature of women.

Schopenhauer, a philosopher of merit and contemporary of modern feminism's mother, Mary Wollstonecraft, wrote in an era when women's rights were increasing. To Schopenhauer (1788-1860), women:

> *"...are dependent, not upon strength, but upon craft; and hence their instinctive capacity for cunning, and their ineradicable tendency to say what is not true. For as lions are provided with claws and teeth, and elephants with boors and tusks, bulls with horns, and the cuttle fish with its cloud of inky fluid, so Nature has equipped woman, for her defense and protection, with the arts of dissimulation."[14]*

Like animals when they defend, women use this clouding *dissimulation* whenever they please, and feel that doing so is perfectly within their rights, says Schopenhauer. He felt women never got beyond a subjective point of view, that women were "thorough-going philistines, and quite incurable." The way Europeans were treating women way back at the beginning of the nineteenth century, *with reverence and notions of gallantry,* irked Schopenhauer. Elevating women, and calling only those who were aristocratically bred, "ladies," only made less-fortunate women unhappy, he says. It caused something he called "the lady-nuisance." And to Schopenhauer:

> *"[the] innate rule that governs women's conduct, though it is secret and unformulated, nay unconscious in its working is this: We are justified in deceiving those who think they have acquired rights over the species by paying little attention to the individual, that is, to us.... But women have no abstract knowledge of this leading principle; they are conscious of it only as a concrete fact."*[15]

Notice how, to Schopenhauer, it is women who are identified with the concept of the "individual." Finally, women are described as having no sense of justice. Thus, their character, "gives rise to falsity, faithlessness, treachery, ingratitude, and so on."[16]

Schopenhauer wrote in the first half of the nineteenth century, whereas things are supposed to have moved on today. However, the word *dissimulation* is so cosmetically apt that it grabs out and pulls the present so-called male *oppressors* right back into the need for a respect for something that is like magic. It's what the "up there and at a distance" respect for the natural awesome talents of these "oppressed" is really about. *Dissimulation* gives a reinstated warning about the power of cosmetics and fashion to manipulate male desire today. Masks aid dissimulation

Feminine pretenses include notions like the divine mother and the exaltation of female nurturing, compassion and vulnerability. These images are ever-shifting, superimposed over women's choreographed sexual presentations—this, from the "sweet" gender, the one, they say, who needs protection because of her inability to resist caring-sharing, she asking for the gentle approach... But the deal can be closed through dissimulation and through sex signals—lipstick beauty and other premeditated physical applications camouflaging true intention. Her aim is power, control, and she will shift the psychological sands between herself and the opposite sex until she has her way.

Immanuel Kant (1724-1804) also comments on the ways of women, in his essay on the interrelations of the two sexes. Acting morally would be difficult for a woman, says Kant, because women are in *service of emotion* and are reactive, having "very delicate feelings in regard to the least offense, and are exceedingly precise to notice the most trifling lack of attention and respect toward them."[17] Kant says women are motivated by the beautiful; men are motivated by the noble. "Her philosophy is not to reason, but to sense."

> *"[And] women will avoid the wicked not because it is unright, but because it is ugly; and virtuous actions mean to them such as are morally beautiful."*[18]

To Kant, women's morality arises not from *principle* but from their *emotional* response to situations. It was the male of the species, he thinks, who could best use reason to decipher duty. And moral action is determined by duty, says Kant. *Dissimulation* makes its appearance in Kant as well, as he writes: "and not forgetting, what one must reckon as a secret magic with which she makes our passion inclined to judgements favorable to her... making her known by the mark of the beautiful."[19]

About education and the professions, Kant says, "Laborious learning or painful pondering, even if a woman should greatly succeed in it, destroy the merits that are proper to her sex and...will weaken the charms with which she exercises her great power over the other sex."[20]

To Immanuel Kant, women who chose a healthy, but pale, facial color possessed a disposition of "more inward feeling and delicate sensation, which belongs to the quality of the sublime; whereas the rosy and blooming complexion proclaims more of the joyful and merry disposition—but it is more suitable to vanity to move and to arrest, than to charm and to attract."[21]

Writing in the mid-1700's, Kant declares that marriage had to be based on *"the understanding of the man and the taste of the wife."* Thus in marriage the right of the husband is to command in matters of *understanding,* and the wife to command in matters of *taste.* If these areas come under question and attack, then the whole union becomes undermined. Marriage will then become "duller" and can "degenerate into familiar love." Then feelings of "indifference and satiety" can put an end to happiness in marriage, because "all those niceties and delicacies of feeling have their whole strength only at the beginning."[22]

Female Influence Today. Today women have become excellent students, and by the twenty-first century they far outnumbered men in college and university enrollment. So have they become less powerful in their charms over males, as Kant predicted? Definitely yes, but pornography, miniskirts and strip bars keep the hard-wired at least salivating and humbled to the female form. And the government-as-husband keeps female interests front and center today, as male concerns are buried underneath the assault of "women's rights."

Feminine charm, beyond the sexual, may not even be much known or appreciated these days. The property of the female that the male jumps to protect is the person of the different sex whom he loves for that very difference. In the past, man approached woman with both fear and sympathy. Though not often seen out in the open, on occasion men glimpsed woman's innate *wildness,* her cunning flexibility and the incomprehensibility of her desires and virtues. And this scared men. They could not grok it all; her nature was a somewhat fearful mystery. But he also found her suffering, discouraged and in need of love. When she yielded to *her* sensitivity, man found his meaning; his sympathy was excited. This display of the feminine, its plea, spurs a man to heroism, but that is going to rapidly evaporate if female sensitiveness and the dynamic influence of the emotional queen bee dies on the vine.

And nowadays many ladies live on their own. But a female body with an animus mentality won't do much "soul-attracting" of the normal testosterone male. Females will have some success grinding on some of the new-age feminized guys whose egos have never really been allowed far off the ground. Also females will make inroads with brainwashed men who have internalized feminist rules and discipline. These are men who produce the touchy-feely words that bring subservience to *her* territory, who now await her instruction because he's given up his masculine judgment.

Other Historical Views on Women. Historically, other philosophers and thinkers have doubted woman's rational powers. Plato (427-347 BC) writes in the *Symposium* that the love of a man for other men, the commitment and trust between the male "brothers," is superior to the male love for a woman. And Plato actually implies in the *Timaeus* that women are closer to animals than men.

According to Aristotle (384-322 BC) and St. Thomas Aquinas (AD 1225-1274), a woman is a "misbegotten male." Aristotle, writing over three hundred years before Christ, claims the female does not share the rational capability of men. And Schopenhauer, of course, would much later claim that these inferior rational powers cause problems concerning women's ability to be *moral*. St. Augustine (AD 354-430) defines *wisdom* as masculine and *knowledge* as feminine, and the image of God is to be found in the masculine.

Tertullian (AD) (160-220), one of the fathers of the Latin church, writing about AD 200, connects the *fall from grace*, the biblical expulsion of Adam and Eve from the Garden of Eden, with the sensuality of Eve. The objects that glamorize a woman's body would have been coveted by Eve, says Tertullian. Thus, it follows that the life of spirit would be expected to be destroyed through cosmetics, sexy adornment and the sexual dress of women. (Tammy Baker is Eve?) And it wasn't enough to avoid sexual impropriety and sexual subversion in one's conduct *if* one still dressed as a sex object. Tertullian asks that "the pageantry of fictitious and elaborate beauty be rejected." Why "excite toward yourself that evil passion," the lust of others, he asks?[23] Even women's natural beauty should be concealed because it is so distracting to men, he says. As well, the female must try not to lead others into temptation.

The Dominican Fathers, responsible for the Malleus Maleficarum, portray the female concern with procreation in terms of her sexuality and this, to them, left woman with close to an insatiable sensuality and close to being in the hands of the devil. Women are constantly identified with nature and men with reason, and this male reason is said to give a shape to the shapeless procreating matter of women.

Rousseau (1712-1778) and Hegel (1770-1831) also equate the masculine aspects as connected to reason and the female aspects as connected to the fecundity of nature. Here a woman's basic concern is reproduction, and thus she is defined in terms of her sexuality.

In the twentieth century, Sigmund Freud (1856-1939) also ties the physical, the body, into identity, saying one's biological functions determine one's destiny. He said women were the "dark continent" and that their sense of justice was lacking. Unlike the males, females had not a strong enough super-ego to keep their morality in check, said Freud.

In the late nineteenth century, Friedrich Nietzsche (1844-1900) wrote seriously about "the fundamental problem of man and woman" and sent up his written warning flares so that the significance of the vexation, this "most abysmal antagonism," would be taken seriously. In *Beyond Good and Evil,* Nietzsche testifies that woman's "great art is the lie, her highest concern is mere appearance and beauty," and that "woman would not have the genius for finery if she did not have an instinct for a *secondary* role."[24]

Nietzsche says feminism will lead its followers away from truthful insight, and he also claims that a woman wanting *enlightenment about herself* may only be in search of "a new adornment for herself." Woman "does not *want* truth: what is truth to a woman? From the beginning, nothing has been more alien, repugnant, and hostile to women than the truth." But women want to become self-reliant, says Nietzsche, and are "beginning to enlighten men about 'women as such': this is one of the worst developments of the general uglification of Europe."[25] Nietzsche said woman ventures forth:

> *"when the man in man is no longer desired...and as she thus takes possessions of new rights, aspires to become 'master' and writes the 'progress' of woman upon her standards and banners, the opposite development is taking place with terrible clarity: woman is retrogressing."*

Since the French Revolution, Nietzsche felt that women's influence had diminished in Europe because women were weakening and dulling their most feminine instincts. The "idea" of feminism concealed an "immense stupidity" that could carry Europe away, thought Nietzsche. And he said:

"Certainly, there are enough of idiotic friends

> *and corrupters of woman among the learned
> asses of the masculine sex, who advise woman
> to defeminize herself in this manner, and to imi-
> tate all the stupidities from which 'man' in
> Europe, European 'manliness,' suffers,—who
> would like to lower women to 'general culture,'
> indeed even to newspaper reading and meddling
> with politics."[26]*

He warned women not to follow the feminist insurgents of their time who advised woman to "defeminize" herself. "There is stupidity in this movement, an almost masculine stupidity of which a woman who had turned out well—and such women are always prudent—would have to be thoroughly ashamed." Fredrich Nietzsche finished these words back in 1895.[26]

Modern Ambiguity about Women. Modern ambiguity in understanding women has fit nicely in with political correctness; indeed, this confusion is a basis of political correctness.

> *Off-balance, modern Jill and Joe are educated into
>   being frozen frigid,
> When it comes to "knowing" their sex roles,
>   all some can do is nervously fidget.*

The female gender feminists try to be philosophers *too,* but they get stuck in retaliating because of the emotionally subjective attraction of the rage *glue.* Thus they react, attacking *often without reasonable objective analysis.* Philosophers who seem to support much that gender feminists agree with are attacked ad hominem over details encountered with distaste in other areas the feminists find displeasing to their conception of the feminist agenda. So, to align with the feminist agenda: *always support women; never publicly show outrage to women; always talk about the unity of purpose for women; don't get caught defending anything but women's advance in society; continually point to abuse of women, blacks, homosexuals and the disabled. Try to carry it off with the righteousness of a woman who has been abused for centuries.*

It's the drive for a feminist utopia by some of the female intellectuals that is holding various *notions of females* hostage. These are the true believers stuck in the word glue. They are telling the young girls and older women that they are missing out on a full life, that they are slaves, that they are persecuted, that they are victims of a misogynist philosophical tradition.

In the twentieth century, the famous psychologist Carl Jung (1875-1961), in *Aspects of the Feminine*, states that modern women were being given the feeling of missing the boat, made to think that too much of life would not be lived in the traditional role as mother and wife, the "...secretaries, typists, shop-girls, all are agents of this process and through a million subterranean channels creeps the influence that is undermining marriage."[27] But, there is another agenda, as Jung continues: "For the desire of all these women is not to have sexual adventures,—only the stupid would believe that—but to get married. The possessors of that bliss must be ousted, not as a rule by naked force, but by that silent, obstinate desire which, as we know, has magical effects, like the fixed stare of a snake. This was ever the way of women...no woman can escape the secret, compelling atmosphere with which her own sister, perhaps, is enveloping her, the stifling atmosphere of a life that has never been lived."[28] Jung thought this out back in 1927.

Spin Salon—Mind Make-up

Purviewing some of the lies and the propaganda used by the "oppressed" today, out of a sheer reactive temper to get "power," it becomes one to consider Nietzsche's statement that man might be evil, but woman is *bad*. Circulating in contemporary rhetoric, claims of female abuse swarm, no matter the facts being trumped up, not built upon any reliable, provable ground.

Domestic violence and Women. *Time* magazine reports that "between 22 percent and 35 percent of all visits by females to emergency rooms are for injuries from domestic assaults."[29] This statistic turns up everywhere, used to bang the anti-male marching drum. But the numbers are contradicting the Family Violence Prevention Fund and the findings of Richard Gelles and Murray Straus (1991), two university researchers working for over a quarter of a century on the subject of domestic violence.[30] They are finding that in the area of domestic violence men and women batter each other in the same amount.

The source for the misinformation in *Time* is, in part, an article in the *Journal of the American Medical Association* in 1984, whose authors had already informed the public that their sample group was *not* representative of America's population as a whole. Ninety percent of the respondents to their questionnaire on domestic violence lived in inner-city Detroit. Sixty percent of them were unemployed. Also, the 22-percent figure of domestic assaults covered *both* women and men, and 38 percent of *men* in the survey were themselves complaining of *abuse*. But into the 1990's, newspaper articles and media reports still irresponsibly misuse the numbers from the flawed 1984 Detroit study.

The gender feminist believes that the average man is a potential batterer. To gender warriors like *Gloria Steinem*, it is a sales job, this snow job, this characterization of men as idiots, buffoons, mental cases that live to beat and batter girls, women. Steinem, who is accused of carrying out assignments for the CIA, is the founder of Ms. *Magazine*. She is at war. Ms Mag, in fact, may be one big CIA operation. Her strategy is to disseminate rhetorical shock tactics (memes), to confuse, overpower and humiliate adversaries. The gender feminists are committed to the doctrine that the vast majority of batterers or rapists are not fringe characters but men whom society regards as normal—sports fans, career employees, former fraternity brothers, pillars of the community. For these normal men, it's said, women are not so much persons as objects. In the gender feminist view, once a woman is objectified she is therefore no longer human, thence battering is simply the next logical step. Of course the guys are rapists, brutes....

In the media it is the gender feminists' propaganda war. And it's made even more palatable in today's world, where coercion is accepted as "normal"—as only the desire to gain power. For example, the White House under Clintonism became a 24-hour-a-day makeover center, employing professional doctors of distortion, circumlocution, traveling in the speed of warp, doing the business of *spin*. Thus all can take shelter in committing some *sin?* So, will society believe that some women are adept at making the phoney look so real?

Feminist activists have a large stake in exaggerating battery and abuse, and they have virtually no conscience in doing so. The plight of the fair sex is the subject area where the spin-as-facts "tacts"—statistics and studies on provocative issues like rape, battery, wage differences, eating disorders—promote women as victims of an oppressive patriarchal system. Their facts may not be true at all, but the gender feminists use this "activist research" for recruiting. They say men are a physical menace to women. End of story. That's the agenda and feminist norm!

Gloria Steinem, long time *spinster*, in 1992 published *Revolution from Within: A Book of Self-Esteem*, which says patriarchy requires violence and "the most dangerous situation for a woman is not an unknown man in the street, or even the enemy in wartime, but a husband or lover in the isolation of their own home." How can Steinem be respected by anyone? These words, spoken by a leader of American women, are shocking. The result of her downright immoral propaganda is today's messed-up, unbalanced society.

Sweet!

Super Bowl Sunday. It is 1993, the year the military hammers out the politically correct "don't-ask, don't-tell" policy allowing homosexuals to serve in the armed forces. In 1993, more danger to women from their live-in "soul mates" was hyped by the disseminators of the anti-male hate hearsay. They planned to get 'em in front of the male refuge of competitive sporting events. Call 'em brutes, bastards that beat the innocent, dirty alley cats that rip bird flesh.

It's the scam of the mean men menace, it's about those who use force over a physically weaker sex and claim it as a right. But here *testosterone* can get mixed up with psychology's take on *power*, and women may be taught to see all male energy as dangerous. The money that men earn through aggressive action, it's just fine to all these women. But after receiving their money, then the men can be painted into a corner as simply violent.

So it goes, as Super Bowl Sunday was proclaimed as "the biggest day of the year for violence against women" by a coalition of women's groups. A large media mailing warned women: "Don't remain at home with him during the game." The *New York Times* refers to the big game as the "Abuse Bowl". And as soon as it's in newspapers around the country, it's like a flash-fire burned into everyone's perceptions. And then just before the game, NBC broadcasts a warning to all the men in America that *domestic violence is a crime*.

Lenore Walker, the author of *The Battered Woman*, claims she had a ten-year record showing a sharp increase in violent incidents against women on Super Bowl Sundays.³¹ It was reported that then women's shelters and hotlines are inundated by more calls for help from victims than on any other day of the year. According to much of the media, boy friends, husbands and fathers are explosive devices on this day. They will beat wives, girlfriends and children. Another number circulating in this *myth* is that hospital admissions rise *40 percent* after Super Bowl games. As soon as these untruths are believed the believer lives in a *false-consciousness*. Falsehood and fiction get a big boost, and brains are changing, causing women *and* men to revile the imagined batterers—the guys. The bomb is dropped that men are very cruel and dangerous in their homes. Like the clouds of smoke that rise from a bomb site, so the false-consciousness grows, spreads, and with enough of an offensive repetition these attacks could replace truth entirely.

But Janet Katz, the author of the original Super Bowl study, says what was really found was no connection between violence and football games, and admission to emergency rooms was not associated with football games.³² All down the line, the authorities for the Super Bowl brainwash deny stating the "facts" that turn up everywhere in the media. There is no evidence that a link exists between football and wife-beating, but the general consensus has been colored. And the gender feminists have won a battle in characterizing men as freaks in the home. It's false, but effective, like masking with Blush-on. Those who know better turn the feminist cheek. No evidence is found but the damage is done. The misquotes and faulty reporting have brought a huge propaganda victory for the enemies of men!

History of Wife-beating: Rule of Thumb. The "rule of thumb" further portrays men as abusers. It's in the muster melody of the gender feminist army. There is an actual myth about where the saying "rule of thumb" came from. It's part of the collective hallucination of history the gender feminists are promoting. And they want to rewrite all the school textbooks too, to give a slanted view of history and women. The expression "rule of thumb" is flogged to the public as originating in an English common law that allowed a husband to beat his wife with a whip or stick if it were no bigger than the diameter of his thumb. The "rule" was supposed to have been incorporated into American law. The gender feminists say this gave the husband the right to beat his wife without interference from the courts.

The system tolerates violence of men against women? It's feminist fiction, but soon the media is again ablaze, and from *Time* and the *Washington Post* to small local rags, the spin " tacts" became the facts. American law predating the revolution prohibits wife-beating. But a writer, a coordinator of the *NOW Task Force on Battered Women*, began the creation of the myth as fact. She says the law "explicitly permitted wife-beating for correctional purposes" and did allow the husband "the right to whip his wife, provided that he used a switch no bigger than his thumb."[33] The spin got official status when lawyers and biased academics embraced the *rule of thumb* as fact. Many, of course, were misled and assumed the " tacts" as actual truth.

Piles of propaganda placed perniciously between the genders, keeps reality at bay and lovers away, the distance getting wider as the sexes become snider, contemptuous of each other.

The deception may serve sadomasochistic females, those who sense they cannot compete with their healthy, effectual sisters, the vital, coherent and centered feminine incarnations. It's the sadomasochists who will decide to take everything down if they can't at least get revenge for their seemingly faulty, imperfect incarnation—and their converts are increasing as their propaganda is now taught in public education.

The *repressed guilt* (shame) from the gender feminists' active persecution of males, combined with the psychosis and paranoia (anger) from their victims—men—probably guarantees exploding neuroses. Over time cynical personalities will emerge in the people who have been "educated" and accept life as bad and people as evil, as each successive brutal and sadistic complaint against fellow humans gets absorbed into their world view. So the future is somewhat guaranteed—terror, persecution, cruelty and smart missiles—to come!

Guilt is like being in a trap. It is evident when women flaunt the physical—sex as the escape, and male passion is bedeviled. So if even this sexy cruelty makes her powerful, then there's applause for more of the same. The trap. In the cycle, it's more neurosis, more "insurance", more assurance that evil rules the world. See, the frustration in contemporary society can be sold as rewarding if one can *ride* the sex neurosis, go with the psychotic flow and call orgasm the denouement, the resolution of hang-ups. Here the environment that counts is *interior*. Women live in the psyche, and here her eros demands company. She gets the power here. The argument is that sex is needed to calm and heal the modern's alienated torment that's over the edge... almost. But sex is easily used for power, not for healing. And each manipulation for selfish "power" carries some weight of guilt, some inferiority. Negativity is being raised up. Soon the *witch* could rule! Power bought with guilt, in each instance, increases the neurotic *insurance*. A self-centered and exploitative world view fosters the perplexing perception that the world must be dominated by some kind of darkened predator.

But the gender feminist conspiracy is real and if it continues to control public policy, it will lead men into a living death, spiritually bludgeoned. They will be mere shadows of men, without a really meaningful, masculine, social purpose, withdrawn from a lot of public life and living in redundant isolation. Is that the feminist utopia? It is getting closer day by day. There never, ever was a rule-of-thumb law in the USA, and wife-beating has always been a crime and a sin. So it's just more violent feminist fiction used to create a false consensus about themselves, to set the stage for the completion of their takeover of society.

Filthy lies, like the "rule of thumb", promote an ignorant and deadly hatred, and women it is you who will be despised in the future for forgetting your men, dumping them, hoping for their ultimate defeat. Many women are afraid to even criticize anything another "sister" says.

Anorexia. To get government funding, some feminist leaders produce reports and surveys that bring on their favorite wounded-bird trepidity. The female feathered in this fiction shows up again as the super-victim. Anorexia, an eating disorder for some women, is painted as "the inevitable consequence of a misogynist society that demeans women by objectifying their bodies."[34] It becomes men's fault these that women are so unbalanced, mentally ill and masochistic that they won't eat food.

It's 1992, and Gloria Steinem (spinster) squeezes out a pungent "tact," no matter that it's so totally false, a blatant untruth: "in this country alone...about 150,000 females die of anorexia each year."[35] Then Ann Landers flogs this meme "tact." And another "tact" disturber, Naomi Wolf, barks out the same lie, then states that these anorexics are *starved not by nature but by men.* She and her gender feminist co-conspirators say that the sick women are only trying to live up to the thin look that men demand in America! It's evidence of the patriarchal society's intimidation of women, and it is killing these innocent women, they say. Professor Joan Brumberg, former Director of Women's Studies at Cornell University, was Naomi Wolf's source. But the American Anorexia Bulimia Association said that they were misquoted – the 150,000 number was not *dead girls*. No, it was the number of females that suffer from anorexia nervosa. But the "boomer bitches" spread the hate-inducing meme and *false* figures. The virulent propaganda rages – its destructive force poisons the mind, spawning the development of more and more false-consciousness, as millions of lives are ushered into misery as a result of the misinformation.

The nation gets instructed—yes, the women as victims, the men as villains. The cup of arsenic called the truth of women's abuse is being drunk from the brim down to the very last drop. The true victims, those inhaling the meme-virus disease, are being devastated. The dead-in-the-head walk pathetically in circles, spun into a politically correct denial. Increasingly their needs are subverted, ignored or perverted into more alienation. This propaganda will hurt and is hazardous to both genders. But the gender feminists, those disciples of misandrist dogma, are scratching, screaming and using fudged numbers to rock any boat that tries to set *sail*, not powered by them—these princesses that model clenched fists and *wail*.

Battery of Pregnant Women. It's 1993 and Bill Clinton, the man without a father, the guy brought up in a matriarchy, is the front man for the USA. It's the year Lorena Bobbitt uses an eight-inch carving knife and cuts off her sleeping husband's penis—and is later acquitted! This was a year after Gloria Steinem wrote that the most hazardous situation for a woman was being with her husband in her own home. Patricia Ireland, the bi-sexual president of NOW, speaks to the nation on PBS: "Battery of pregnant women is the number one cause of birth defects in this country."[36] That's her message. That's her statement of truth, of the facts, as one of the most powerful leaders of modern American women. That's her leadership and guiding voice, her voice of responsibility picking the issues with which to focus the masses on her watch.

Another female, president of the Women's Studies Association, had earlier posted a message on an electronic bulletin board about the March of Dimes. Apparently the March of Dimes reported that domestic violence against pregnant women was responsible for more birth defects than all other causes combined. The report was circulating all around the country. It was in the *Chicago Tribune* (April 18, 1993), *Arizona Republic* (March 21, 1993), and *Time* magazine (January 18, 1993). But the March of Dimes denied any knowledge of the report and asked *Time* magazine for a retraction. The author of the *Time* article, Jeanne McDowell, said she just didn't check her sources. She said the San Francisco Family Violence Prevention Fund gave it to her, and they in turn received the "tact" from Sarah Buel, a director of a domestic abuse project in Massachusetts and a founder of the domestic violence advocacy project at Harvard Law School.

> *It's up at the top and in the establishment; production*
>   *of the inexact,*
> *Information raked across the male to constrain,*
>   *to impel and to infract –*
> *It's in the system, this control and tact,*
> *Lies twisted to excite, and then to attract*
> *A target for true believers, those setting up the men*
>   *to swack.*

Eventually, on December 6, 1993, *Time* magazine retracted. The thought that domestic battery could cause more birth defects than all other causes combined is hyperbole for sadists. All the young minds that assimilate this meme—what will their future love life now be? Voltaire left us with: *"if we believe absurdities we will commit atrocities."*

Rape by Numbers. Naomi Wolfe, in the *Beauty Myth,* cites a *Ms. Magazine* survey that claims that one in four women respondents had had an experience that met the American legal definition of rape or attempted rape. *One in Four* became the media headline that soon had found a home in people's heads. Wolf and *Ms.* claim that women may not even know they are raped. So they are helping them realize their raped condition in a society where "sexual violence is seen as normal by young women as well as young men."[37] A woman or girl who feels "regret" after sex, or feels somehow "violated," can qualify as a rape victim—even if she went through the sexual intercourse without any complaint! Weeks, months, years later she can charge her male sexual partner with rape. And it has become popular, this whipsaw surprise that today's "princess" can present to her contemporary "beastly male" partner. And some serious college students believe that the number of young women raped is actually closer to one in two. It seems America is a "rape culture."

Rape serves the gender feminists because it gets sympathy and support for females. By fudging the numbers through their unaccountable *advocacy research,* a huge political victory is won by these self-interested enemies of men. Many gender feminists seem to carry utopian visions of sexual relations, where there is sex without power, sex without persuasion and sex without pursuit. This is unrealistic, but "reality" is not their interest. Power is, and it seems there are no rules in their pursuit of power.

Studies have demonstrated that up to half of all rape allegations are untrue. And this 50-percent level of rape fraud is based on women who have actually *admitted* to lying![38] So the real numbers must be even higher.

As Hugh Nations has stated: "Rape is frequently described as a crime of violence, not of sex. Yet a woman 16-19 years old, the age of greatest sexual attractiveness, is more than 84 times more likely to be raped than a woman 50 or older."[39] Nations' summary of facts about rape has led to more insights in the truth about rape in America. A survey of 610 female college students whose average age was 19 years found that 39 percent said they had said *no* to sex when they meant *yes,* and 69 percent said that they had said *no* when they meant *maybe.* Of sexually experienced women, 61 percent had engaged in token resistance. And in a survey of 507 male and 486 female college students, 63 percent of the males and 46 percent of the females said they engaged in unwanted sexual intercourse.

A Purdue University study reported in 1994 that false rape allegations provided three major functions for the complainants: an alibi, a means of revenge and a platform for seeking attention or sympathy.[40] Students who recanted their claim of rape admitted to these motives. From the accumulated data, the study concludes "false rape accusations are not uncommon." The Purdue study also states that "university women, when filing a rape complaint, were as likely to file a false charge as a valid charge."[41]

The one in four rape figure is based on the Ms. *Magazine* Campus Project on Sexual Assault, conducted by Mary Koss. She had once stated that rape "…is on a continuum with normal male behavior within the culture."[42] Gloria Steinem takes her to lunch, and Koss is chosen to do the Ms. *Magazine* national survey on rape. The "one in four" rape probability is now history. It became virtually the official figure used in women's studies programs, rape crisis centers and in women's magazines. Susan Faludi supported the survey. Naomi Wolf uses its findings.

"One in Four" is chanted during all the Take Back the Night spectacles and processions that keep young college girls and their mothers alerted to a threat that isn't there. Politicians jump through hoops railing against imaginary criminals. And large sums of money come from public funds to combat rape on campuses. But the majority of women Koss had classified as having been raped did not believe they had been raped; 73 percent did not say that they had been raped, only 27 percent thought they had been.[43] And 42 percent of those included as raped women went on to have sex with their "attackers" on a later occasion.[44]

Female Click Experience. At another time the women of America are asked by Gloria Steinem's Ms. *Magazine* to try and locate their own personal "click experience." That's when a light "clicked" on in her head at the moment of her epiphany—when she first realized her society, her culture, *cheats her* in favor of men! So, it is taken for granted that men have cheated her. She is made now to see: men are self-serving and dangerous; men dominate and oppress; men write official versions of history; men have designed the whole of the college curriculum to focus on men's aptitudes and perceptions. In a single "click" the game is considered over! Men are castigated, the woman now to burst out, having had her flash, re: being cheated, re: being in danger from her culture. And now she's supposedly ready to create a society to serve herself.

Believing in female oppression is what the zap is about. Ms. *Magazine* makes it a contest of sorts. *Have you realized the truth? Seen the light? Reached a level of consciousness that can handle reality, actually had a click experience? And are you now totally anchored in the knowledge you have been cheated, silenced?*

Revisionist History. Filler feminism is now filling school textbooks with *herstory*, this pat-on-the-back crony feminism creating fantasy *history*.

> *This "non-sexist" history teaches lessons many*
> *feminists wish to impart,*
> *Even though the facts just aren't there from the start.*

Some states in the US are demanding "gender-fair" history be taught, insisting the women be given 50 percent of textbook content for *their* female contributions. This dishonest approach focuses on *notions* of fairness—that is an equal numbers of pages, equal ink going to the genders—more than on historical accuracy or faith in historical truth. It's politically correct. What many education departments around the "land of the free" are instituting today is a force-fed feminist revision of history. It will obviously bolster the false-consciousness already filling the students' cranial cavities, and raise embarrassingly to the fore the fantastic cultural illiteracy being championed all over the country.

The idea is to elevate some female creations so as to give a democratic-egalitarian representation in textbooks—for example, to bring some female work of art into art history so that the masterpieces by men are offset by something, anything, from the female. It could be a leap into mediocrity at the expense of the genius of another work by a male, a work that may be just short of being an accepted masterpiece. So the male work is trashed, turned out, so a female can have an equal quantity of representations—quantity perhaps devoid of comparative quality. Here today's society is cutting its own throat. Women have been freed up from many of yesterday's tasks through inventions that have made her life easier. Name one invention that has helped "liberate her labors" produced by a female....?

Self-esteem Propaganda. Another area in which the gender feminists' propaganda shows its deplorable and vicious agenda is in self-esteem studies about girls. The evidence actually shows that it's boys and not the girls who are losing "voice" and declining in self-esteem.

Shortchanging Girls, Shortchanging America—that's the title of the American Association of University Women's (AAUW), report in the early 90's.[45] The AAUW report claims that girls' aura of self-esteem descends between the ages eleven to sixteen, which hinders the girls' learning and achievement. This report caused headlines around the country and provoked hundreds of conferences and regional group responses. The AAUW then got politicians, business leaders and the media on board. Fifty US congresspersons sponsored a $360-million bill, as bleeding hearts ran to nurture the "shortchanged girls." The young girls, according to some, "no longer like themselves," "doubt themselves" and, of course, now *needed to learn* "that their lives are valuable at the same time that they learn their ABC's." At the time, men had virtually no base of support, no lobby groups promoting their well-being.

An enormous impact, this self-esteem propaganda had, but its methods, analysis and conclusions once again get the verdict: "tact"! The 140,000-member strong AAUW promoted its report through press conferences and thousands of "calls to action" brochures distributed to its membership, to politicians and to journalists. And the AAUW made a polished media documentary to show all over America.

Their tale: the torture, defeat and deprecation of America's young females. The AAUW documentary claims that eating disorders, depression and dislocation result from "undervaluing" girls. Everyone bought right in, freaking from these gender feminist " tacts." From schoolboard bureaucrats to politicians and the media, all focused on addressing the needs of the girls.

The devil and all went right along believing the AAUW because of its prominence as a major professional group, and therefore as credible. No journalists ever got to the nuts and bolts of the report. And like the seemingly low-IQ people today hired to read the *official* network news, the dummy reporters go flat straight ahead and report the spin as news. They simply print the news releases handed them by the AAUW!

A National Council for Self-Esteem was soon established as the nation chased its tail, scampering to help the girls *feel* like they do belong, and like they are competent, that they have possibilities and that they, indeed, are a somebody. It's like the elevation given women in the nineteenth century, so much time and attention focused on women having it all go so right for them.

According to Christina Hoff Sommers, Ph.D., when the self-esteem report was being flogged all through the 90's, the leadership of the AAUW made: "the association into an activist arm of gender feminism. Its current group of officers—Executive Director Ann Bryant, President Sharon Schuster, and Alice McKee, President of the AAUW educational foundation—are committed gender feminists who had expectations of what they would find when they initiated the self-esteem study."[46]

Carol Gilligan, Professor of Gender Studies at Harvard Graduate School of Education, and her theories had been behind the AAUW self-esteem survey that she also helped design. Gilligan claims that during adolescence females are pushed aside and are kept in the background by society—girls are silenced and go underground *not knowing what they know.*

Girls, to Gilligan, are silenced by a "male-voiced" culture, the *patriarchy*, and she claims that she has the evidence. It's not puberty that brings on female turmoil; oh no, instead it's a girl-destroying society that is at fault. In 1990, the *New York Times* ran the Gilligan theory of girls' self-esteem being shredded. Next it was Gilligan working with Ms. *Magazine,* alerting the world to the plight of the girls, who are confident at eleven but just plain confused at sixteen, or so the story goes. Girls are portrayed as coming up against the wall of a culture that values women less than men.

As Hoff Sommers summarizes: "The gloomy picture of adolescent girls that she [Gilligan] presented to Ms., the AAUW, and a concerned public is every bit as distorted as any ever presented by social scientists using (in Gilligan's words) 'androcentric and patriarchal norms.'"[47] The AAUW report stands as a classic example of advocacy research. The artful way in which the questions were asked and the answers were marked got the conclusion that the AAUW wanted: fear of a national crisis in the self-esteem of adolescent girls. Once the " tacts" were out in the public domain, as one researcher said: "the whole thing is being carried on in the court of the media."

In 1993, the Ms. Foundation for Women declared a *Take Our Daughters to Work* day. A great success, more than half a million daughters went to work with their mothers and fathers. The teachers' guide handed out by the Ms. Foundation reiterated: "recent studies point to adolescence as a time of crisis and loss for girls. While most girls are outspoken and self-confident at the age of nine, their level of self-esteem plummeted by the time they reach high school." Gloria Steinem was involved in *Take Our Daugh-*

ters to Work day, saying the young girls, when they must take on their feminine role at age twelve or thirteen, will have to go underground, making them vulnerable to depression, pregnancy and eating disorders. But what about the boys left behind? Why aren't they being catered to, encouraged to be "visible, valuable and heard," and taken to work by a parent? Well, the Ms. Foundation proposed that the boys spend the day *doing exercises to help them understand how our society shortchanges women.*

The AAUW then gave money to Wellesley College, and it produces another report that dramatically buttressed the AAUW report on self-esteem. The Wellesley Report, *How Schools Shortchange Girls*, rants on about a "wealth of statistical evidence" that shows girls are persecuted in school. The media again buys right in, reproduces most of the propaganda verbatim. Christina Hoff Sommers states: "What is highly questionable is the value and integrity of the research and the way the advocates have deployed the 'findings' to activate the United States Congress."[48]

The Press Buys In. Just how do the nation's reporters and news anchors allow this *merde* to pad their promotions? Except when in the camera's eye, they are so often beyond any pretense of professionalism. Do many graduates of journalism regularly check sources, or has the truth imprisoned them instead of setting them free? Chirpy, lean male and female script-reader television mouthpieces spew out words. They are getting paid to say anything that is written and stands in front of them.

> *Messy major issues are diced through,*
> *These obvious orators haven't a clue,*
> *Or give a damn...*
> *If their spiel is totally untrue.*

Spin, " tacts," private agendas, created mass consensus, ownership of all major media by the few—and the talking heads fall into line. They read the word prompter scripts prepared to induce mass hypnosis, and apathy about neuroses. Jill and Joe public are forced at odds, off-balance, able only to work and then flake out after all the meme assault.

New Feminism and Academia

Testy and unpredictable, the new feminism has renovated the

university of today. A huge victory for the gender feminists as the male professors and university deans have more than accommodated these "oppressed" females.

Some of the males are sincerely affected by the tacts,
Others following the political denial of the times
see all creatures in abstracts.

It will probably only get worse as the women outnumber the men in the universities. This is a done deal. And as females support anything "female" today, many gender feminist types, a number of them male bunglers, are in large part controlling the educational system. Perhaps they *will* rewrite all of history.

Female Gender Bias. Evidence of female gender bias is witnessed in politics in the United States of America. In elections, women of the Democratic and Republican parties will never run against each other on the same ballot. To them it is more important to have *any* women in power, no matter her party affiliation.

It's for the nation's future that this gender-serving skullduggery is believed to be able to bring such wonders. It shows the agitation around control that is going to have to be squarely faced. What a scene this propaganda culture is: sirens, babes, cruel postmodern male-bashing meme-warriors ride roughshod, thinking to get their licks in and, like rock stars, dig the revolt. But some may as well be riding broomsticks. They are as unaccountable as phantom market forces. They may claim *unconscious* reasons as excuse for their behavior. The people of the West are reeling under a witches' spell and the power of a witches' spell—the *Great Gender Conspiracy Theory*.

Psychology departments today brim with females. It's *she,* the psychic, emotive one, in relationships all over the map, looking basically for more sympathy, a misplaced sympathy perhaps, and that unfortunately could become the end in itself; it's addicting.

Magic, tarot card readers on TV, the Potter books for the kids a rave, as the mystical feminine is disseminated into the young souls. Enchantment, dissimulation, fantasy and faulty facts fixed, made over and dished up as the rational....

Replacing Males. The simply rational is now called reason, and then logic as well. Soon the will of the human hammers it into some seductive sales pitch or law. Is justifying the nuking of enemies that difficult? And just what could *getting the government off of people's backs* actually do, if not to give people less protection, less security from corporate greed?

Corporate greed and government non-action caused the stock market crash of 1929 that ushered in the poverty and suffering of the Great Depression. Mussolini, the leader of the Italian fascist party in the 1920's, held power promising an anti-government government. He was the first of the *anti-government* political leaders, promising less government in people's lives. The fascists are corporatists, and they plan to enable big business's profits to grow. Removing government's watchdog role must remove people's participation in democracy as well. The corporations want to sell products as solutions for people's needs. So who will keep the corporations in line, if not the government? The Green Party and Ralph Nader point out the insanity of many of our rationally portrayed solutions. But who's listening?

Can innocent plebs be forgiven if they don't have a clue?
Is their role to buy and die all that they are asked to do?

Never matter children the name, sorrow's showers surround the gratifiers, the shoppers reaching for answers, searching with wry grins. Things, stuff, products are bought. It's more their thoughts of self-improvement that they really like, thoughts of themselves, featuring them becoming salaciously improved so to speak, and their self-respect going up. Envy is the main motivator.

Envy also leads the conspiracy to capture what is seen as the power positions of men. The gender feminists have taken over the universities without braving any eye-burning *mace*. They are succeeding at control of the schools and all workplace environments, and soon society may just more or less replace men, as gender feminists further win their *case*.

Boys Lose Out

In reality, boys are in the pits compared to girls in the school system. Twice as many girls as boys are involved in student government, drama, band and orchestra and service clubs. More females intend to go to college, with a tripling of women focusing on higher degrees in less than twenty-five years. More boys cut classes, fail to do homework, have discipline problems, have been suspended and have been in police trouble. And boys drop out of school more often. Boys are more likely to be victims of violence in and out of school, be robbed or be threatened. Almost every syndrome, including alcoholism and drug abuse, hits boys harder.[49]

Data on suicide during adolescence is also skewed by the gender feminists. The Wellesley Report states that "adolescent girls are four to five times more likely than boys to attempt suicide." And according to clinical psychologist Mary Pipher, clinics are inundated with girls who try to kill themselves. Pipher says: "The Center for Disease Control in Atlanta reports that the suicide rate among children age ten to fourteen rose 75 percent between 1979 and 1988. Something dramatic is happening to adolescent girls in America, something unnoticed by those not on the front lines."[50]

But the Center for Disease Control's suicide statistics about children show that for *boys* aged ten to fourteen, the suicide rate had increased 71 percent between 1979 and 1988. *For girls the increase was just 27 percent!* But Mary Pipher says girls are terminating hope and their lives in America. Is an increase in suicides by girls from 48 in 1979 to 61 in 1988, an increase of thirteen out of a population of nine million girls between age ten and fourteen, evidence of a "girl-destroying culture"? On the other hand, the boys suicide numbers go from 103 in 1979 to 176 in 1988, an increase of seventy-three. The fact: five times as many boys as girls killed themselves. This is close to the adult ratio for suicide and gender as well.[51]

And who cares about the boys anyway...or the real facts? It's like hearing Immanuel Kant again, this time on the loudspeaker coming from the school principal's office: "Nothing of duty, nothing of compulsion, nothing of obligation! Woman is intolerable of all commands, and all morose constraint. They do something only because it pleases them, and the art consists in making only that please them which is good. I hardly believe the fair sex is capable of principles...."[52]

The gender feminists have been busy trying to socialize boys. Carol Gilligan calls for "a new and healing pedagogy to free boys from an errant masculinity that is endangering civilization." Society, she claims, needs to free boys from "cultures that value or valorize heroism, honor, war, competition—the culture of the warrior, the economy of capitalism."[53] Very interesting, but in their culture, American women have been brainwashed to compete and fight in an economy of capitalism, and they call their participation "liberation." And a big problem to Gilligan is that in western culture the boys are separated from their moms! She wants to reconstruct boys "imprisoned by masculinity," and feminize them. She's visioning a future by ignoring the biological factors that distinguish the genders. Her word glue will emotionally hook many, but she's speculating without much common sense. Gilligan's "buddies" can be found in the departments of education where her propaganda has been disseminated to the school boards, and where they are using it to construct the new learning curves. With 73 percent of teachers being female, the curves demanded by Gilligan's ideology are basically in the hands of the gender of curves. As Hoff Sommers says:

> *"Her ideas were successful in the sense that they inspired activists in organizations such as the AAUW and the Ms. Foundation to go on the red alert in an effort to save the nation's 'drowning and disappearing' daughters. But all their activism was based on a false premise: that girls were subdued, neglected, and diminished. In fact, the opposite was true: girls were moving ahead of boys in most of the ways that count. Gilligan's powerful myth of the incredible shrinking girl did far more harm than good. It patronized girls, portraying them as victims of the culture. It diverted attention from the academic deficits of boys. It also gave urgency and credibility to a specious self-esteem movement that wasted everybody's time."*[54]

Now Gilligan promotes an aggressive re-socialization of boys, a feminization to save them from the *patriarchy*. Some say boys *already* express themselves verbally like girls. Just listen to their intonation and speech rhythm, it's become like the females', they say. Many men talk like women today. But Gilligan must be a control freak. She, too, has got the girls up there and at a distance, idealized and polished in mind. Now she's going to box in the boys? How square.

Meanwhile, over and above the propaganda and pathetic claims, all bow and heed the transcendent, all-powerful God Market (GM), the voice of the people reduced to what can be bought or sold, for how much, when and where. Shopping perhaps, the body to adorn, searching for all types of improvement, the plebs are out of the way, programmed to pursue anything to stop them from seeing things as they really are.

Effect of Affirmative Action

Are there problems in education for the saintly gender? Females have flooded the university campuses and are the majority there today. The government's Affirmative Action (AA) policy will keep it that way, even though the intent of AA was to get African-American and other minorities some support in the US—rather than the dominant class of white women. Will women identify with anything, to get free rides? Master's degrees at the universities—currently 61 percent of those enrolled in these superior degree programs are females. In the social and psychological sciences, and in the humanities in general, women receive approximately 55 percent of doctoral degrees. At Yale Medical School, in 1996, women were 54 percent of the entering class. Half the law degrees awarded in the US go to women. And at Harvard Law School female enrollment has jumped from 18 percent in 1975 to 42 percent in 1997.[55] Female enrollment in 2000 is up 700 percent from the 1970 level at Harvard Law. By 2006, according to US News and World Report, Harvard Law School has 56 percent male and 44 percent female students. The trend grows for higher admissions. The proportion of women physicians has tripled in the last twenty-five years, and women have become the majority in pharmacy and veterinary medicine.[56]

Legal policies snuck in by the feminist camp through Affirmative Action favor women in employment. And so police and fire departments and the military are forced to hire both sexes; they have to meet quotas in spite of the quality of the candidates. The new elite members of the foreign office in Great Britain are predominately women. In the US, 30 percent of senior officials are women.

Portraying the man as a violent low-life really has worked wonders for some feminists, getting money from taxpayers to protect against claimed male furor and the male tearing up of the earth. And men have lost jobs while their image as provider has been demeaned. It's *everyman* the gender feminists are after, *not* just the criminal ones who break laws and commit aggressive assault. No, not just the fringe characters, but men society regards as *normal*; these men are the focus of the anger of the gender-benders who see women "objectified" and thus soon to be battered. Some say that to people like Gloria Steinem and her group, the task is to "persuade the public that the so-called normal man is a morally defective human being who gets off on hurting women."[57] And women are having tremendous success using this type of unjustifiable assault. They ridicule all men for crimes some criminals *commit*. By lumping all men into the garbage can as criminals, all males are made to wear the same *outfit*.

Domestic Violence Again

Memes of rage, memes of hate,
Paint the male into corners, and there is no escape,
The propaganda war has been won, and the guys
  put through,
The males tarred and feathered with "numbers,"
No matter they are untrue....

Published figures of battering and abuse result in an arson on the living minds of readers, as the whole of society seems held hostage by men's physical torture and scorching cruelty to the female. So much of it is about domestic beatings, battery. The number of women beaten varies with these studies, but the studies get prime-time coverage. And thus the message gets out, even if false. It would seem men are pounding women, wives, at an awesome rate. *Time*, in 1983, said some 6 million women will be abused by their husbands each year in the US. *The New York Times*, in 1993, said every fifteen seconds an American woman is beaten by her husband or boyfriend.[58]

And on and on the numbers go, painting the picture
  of the woman's foe.

But responsible research shows that women and men batter

each other about equally. Murray Straus and Richard Gelles find women were just as likely to engage in it as men. But what is not promoted or appreciated in their professional studies and results is the fact that 84 percent of families are not violent. Of the 16 percent of families who are violent, approximately half the violence is perpetrated by women, according to Straus and Gelles.[59]

Martin Fiebert of California State University produced a bibliography that shows that violence is an equal gender issue. The collection covers 117 scholarly investigations, 94 empirical studies, and 23 reviews or analysis which demonstrate that women are as physically aggressive, or more aggressive, than men in their relationship with their spouses or male partners.[60]

It is more than foolish to skew some of the numbers, as some surveys do—considering an insult or swearing at a spouse as domestic abuse. Or if a spouse was "pushed, grabbed, shoved or slapped," it is automatically considered domestic violence, without regard to whether the aggression was natural or whether it was harmful or seriously intimidating. Or induced (provoked). Minor and severely violent acts are all blended to give high numbers. If a spouse stomped out of a room or the house or the yard, this has been—yes, indeed—fictionalized or imagined as more domestic abuse!

Thirty-four percent of women in the 1993 Commonwealth Fund telephone survey, designed and carried out by Lou Harris and Associates, answered "yes" to the question of whether in the past twelve months your partner has ever: (1) insulted you or sworn at you, or (2) stomped out of the room or house or yard. All 34 percent of women who answered "yes" are classified as victims of "emotional and verbal abuse." The numbers are used like recipe ingredients, thoughtfully added to the stew that the gender cannibals prepare—male stew with baked numbers, the spicier the better.

Although *Time* reports 6 million wives were abused, Straus and Gelles, in *Behind Closed Doors: Violence in the American Family,* report 1.8 million women assaulted each year by husbands and boyfriends. But then the National Coalition Against Domestic Violence reports that 50 percent of all women would experience violence from their spouses, and that one-third of all women are battered each year. The "facts" can also be measured in assaults per second. For example, Brother Peace, in 1993, said

6.5 million women are annually assaulted by their partners, one every five seconds. As previously stated, the *New York Times* (1993) had a woman beaten by her husband or boyfriend every 15 seconds. The *Annals of Emergency Medicine* claims that every 7.4 seconds a women is beaten by her husband. But, Straus and Gelles state that fewer than 1 percent of women experience severe violence.[61]

In our cynical age of accepted cruelty, all the nasty and often contradictory claims can drive a person nuts. Journalists and the media seek the sensational, the sadistic and hyper-realities to attract the piranha-souls seeking reassurances that, yes, everything is more or less a total mess, totally sick, violent, perverted and shocking. Thus one's own personal living mess can be accepted as not so bad, etc. It's the *insurance* neurotics need to maintain their addictions to low expectations, escapist solutions and Hollywood distractions. And it keeps lasciviousness and copulation, the sexual, up there and ranked as a premier method to flaunt one's full life of alienated stress. Randy and musty, the carnal as a means to *ride the stress*. But will it also guarantee the Nuclear Bomb?

Many begin to relate to sex as an escape from all their frustrations, as a focal point to obsess upon and as a detour when life gets strained or uncontrollable. Luckily, pleasure brings a cleansing of all the "freedom of speech" that's got the plebs in a titillated but neurotic condition. The world's been screwed over anyway, it says so on the *news!*

Entertainment and Sex as Escape

Unfortunately, many escape from the reality of contemporary society and its lunacy through an entertainment world that's obsessed with hyper-cruel and sadomasochistic sexual themes. Civilians' brains are figuratively blown out reveling in Hollywood productions about the violent, brutal, unredeemable world they themselves are increasingly shrinking away from having anything much to do with. And the peace process between the Israelis and the Palestinians—people may soon think it too can be fixed by a big explosion.

Everybody's stressed. Most can barely deal with all the bits and pieces of the transmitted signals flying through the air. For personal escape, entertainment, a modern woman or man can sit and just *watch,* go blank, and leave their need for peace to those on the TV screen. But watching TV doesn't guarantee the truth, and our controlled contemporary compatriot's brain is maybe going to rot, struggling to get the reasons about why we're all so fagged out.

Insurance and its negative world view is the neurosis that is in part due to the group allowing life to be controlled by the sadistic, negative spins and propaganda. It can be propaganda so false it's psychotic—denying compassion—this seen in the worship of a brutal, impersonal God Market. People endure all the lies, cruelty and the phoney sanctimoniousness of hired actors and the politicians. They endure the trashing of the human soul by the greedy beings in charge. *Huge anxiety, shock and guilt force the brain into overdrive.*

The tension swells bringing on desperation for release. Welcome in! Sex has become the ride of the century, the neurotic express that stretches over the mundane cemented structures of modern civilization. It's the muscle used to cope with all the neuroses everyone is coming around to expect and take for granted.

> *Sex has got the serfs obsessed,*
> *Undressed*
> *And starting to itch and pull at their flesh.*
> *Alone, with the TV*
> *Or with some body,*
> *Sex is the simple way to get to free?*

This society can be counted on to make everyone sick. The moderns are infected from ingesting society's psychoses. But can they use this neurosis as their *guiding weight*, mesmerized like selfish dogs in heat without concern for the future? Or for others. The moderns will even consume sex toys and orgy videos to help boost this neurotic guiding principle, to break any outside demands while working so diligently, trying for sex that can supposedly *take them out of this world....*

Punishing Males

Unfortunately, much of today's wholesale sickness and sadism is directed at males. Punishing them is popular. They are criticized and blamed for virtually all of society's problems. They are forced onto the altar of modern sacrifice, as cruelly they are hurt, regardless of innocence. The abomination of sacrificing males brings on more belief *(insurance)* that darkness rules, as the moderns now tilt toward their masochistic side—and take their governments' mistreatment as if deserved!

But the escape into sadism and masochism leaves guys as the scapegoat; the real victim here is the man who is taking it in the *ear,* painted as the one to *fear*! America and western civilization has always had a lower esteem for the males. It is males who in war have been slaughtered by the hundreds of millions. Our society is used to depriving boys and men of dignity, but it respects women openly. There are few support agencies for men like there are for women. And so, in divorce today, the money and the children are taken from the men, given to the women. We are used to ignoring the humanity of the men; it's been that way in our history. So today we let the gender feminists torture the men.

In North American culture there is isn't as much respect for young men, nor does society promote anything near the caring or catering that is given to the girls. For example, in the movie *Fight Club*, the guys are left alone, many without the father that his mother may have deemed disposable, and then they resort to the crudest male stereotypes. They escape their boring jobs and their educated public-school dysfunction by beating up each other in the secret surroundings where they meet each week. These guys, while typifying the male jockeying for a dominant role through physical challenge, are not emotionally well. The fights serve a modern inner cruelty, a sadomasochism derived from the male-trashing going on.

Playing *smash face* (American football) at college or school is one thing, in front of audiences and under game rules. There the boys rip and tear, physically confront their "buddies" for glory and girls. Sure the boys are thus being trained to identify other boys as enemies, but they have been trained for many centuries to sacrifice their bodies for society and to protect the females.

If the enemy would become "girls," then what? In *Fight Club*, there is no big audience, but it's the competitive market-economics society in microcosm, and like the corporations themselves the boys have rights, but they might not have dads. Desperate for the bottom line, they are brave enough to seek solutions. *Children of the single momhood*—they are a big part of the nation's future.

Social Consequences of Single Motherhood

Is a woman better off without a man, going it alone, even to the extent of withdrawing a man's biological child from him? That is what the newly minted feminist calls for *reproductive freedom* could end up being about.

Divorce casino. Divorce is today initiated by women at twice the rate that it is initiated by men. Our society actually gives women incentive to divorce! Women get benefits from divorce. They usually will get the children, child support and the family home if there is one. Research shows that about 50 percent of mothers see no value in a father's contact with his children and try to sabotage it, or resent the father's contact.[62] Both tax-free child support and dependent exemptions go to the mother in the US. With the help of feminist organizations, many city agencies and even bar associations give free legal aid to women in order to take children away from men.[63] Society gives women emotional and financial reward to divorce. Divorce is hailed in front page newspaper stories as the way for "alpha" women to "build coping muscles." Divorce as the road to building a women's strength!

A divorce can mean a man's loss of his job as a father. But he is forced to pay for his "firing" by subsidizing his own removal through money given for child support—a mother subsidy. Today many biological moms think that they can be fathers too, and the government is supporting them to think so. In 1960, there were 5.1 million single moms in the US. By 1996, it was 16 million.[64] In 1970, about one in ninety homes in the US were mother-only homes. By 2000, it was 22 percent.[65]

Divorce can leave men in big trouble. They can end up alone: no family, no one needing them, no hero role to give superior meaning to their lives. They are often rebuked as if they are the problem itself. Then his money is expected and that helps his ex-wife fulfilling *her* "psychic" life with *his* children. It's a special hell, for men only, and it's brought to them by that extra-special somebody—the wife he married. In fact, after a divorce, a man's risk of suicide rises to ten times greater than that of a divorced woman's.[66]

Men's needs as fathers are ignored. One Alley McBeal TV show had a mother offer to sell "her" baby to its unwed biological father for five million dollars! Our society is programmed to disregard, pass over the men. When a woman with children takes the notion to divorce and to dabble in different lifestyle choices available only to her, she receives support from the government and from the ex-husband, and often from her parents. But the man, the father, is virtually ignored—except for his wallet. His children are taken from him in most cases, and the woman gets custody. But the loss of his children is like a death to the man. In *Father and Child Reunion,* Warren Farrell, Ph.D., elaborates:

> "When we demand a dad give child support and wife support, then take away his children and home, we kill his soul, his reason for earning, his reason for living...when we drive him into a deadend, he becomes a deadbeat, dead broke, or just dead....[67] When a dad's child is dead to him, but still alive, he can never begin the process of mourning; he can never heal. We feel this unhealed hurt and bitterness when we meet dads who are denied their children."[68]

Many women have off-chucked their childrens' fathers. Our society rewards them, really—for this. The women's network, when working for women's needs, encourages *psychic relationship,* both intimate and emotional. Women *need* this psychic relationship; it's something they are simply unable to run away from. It's available with their children. So if it isn't working out well in the *psychic relationship* that she *married* her *husband* to get, she eliminates him. He may have become an insensitive boor, an emotionally crippled failure in her eyes. This may become his described identity and its promotion may help build the story of her claimed demise. But her psychic relationship continues as she feeds off the kids. With *his* children she approximates emotional health! He usually pays, may get some visitation privileges, but his needs are simply not a big part of any solution in our society. Today, it is all set up for moms to live somewhat happily, and without husbands. The law forces large numbers of men to pay more money than the mother does for children they cannot see as often as she does. As Farrell states: "In the case of fathers, economic hurt and emotional rejection are joined by a sense of legal injustice."[69]

The single, unmarried mom phenomenon. Climbing through the inferno of men's anguish brought on by their separation from their children, there seems to be never-ending evidence of women further corralling-in their children. In the US, in 1960, only 5 percent of births were outside marriage. By 1990, the national number had increased to 24 percent.[70] But it was estimated that this number would increase dramatically in the new millennium to more than one in three births. One in three! Yes, and by 2005 it's 36% of all births to unmaried women. (*USA Today*, 10/30/05 S. Jayson). This trend towards unmarried single-parent homemakers is a major social phenomena.

In 1993: single women accounted for 71 percent of births in Detroit, 65 percent in Washington, D.C. and 45.2 percent in New York.[71] The stigma around an unmarried parent has receded. The popular idea of the day implies that the modern woman is a self-sufficient, resourceful type that can, and maybe should, go it alone. Governments back her up with public money, and the courts back her up by taking what they can get from the children's biological dad. Unwed mothers used to be shamed, their children called bastards and illegitimate. Now the gender feminists' rally call is *women's reproductive freedom.* And like the pro-life and right-to-choose debates, neither side in the debate of whether women shall have exclusive control of any pregnancy is really interested in involving many dads in the discussion. It's the postmodern obsession with separate power.

Pregnancy yields a solution for a female sensing that the new globalized economy and its low-paying service-industry jobs aren't really going to solve her needs. Only one-tenth of unwed mothers now put up their children for adoption than they used to just thirty years ago. Getting pregnant is a way out, a way to get money from relatives and welfare benefits. Originally these welfare benefits had been put in place for widows with dependent children, to get them funds. But today they subsidize lives of single and divorced moms, giving them a more cozy lifestyle than that of a "free-market" warrior slugging it out in the unstable, poorly paid service industries. Pregnancy gives status as an adult, gives an object, a child, for women to project their emotions on, helps women get subsidized apartments and gives women a sense of *purpose,* a reason to live. They can dodge depression, low self-esteem and ugly work. They can find a purpose, a calling in life. They are needed! As Tiger states:

> *"In one pleasurable act and then in the rewarding process of pregnancy, these young women achieve both productive and reproductive success at once.... Whatever other people may think, from their standpoint they have achieved an upgrade...they have aced an unpromising system."*[72]

In some African-American communities births to unwed women are as high as 80 percent! In Great Britain, among fifteen- to nineteen-year-old white women 87 percent of births are to single moms, and in the US 62 percent of teen births are to single moms. And even with all these births to unmarried women, another expert had already testified that the national average would rise to at least 40 percent by the year 2000.[73]

Reproductive freedom for Whom? Does the future hold a place for husbands as fathers anymore? Some activist females have been planning for years to eliminate women's dependence on men, for anything. Reproductive freedom means women choose again; the men will be without rights, even to their own children. Women's claims of *our bodies–our business* can leave men working and paying for the children produced through his "business" with her body. She can do what *she* pleases with his child—abort it, or keep it. For her it can mean *freedom* through reproduction. He may never know that she had his child, or he may be told the news years later, told that he is a real daddy all right—just send his money, be a good fellow, it's his duty, etc. And it seems that males were mistreated by societies for ages. The men have been sacrificed, sent to war to protect women and *his* children.

Today we still ignore men and their humanity; we are used to it. Now we allow their children to be taken away, or for men to just be wallets for biological moms who have got the children under control, sometimes covertly. But this lack of respect for men and their needs really hits home when it's realized that 15 to 20 percent of dads may be *unknowingly* raising one or more children that are not even their own![74]

Marginalizing Men. The future for men is frightening. They are marginalized and are being pushed off the stage of our communal life. Watch virtually any Hollywood movie and you won't find any single dad raising kids, unless his wife in the movie is dead. This role, the male as caregiver, is not given much support in our pro-female culture. Even when a man and a woman create an embryo in a petri dish, it's the woman who will get custody or legal benefits in lawsuits over their embryo.[75] Women's rights are more important than men's rights today, and the law is designed to protect women more than men.

Single Parenthood. In 1996 in Canada, 826,000 children under age 15 lived with single moms; 117,000 lived with single fathers.[76] And with over 80 percent of US single-parent homes being controlled by the children's mother, it is obvious that the future adults of North America will have to deal with the influence that these single moms will have had. Male single- parent controlled homes have risen from 10.2 percent in 1980 to 18.9 percent in 1998.[77] This is almost a doubling of single-parent fathers in a short time. As Warren Farrell states: "Moms moving out of the home has been a headline-creating revolution, dads moving into the home has been the quietest revolution."[78]

The US Census Bureau reveals that one-third of lesbian households and one-fifth of gay male households have children. What does all this "new age" and single parenting reveal today? What types of people are being raised in these homes, and can society feel positive about a future for the children of "new age" and single parents? The evidence points to a crisis ahead, for parents, children and the whole of society. Objectives and intentions for our children need to be made clear.

In a society where employment income is steadily falling, with take-home pay declining, many single parents are under a lot of pressure. Women, traditional at-home parents, now attempt to be both provider and protector as well. The well-being of her children, and that of the nation, will depend on the woman's ability to cope in society today. But the picture looks bleak, if it is health, well-being and holistic integrity that is being looked for in these single-mother households.

A Case for Single Fatherhood. With regard to domestic violence against children, *single-mother households* account for 43 percent of all abused children.[79] The mother in control of a household is one of the most important single predictors of a battered baby—"a more important predictor than poverty, illegitimacy, and almost all of twenty-nine family characteristics."

A 1999 US Department of Health and Human Services report showed that almost *two-thirds* of parents who kill their children are mothers. And almost two-thirds of those killed between the ages of eight and fifteen are boys. Children are also *twice* as likely to be victims of neglect by their mothers as by their fathers. Children are 88 percent more likely to be seriously injured from child abuse or neglect by their mothers than by their fathers. People living in a feminized culture may have trouble believing these statements about females. But ignorance about females will only set up one's life for disaster. And single moms are twenty-four times as likely to kill children as are single dads.

Here are some facts about schooling a child.[80] Elementary-school children living without their dads did worse on twenty-one of twenty-seven social competence measures and eight out of nine academic measures. They were more likely to repeat grades, had higher absentee records and were less popular than their peers. Another study shows boys who have lived at least six years with their single mothers scored low on ten social and ten academic measures. First-grade black and white children without fathers in the home recorded lower IQ scores than those with fathers present. Fathers improve their children's mathematics and science ability. By the third grade, boys scored higher on every achievement test and received higher grades—if they had fathers present in the home. A child living with both biological parents has a one in nine chance of repeating a grade; living with a single mother the chance increases to one in four. And the more years a child spends with a single mother, the fewer years of school are completed. As well, living without a dad doubles a child's chances of dropping out of high school. In a study, students from father-absent homes scored much lower on college entrance exams.

A psychoanalytic study by Pruett and Litzenberger published in 1977 found positive benefits from males raising their own children. The study, over an eight-year period, showed that children nurtured by their fathers were normal, actually smarter than average and secure in their gender.[81]

But the popular consensus is the opposite. Why?

The media is awash with misinformation. Those who gather

statistics can be biased or irresponsible, or both. Why does the US census bureau ask only women about support payments, how much was paid, or why it wasn't paid? The census bureau doesn't ask only men why the mothers of their children deny or block access to their children.

The bias towards protecting and elevating the female takes place behind what Farrell calls the "lace curtain." Farrell describes the lace curtain as "the tendency of government, the media, academia, and the helping professions not to print anything that makes a woman look like less of a victim than the public consciousness holds her to be...."[82] Socializing our citizens with female values and gender feminist propaganda has helped bring this protective but artificial bias. The "lace curtain" keeps public understanding away from the truth, while it promotes female-only agendas that will result in increased social and emotional illness. How can healthy solutions result for a society if people are left wallowing in the denial, lies and dysfunction found behind the "lace curtain"?

In 1995, in Denmark, a study was made of one-quarter of all three- to five-year-old children who lived only with their single biological *fathers*. They were compared to an equal number of children who were living only with their single biological mothers. The information from the study presented to the Social Research Institute in Stockholm, found that children living with their dads were much less likely to experience the problem of feeling like a victim. They were half as likely to have frequent nightmares, feelings of low self-esteem, and lonesomeness; they were one-third as likely to feel victimized by other children and one-quarter as likely to experience frequent seizures of fear. Can living with the gender who has been educated to see herself as a victim rub off on the children? Obviously, yes.

The children living with their fathers were only half as likely to experience problems with concentration.[83] This resonates loudly for many fatherless boys put on medication for Attention Deficit Disorder in North America. Males are increasingly being raised in a society that exclusively applauds female values. Young boys are receiving a female socialization, and *those* boys from *single-mom homes* are over 300 percent more likely to see themselves as *victims* of other children. Farrell: "...when female values are so dominant in raising boys, I believe it leads to boys not feeling lovable for their core energy, thus tempting feelings that they must perform to be loved rather than love to be loved."[84]

Undermining Males—Sexual Abuse and Propaganda. President Bill Clinton was a useful male for the gender feminists to debase, ridicule and squeeze money out of. His political life counted heavily on female and feminist support. Even though, in general, he stood for an attitude toward women that they hated, the gender feminists found his sexual scandals opportune. His numerous disgraces painted the male as a sexual pervert, and this was useful to those determined to destroy the "patriarchy."

Clinton was just another *mentally challenged sex addict* to them, perhaps just how they see most American men. He used women as sexual objects, mere receptacles. He was rude, gruff and perhaps violent with them. The focus the gender feminists promote is men as molesters rather than men as caregivers for their children. As long as males can be hung out to dry, seen as sexually dangerous predators, then women can control and keep the children to themselves. An irresponsible sex-crazy male is useful. He allows *feminazi propaganda* to grow. He is evidence of the warts covering the patriarchy. So Clinton was the gender feminist's meal ticket. He sold the nation on a much lower standard for the man at the top. And during his term of office the feminists have taken control of much of the working apparatus of the government itself.

A psycho sex maniac as the highest male in the land—this image produced gift-wrapped white-hot memes, used to assault male integrity and accountability. Male sexuality became more debased than was usual when Clinton incarnated as the feminazis' patsy. They made the President into their talisman, leading the nation toward the visioned feminine oasis: reproductive rights, selling their eggs among themselves, government subsidies for moms only, housing for women only—for women and children only. It helps for the radicals to have men presumed to be perverts. The presumption of perversion, if believed, keeps the female elevated above the male, enables women to get privileges and protections denied the men. And it gets children separated from men, and then the assumed guilt from their "maleness" may keep men in a self-doubting and confused state of mind. Out of the way!

Men may feel unworthy of becoming caregivers, that is if they believe the lies told today as truth, that paint men as perverted sexual beings. At present, the Boy Scouts of America's national policy bans any scout leader from being alone with a boy! But in Canada, a public school district employs full-time a self-outed *lesbian* to teach a women's studies course to *grade eleven girls*. Go figure....

Sexual abuse of children has been headline news for decades. But it seems that it is always men's fault. With biased judges and increasing credibility for accusations from females, men are being sketched as sexual criminals. There is a 2,000 percent increase in sex-abuse allegations in the past ten years.[85] Scores of men are being falsely *accused* of child sex-abuse, and many men lose their jobs even if they are eventually found innocent. During a divorce it has been found that up to 94 percent of those who make *false accusations of child sexual abuse* are women, and 96 percent of those falsely accused are men[86] Mothers making these false accusations are characterized by their anger. Interestingly, 80 percent of all child sex-abuse allegations are found to be without foundation.[87] Lying, fabrication and character assassination surround much that some women claim as *the truth, the whole truth and nothing but the truth.*

Men don't defend their sexuality. They've been made guilty; they just take abuse. Ridiculing men and their sexuality as dangerous to society may give the females unopposed grounds upon which to build their version of the female alternative to their "spin" about the country being inhabited by perverted males. In New York City, *unfounded* child sexual-abuse allegations against men increased from more than a half to more than three-quarters from 1989 to 1993.[88] The evidence shows *false claims of sexual abuse and assault* are so high that these claims are unprincipled attacks on men, used to gain rewards—money, child custody—and to punish men. Whether they did anything or not! Our society is letting men take the rap, even if they are innocent.

A study of male sexual offenders found that 30 percent had themselves been sexually abused as children. Of these, 78 percent had been abused by a woman.[89]

Shocking. But can our society cope with this and other information that doesn't bolster the consensus image of women as caring, innocent victims?

Nearly 60 percent of convicted rapists were sexually abused as children by women.[90]

Child Custody. When mothers have custody, their children's relationship with their father deteriorates. When children live with only their mothers, their parents are nine times as likely to have conflict as they do when children live with their fathers.[91] In the US, it has been found that 42 percent of all children living with their single moms reported that their moms tried to stop them from seeing their fathers.[92] Results from interviews with children on average of eight years after their parents divorced showed the following: 54 percent of the children said that only their mothers spoke badly of their fathers in front of them; 12 percent said that only their fathers spoke badly of their mothers.[93] In the Danish study it was found that when mothers had custody the children were more than twice as likely to have no contact with the other parent; and that in part must be due to moms being almost five times as likely to bad-mouth dads as dads are to bad-mouth moms.[94]

Child Support. Even though 75 percent of custodial mothers will likely move at least once in four years, 54 percent of separated dads see their kids weekly.[95] And 85 percent of fathers with shared parent time (joint custody) pay child support on time. When mothers have custody but are open to fathers seeing their children, 79 percent of these fathers pay in full and on time.[96]

The Reality for Children with Single Mothers. For children living in a single-mom home their future is warily confronted by the facts:[97]

- 65 percent of juveniles and young adults in state-operated institutions come from father-absent homes.
- 80 percent of pre-school children admitted as psychiatric patients in two New Orleans hospitals came from homes without fathers. Similar percentages are found in Canada.
- 90 percent of homeless or runaway children are from fatherless homes.
- A close relationship with dad is the most important factor in preventing drug use.
- 73 percent of adolescent murderers come from mother-only homes.
- 80 percent of rapists who rape out of anger and rage came from father-absent homes.
- 90 percent of young repeat arsonists lived with only their

mothers.
- Daughters of single moms are 92 percent more likely to divorce than daughters of two-parent families.
- In Baltimore, a study found one-third of daughters *of* teenage single moms also became teenage moms. No daughter with a good relationship with her father had a baby before age nineteen.
- Students without fathers at home are 1.5 times more likely to be unemployed in their teens through their mid-twenties.

Being with their fathers has proved to help children manage their emotions, develop intelligence and attain better grades in school. These children are socially better adapted and have better relationships with the parent they aren't living with than the children who live only with their biological mothers.

Domestic violence and Murder in Canada

In Canada, the *Vancouver Sun*, a newspaper servicing a community and province with two and a half million people, on December 6, 1999, published a *front-page* story written by two women, stating: "In 1999 Canadian women constituted 98 percent of the victims of spousal violence, kidnapping and sexual assault." The editor himself, when confronted with this misrepresentation of the truth, was not swayed at first. Maybe men didn't report many assaults on themselves, he said. But after seeing some seventy studies on domestic violence he began to understand the picture, see the abuse of facts. Otherwise male editors probably want to give women the benefit of the doubt because, after all, it is what they were probably raised to do.

Even at Statistics Canada, it's found that whoever compiles the data can determine what is seen in the numbers. Much of the statistics are incomplete, based on samples that can't be taken as representing anything like the true picture. *Gender-benders* are getting into the research and the data banks, and some numbers are going to have had their "face" put on. Believe it or suffer the consequences!

Statistics Canada has not been a reliable source for information in the past. As F.A.C.T. (Fathers Are Capable Too) has stated:

> *"Statistics Canada, one of the world's leaders in producing one-sided gender-specific statistics in their 1993 report on Violence Against Women has been largely panned, criticized throughout the world for their politics over real analysis."*[98]

After much criticism, however, by 2000 even Statistics Canada produced a 1:1 ratio of violence between the genders—this time they asked both men and women the same questions![99]

And the Father's Canada web page states: *Men and Women are Equals in Violence.* In Canada, 400 publicly funded shelters exist for battered women, but not one single one has been established to help battered men. "Researchers without a feminist axe to grind have long recognized that about half of domestic violence is a two-way street—with both men and women doing the shoving, pushing, and throwing."[100]

Without surveillance, the feminazis are free to get away with *info-murder.* Imagine, 98 percent of spousal violence being initiated by males! It's front-page power – in the dominant newspaper, the *Vancouver Sun* – for who? Every young boy who reads this is now not only *armed* with false-consciousness, but also must become somewhat self-hating and self-deprecating. Just as the gender feminists want them? These " tacts" just bring more ammunition to coax money, support, protection and favored status from society at large. Maybe milking the cash cow of women's claimed victimhood should be a degree program at university? Or is it already? Check out some women's studies programs!

According to Statistics Canada, 8,389 men and 4,475 women were victims of homicide between 1978 and 1997. The 1998 Canadian Crime Statistics showed that: for every female victim of an *attempt/conspire to murder* there were 2.7 male victims. For every female victim of *aggravated assault* there were 3.7 male victims. For every female *assault with a weapon causing bodily harm* there were two male victims. For every female victim of *discharge of a firearm with intent* there were 3.4 male victims.[101] Even from these statistics it's obvious that women, far from being the victimized gender, are actually avoiding a great deal of the violence in Canadian society.

Female Violence

In a letter to his union newspaper, Keith Harris writes in response to "discriminatory lies" and "this official scapegoating and marginalization of men" in the media. Here Harris reports that: "the majority of homicides of children under the age of one year are committed by their mothers;... that mothers kill more male children than female children; that siblings of both sexes kill their brothers more often than their sisters." And in British Columbia where Harris lives, he reports that the 125 workers killed on the job in 1998 were all men![102]

In the US, Harris points out that the FBI Uniform Crime Report on Murder and Non-negligent Manslaughter in 1998 reveals 3.1 male victims for every female victim of murder, and that females perpetrated homicide at a rate of 3.3 male victims for every female victim.

Next, in his letter to the newspaper, Harris offers some reality therapy. The "sugar-and-spice" gender, these so-called nurturers, do possess a mean streak, relatively unknown to the public. Harris printed some women's names who our society does not want to recall: Susan Eubanks, 1999, stalked and murdered her four sons by shooting them in the head. Aileen Wuornos, 1992, stalked, shot and killed seven men—all strangers. Dorthea Puente, 1990, murdered eight men and women in her boarding house. Gwen Graham and Cathy Wood, 1988, suffocated six patients. Marybeth Tining, 1987, suffocated nine of her children. Velma Barfield, 1987, was executed for poisoning five people. Carol Bunday, 1980, shot and killed seven women and a man, whose head she sawed off with a boning knife. Delfine and Maria Gonzales, 1964, murdered eighty women and eleven men.

And on the list goes, way back: Susanna Fazekas, 1929, involved in the murder of as many as 200 hundred men and women. Amy Archer-Gilligan, 1916, murdered forty-eight people. Belle Guinness, 1908, murdered sixty-seven people. Then leaping centuries back to around 1615 reveals the mass-murdering "celebrity" of the fragile gender, Countess Elisabeth Bathory, who beat, tortured and bled to death some 650 women.[103]

The media tend to jump all over the news about a man murdering a woman. The respected image bestowed on women in our present society, and our dedication to women's protection, can inhibit focus on female dysfunction. But men are fair game. Husbands who become victims when their wives kill their children, like Rusty Yates (five dead children) and David Smith (two dead children), what sympathy is their for them? David Smith found out the unbelievable truth on the television! The police had not even told him. And many seem bent, against all evidence, to finger Rusty Yates as the cause of the murder of his children. For murders within the family, 54.5 percent of victim's (including children) are male.[104]

According to *Behind Closed Doors: Violence in American Families* (Straus, Gelles and Steinmetz, 1980), out of every 100 families, 3.8 percent experience severe husband-to-wife violence, but 4.5 percent experience severe wife-to-husband violence.[105] In Canada, the *Canadian Journal of Sociology* (1988) reports that the rate of severe husband-to-wife violence was 4.8 percent, while severe wife-to-husband violence was 10 percent. To some researchers the most "unreported crime" is not wife-beating—it's husband-beating.[106]

The US Congress is to spend billions in its crime bills to combat violence against women. Most of the money will go to advocacy groups, to sensitivity training, to educational programs for everyone from judges to school children and to shelters and publications. The issue of domestic violence is a political football, used to keep the female voter onside, while more serious study and comprehension are ignored. Politicians again mouth the words, and the female responds to those who will give them protection, status and money.

> *So women are courted through scare tactics and*
> *false facts,*
> *While politicians get elected as this confusion distracts,*
> *But misrepresentation is being loaded onto*
> *women's backs.*

Over and Out

Guys are being pushed out of reach. Through advocacy research propaganda and lies, through media control and through government courting of the authority-accepting female, the nation will be made weaker. This could effectively kill the impetus for some of those—many men—who would take issue, stand up and *fight* the perpetuation of the false, politically correct consciousness and official versions, those who would persist in hounding the criminals till they are run right out of *sight*.

In *The Decline of Males*, Dr. Lionel Tiger, Professor of Anthropology at Rutgers University, examines contemporary society and writes of the unexpected new worlds facing the genders. A novel economy has to be faced, says Tiger: "Lester Thurow estimated that the number of males who could not find work sufficient to support themselves and a family doubled between 1985 and 1995. They are simply unprepared for the new economy. They may never be unless successful government and private initiatives are introduced. Meanwhile their means and status do not commend them to potential spouses and parents-in-law. They are threatened with both productive and reproductive oblivion."[5] Because they can't be productive, earn a good living, they are unable to find a mate to reproduce with. The number of guys in this boat *doubled* in the ten years between 1985-1995.

The real news about a man's changing role in society is shocking. Lionel Tiger in the *The Decline of Males* again: "In 1955, in some *60 percent* of American families, Dad worked, Mom stayed at home, and there were two to three children. Thirty-one years later barely *4 percent* of families boast this form."[107]

The False-consciousness of Pipher and Giligan

Mary Pipher, Ph.D., clinical psychologist, drives girls crazy cramming the false-consciousness down their throats. She is so far out there, insidious about a land scarred by permanent warfare against females. In her book *Reviving Ophelia*, 1994, she followed up on Carol Gilligan's scare tactics, and she has used fear to market her writing.

> *Her claims made one wonder—Mary Pipher,*
> *The living truth can she decipher?*

How can she equate females with the disabled or the "slave" minorities—with all those possessing today's criteria for Affirmative Action jobs and money? But this professional psychologist has marketed a hyena rage and spread hate memes. What did the Nazis tell their people about the Jews? And Pipher, where did she get her information that she uses to brainwash society? She spreads the false-consciousness and promotes the persecution of males—that's the gist of her drama, the results of the spin.

Pipherisms:

Why do so many girls hate their parents? Many are the victims of sexual violence...Girls are less protected...Girls today are much more oppressed...I was struck by what a girl-poisoning culture it is...America today limits girls' development, truncates their wholeness and leaves many of them traumatized...Hillary Clinton, Tipper Gore, Janet Reno and many others are sounding the alarm...

Adolescence is when girls experience social pressure to put aside their authentic selves... adolescent girls are saplings in a hurricane...Girls are expected to distance from parents just at a time when they most need their support...American culture has always smacked girls on the head in early adolescence...

Simone de Beauvoir believed adolescence is when girls realize that men have the power, and that their only power comes from consenting to become submissive adored objects. They do not suffer from the penis envy Freud postulated, but from power envy...

Guys would grab me in the halls... Later I got used to it...

A health department study showed that 40 percent of all girls in my midwestern city considered suicide last year...

It was impossible to score [on a test] as both a healthy adult and a healthy woman...

Girls who speak frankly are labelled as bitches...The rules are enforced by the labelling of a woman like Hillary Rodham Clinton as a 'bitch' simply because she's a competent, healthy adult...

Girls come of age in a misogynistic culture...they make less money baby sitting than their brothers do mowing lawns...[108]

So this Mary is a raver too, throwing flaming hate-memes and bags of the *tact* glue.

Anti-male Media Propaganda. It's war and propaganda against the man. Well, what is a victim left to do when their *true selves* are under attack? When: *everywhere girls are encouraged to sacrifice their true selves* in a *culture that is all too happy to use them for its purposes*.... But it's Pipher who is doing the victimization of the girls through her lies and emotionally-charged accusations against the male.

She isn't really worthy of a doctoral degree because
   she is sinking so low,
Mixing fact and fiction
To give the men a licking,
Thinking to give all of America a knockout blow.

"America today is a girl-destroying place," so says Mary Pipher, Ph.D., as the scholarly community now *neurotically— (Yes! It's more insurance for to grow the blackness the future is sure to bring.)*—must duck out, somehow from her work, trying to save some face. Most just keep quiet. Professors tell the truth? Power privileges female aspiration, and the academic staff fall in line. Many teaching "brains" working in universities must feel like cowards. But there are others who must also be appalled, observing how the feminist spin " tacts" encourage so many to settle-in, and sink in the poisonous "tact"-ful muck like pigs in mud. Real knowledge decreases with their politically correct silence.

It's so unprofessional, this Pipher-type research. When Faludi and Wolf and the rest wrote of the backlash, they contended that the patriarchy-controlled media itself printed lies and broadcasted misinformation to stop feminist liberation. The media was identified as the problem, and the gender feminists set about screaming loudly to get attention. It has worked, and the media is now their acolyte and pimps their " tacts."

The gender feminists have assimilated behavior they say they hate—media control of " tacts"—and have proven themselves very adept at the subterfuge of truth. Pipher has a large, willingly *victim-oriented and victim-educated audience,* and she is filling their boots with postmodern sadomasochism, as crisis is created, but the facts, ma'am, aren't really there.

Pipher and Gilligan want to assume society is unsympathetic to women, and to feed their psych-out victimization claims to women looking for something or someone to blame for their personal predicaments.

The church found a devil to blame,
Gender feminists have the men to shame.

The Plight That Does Not Exist. Gilligan and Pipher may get on the lecture circuit, sell books and become important today. No doubt the judges of the future will have even more to say and will take no mercy in exposing their aggressive, hurtful agendas. For example, Gilligan is doing more of this "research" about the development of girls and how they are drowning in the sea of western culture. But she lumps the girls in with people of color, gays and lesbians, the poor and the disabled. Although American culture is where girls are the most outspoken, to Gilligan, it is *in* America that girls are silenced.

A lot of research contrary to Gilligan's is available. Material that shows no evidence of loss of voice in girls. Perhaps Gilligan is only a developer of pathological science, the science of things that aren't. Her work has convinced many educators of a plight suffered by girls alone, a plight that does not exist.

Andrea Dworkin

Andrea Dworkin, once a college lecturer, helped make up many of today's female minds. She has probably been studied in most women's studies departments in universities, and has had a profound affect-effect upon contemporary society.

Propaganda and Inequality. To Dworkin it is: "a woman-hating society where women are sex and dirt in one human body; the screwed one: passive, inert, and open...."[109]

Andrea Dworkin feels somehow that equality between the sexes *is* reality, and that there is abuse going on, *abuse* of this equality. Dworkin was educated in a proudly "democratic" society that claims to possess: civil equality, human rights and freedom of speech. That's the USA.

The two-party system, and the other grand narratives and "enduring truths" about America's mission (to protect the world from evil and to raise up the Holy Grail of democracy and market economics) were all included in the common public educational fare served up to the "equals" of Dworkin's time. It's been called the *rant of the mediocre,* these claims of rights and privileges, the "tunes" that indoctrinate those in the *land of the free.* Dworkin wails and bitches at the males, who she says are running the show and ruining the realizing of all these normative assumptions—equality, civil rights, freedom, etc. She says the men dictate to women just where they can go, what they can be.

But Dworkin's anger is overly reactive, simply more of the victimization siren song. Wanting the world to be like sugar and spice is useless; the real world needs *attending,* and Andrea—democrat, egalitarian, gender feminist—into hell many a young lady is *sending.* Like countless new-ager chicks, Dworkin has gotten matronly make-believe, wish-thinking fab phrases (advertisement socialization) and government propaganda all mixed in a deceptive brew. Here the hungry heart is an organ of compassion, tenderness, heavenly and brotherly love—the chaste forms of love.

On Sexuality. Of course Andrea, who tries to force a warm heart-centered equality between the sexes, seeks to find a level ground where this can exist. But *virginity for women, chastity for men* may be the only level upon which her idealism can avoid broad neurotic chagrin. She has told Jewish women to betray their husbands.

Sex must be like some smut to Andrea, with men trained to initiate this dirt. Of course, Dworkin reads, as a college English teacher, and then the fiction she perused gave her a third-party mental picture of emotional, moral and sexual themes. She then used this fiction as a backdrop to do her male rape, the assault upon gender. She paints males as cruel, violent, suffering a loneliness they can't endure. They are alienated, she said, because of their own detachment or abstraction, and they are self-obsessed and in need of women to help them cope with their male nakedness which is loathsome to them. "For men, the meaning of a woman's naked body is life itself," said Andrea.[110]

Numbed abstraction—that is what Dworkin calls male sexual desire, a desire of *watching*, displacement. Does she, through this reading, studying, analyzing, through her appropriation of "meaning" from *fictionalized* dramas and characters, become like the men she terms prisoners of a numbed abstraction? Or does she have a life that supplies her the answers? Neurotic feelings of victimization inhibit the heart. The heart shrunken by lust or hate could go for actions violent. And swiftly.

Is it sad that Andrea will never get her wish, to live in a permanent fantasyland where all are equal and able to do as they *please*—just like her grade-school teachers' storybooks pretended it to *be?*

The Female "Antibeing." But when a male can slice into female flesh, well, equality to Dworkin just disappeared: "Male authority, religious authority, and civic authority all converged, indistinguishable, at the point of entry into a woman's body...."[111] Ms. Dworkin thought being inside a woman's genitals is ownership, possession: "deeper, more intimate, than any other kind of possession." To her having sex and being owned are inseparately the same, "they are sex for women under male domination as a social system." A woman's insides become part of the male's domain and, "he can thus possess her as an individual—be her lord and master." Andrea Dworkin even declared that to most men most women are not considered private, distinct individuals. Then strangely Dworkin went on to claim that females have to *learn* to respond to male touch, as sex, as love! But this ability to even feel sexual pleasure is learned, she said, within the "narrow confines of male sexual domination."

All women know, said Ms. Dworkin, is they are to restrict pleasure to being owned. This "pleasure" will become an erosion of the self and the erosion of *her physical reality*, according to Ms. Dworkin, as well as a psychological possession and domination. This possession is so severe that it's described as *antibeing* for the women—her body used, her will raped.

Sexual intercourse means the disappearance of the woman as an individual, because the individual is possessed and

> *"ceases to exist as a discrete individual; is taken over.... Being owned and being fucked are or have been virtually synonymous experiences in the lives of women. He owns you; he fucks you."*[112]

Natural intercourse seemed to amount to some notion of *trespass* to Andrea Dworkin, since she described intercourse as turning a female's insides into part of a man's domain, over which he asserts a feudal dominance. And "her insides are worn away over time, and she, possessed, becomes weak, depleted, usurped in all her mental and physical energies and capacities by the one who has taken her over." To Dworkin this amounts to the stunning logic of male supremacy. Will Andrea's lack of personal fulfillment be analysed as being produced by an inferiority complex resulting in a repressed sexual desire, and will this be said to have stimulated her anger?

Men as Beasts. To this feminist icon, Andrea Dworkin, whose writings are now being taught to millions and millions of teenagers and university women, men were the beasts, the users and conscious abusers. Men she degraded as unmotivated, even by beauty, quoting Lenny Bruce: "You put guys on a desert island and they'll do it to the mud."

The way Dworkin pictured the male sex drive brings a view of the male sex drive as something akin to the *insurance* of neurotic collective guilt. She perceived males as the cause of society's self-destructive behavior and helplessness.

Dworkin, along with Pipher, Gilligan, Faludi, Wolf and Steinem, and their numerous gender feminist co-conspiritors—Patricia Ireland, Mary Koss, Lenore Walker, Joan Brumberg, Jeanne McDowell, Sharon Schuster, Ann Bryant, Alice McKee, Sarah Buel—are responsible for many women forsaking marriage and relationships with men; and for the ever-increasing and wide-open lesbianism that is becoming a symbol of American culture.

Attention Men

Ever listen, men, to Eve Ensler, writer of the *Vagina Monologues,* talking about the *vagina brain,* a separate brain where knowledge of the world comes through the body? And the reason the earth's in so much trouble is because the vagina intelligence has been damaged. By rape, battery, sexual abuse and terror.

So all you western feminized guys, are you now alerted and with chagrin making moves to protect yourselves from this scathing rebuke and insult? You are demeaned as dog-men—dangerous, violent and ignorant abusers of the female. You are scum to be stepped over, ground from society and kicked about—this the message, what it's about. The women have organized, and they'll take all you have got, your job, your kids and your future.

And you'll be further *taught!* That is why Feminist Expo 2000 came! Expo 2000 was to ignite...*fighting for women's empowerment, expanding feminism globally, promoting a gender perspective...and the rights of women, lesbians....* Any clue guys?

Most of you have been raised by females. The first seven years always mold the person, and many of you guys were locked in the home with mom. Your whole world revolved around her. She told you just what to be, and pleasing her gave you rewards. That was many men's early training. And elementary teachers have always been mainly female, and thus feminism has flushed all around our western society for over 200 years.

> *Your "truth" came from mommy and from teachers*
>   *professionally sincere,*
> *And have you bought in, been washed away in their tears?*

19
Purposeful Incarnation

Is there a crisis when the bisexual President of the National Organization for Women (NOW), Pat Ireland, appears on TV begging the nation to embrace marriage? Like a juvenile delinquent asking others to go straight, she's asking others to wed while she is in breech of the very exclusiveness that marriage represents. She may be seen by many as the devil incarnate. Who cares what her hubby thinks, knows:

He's just a *male* and can follow at her *tail?*

Marriage Breakdown

It is rather easy to witness the burgeoning breakdown of marriage in contemporary society. It could be called a crisis because it is changing the behavior of men and women and begs the question—what will their future society be?

There are numerous points of consternation that tear at the fabric of marriage today. Women's liberation has given women rights, protections and permission to self-actualize, if that is what they think they want. But it's obvious—their *liberation* perspective developed into women rushing to get themselves some "power," in the process trashing men and marriage as things that are not power-conducive. This women's stance is still popular, but the truth underlying women's action today may not be quite so simple. Women are invested in making this human life system go, and their actions and their responses may belie the esoteric strategies that are really motivating them.

The coaches screaming from the sidelines only
   think to win,
Likewise in the gender-hate field of play many aren't
   above tactics
Some would call plain sin.
The coaches they've been operated on too,
And maybe just don't know what they do,
It might look like the height of western civilization's
   Socratic wisdom –
To debate, allow two sides to spin,
Hoping you can bring a winner in,
But it's much ado about plain alienation of the masses,
Since most give up, simply listen,
Grasping little, the time passes.

The people at NOW have caused so much suffering with their partisan and ruthless attacks on males, that distrust skyrockets between the mainstream adherents who've assimilated NOW's memes and the rest of society—the innocent men and the "uneducated" women NOW hasn't got a hold of yet. The academic community (the brains?) have jumped on board. As women's agendas dominate educational institutions for funding and political contingencies, *the brains* have obviously sunk into being bought advocacy researchers and pollsters—they who can produce any result by simply constructing suitable questions, and then it's a wrap.

Today the gender war is symptomatic of the prevalent social-breakdown syndrome that's permeating the social body, and it is fueling the postmodern alienation that crops up in *political correctness.*

It is desirable for some to keep the people off-balance and looking for solutions through shopping, out of a private self-interest to keep consumers consuming with built-in *needs* for items, things. The "educated" shoppers' propaganda-inserted (brainwashing) meme kits are pre-wired to serve and to promote consumer goals. Freedom to shop, free markets, free country—these white-hot "ideas" influence behavior. As well, the meme kits, ingrained by western culture in each consumer, bring a perceived (trained) *internal need to immobilize opposition* to the status quo. That *is* political correctness. The consumers are educated to see "progress" as a new can opener, not humane social programs.

A Foucaldian frame of reference, these internalizations support the normative assumptions of the *majority consensus,* producing the *false consciousness,* and they direct focus. People can then be used to promote antagonism, or to neutralize opposition to "official truth," as people are thus given the information that will back up only the status quo. The hundreds of hours hurled mercilessly into new thoughts, new fantasy, new desires by continuous television manipulation and hypnotism, this wastes people. Slick TV comercials keep consumers watching, dreaming of solutions that can be bought. But the glue here is often envy, an envy that's like desire, but more (wantonly) submissive. Envy need not act. The envious can simply be entertained!

But to find the impetus for women's real agency as of late, a pilgrimage is necessitated through the victimization spin that on the surface she's been *prone to mention*, to get to the foundation of her purposeful incarnation. Nothing can be gained by destroying an ideal like marriage without replacing it with something better.

> *Going below, into the morass of personal affliction,*
> *Needs an ego that can take a lot of pain,*
> *But that is what is needed for to fix the gender game.*
> *It may not boil down to simply wrong or right,*
> *Where philistine enemies clash by night.*
> *Instead, underneath the brainwashed-battling*
>   *misinformation,*
> *Pompous and reactive victims stew in pious fiction,*
> *Boiling egos rage to get it right,*
> *Swept by the confused alarms of struggle and flight,*
> *And needing some professional help, perhaps,*
>   *to see the light!*

Invitation to the Collective

There is an instinct for survival of the species that demands an acceptance of and a respect for the collective, the group. It works in mysterious ways at times but this instinct brings people into the coherence necessary to work to align society for its own continued survival.

The distrust of grand master plans, whether church inspired or hailed by popular leaders of the state, has brought the modern person to cry "no more absolutes!" After the failure of Christianity to solve man's inhumanity to *man,* women have come to attempt to fill the gap with an internal focus and a psychic *plan.*

In general, the feminine is drawn to relationship, and her ego here gleans knowledge of interpersonal skills. She is found dealing with high-frequency emotion and feeling around various details that she picks up in respect to making her psyche healthy and whole. Since early youth, all her soap-opera obsession comes from her need to know answers about interpersonal relationship. This is what matters to her. *Relationship* to her is psychic anyway, so in this area of human experience she's the one in the know, or at least the one who wants to be.

> *But, the males are learning too,*
> *What female understanding can do.*

Beyond good and evil, the deep motivations of the contemporary female can be seen as positive, as an attempt to rectify the ills of a society beset with so much suffering and needless cruelty that the society itself could be seen as terminally, even suicidally, inclined. *She* and her nurturing-collective *love* may want to swamp the male into the collective whole and give him the goods that she can see—the healing of pain, the empathy for others and respect for the individual. But most of all she just wants to get him in the game, to *deal with the feel* and to rebuild in the name of her "love"; that is, in the spirit of relatedness, in psychic relationship.

Christianity Fails

World War I was, as D.H. Lawrence said, "Jesus' War," the war of the lamb, the war brewed of a Christian "love." All the sermons throughout Europe did zip to halt the screaming bloodbath and oncoming stench of human inhumanity, as scores of millions of basically young men were raped by the war industries, left dead in more mud, fighting for some king or queen's imperial business. The warring countries all had strong Christian institutions, and prayers were probably said each day in their schools. With their love of *belief,* these societies are induced to war by upper-class rulers. They used religion like a drug to humble independent understanding.

Membership in the Christian church, with its emotional sing-ing-praying activity, induces group loyalty and a security through belonging. It also brings on the *insurance* of the collective. Memorizing the memes, glued to their congregations, the plebs make their beds. Most Christians have *no idea* what another religion promotes or believes in. They are taught only that other religions are wrong.

> *It's blinders to the left, blinders to the right,*
> *Straightforward are sent the believers to fight,*
> *And to herald the example of Christian might!*

Jesus had rebuked his followers because they mistakenly believed that *He* was here on earth to bring peace. But *He* told them, *He* had brought a sword, *He* was here to spread war and to disturb human relationship and even to divide family members—father against son, mother against daughter. Jesus's statement here seems to have been lost or did not fall on listening ears. Maybe the rulers of society prefer a meek Christ, as an antidote to their violent capitalist-imperialistic drive for world domination. Thus the spin of brotherly love, turning the other cheek, care of the lowly gets prime time. Subsequently, the incomplete teachings of the "savior" don't save the day. Instead they facilitate a righteous blackmailing of the believer's ego, because to the Christian, "belief" is everything.

Christians have been told by priests that if their belief is to prove to be righteous and strong, they must stand up to the devil that is portrayed as their "enemy" in a war. Then the true test of Christian willingness to go with the "word"—*letting belief go to war*—will be their salvation if the body is killed, as the pure and strong spirit is believed to go to heaven. For the believer, death is decertified, overcome.

From 19th Century Women to Gender Feminist Victimhood

The nineteenth century brought women many safeguards for their position in society. Some women scoffed at attracting any more attention, thinking women could cope quite well on their own. But laws and "reforms" gave an external, legal and societal boost to some women to try something *new,* and a hope that, as "individuals", not just as women, they could now pull right *through*.

The women became enfranchised not long after men. But there were those women, however, who did not think that being classified exactly like a man was the route to power. To them their gender has unique strengths. Some women felt their gender was doing quite well for itself, and that making them equals under the *law* would only bring them down. And not a few must have feared they could lose their idealised and protected positions, from where they dissimulate, from where their emotional-sexual and sentimental worlds are able to control much and bring power. What good, said these women, to be on par with a man?

But if the popular belief is that *power* is with the men, then what the men have is *thought* to be what will bring liberation.

> *To bring in more power,*
> *To be more than only a wife,*
> *And an active participant in all social life,*
> *Thus to the medieval marriage, she has taken the knife!*

Some women may not acknowledge a necessity for women to break marriage somewhat down so that the world may evolve minus man's inhumanity to man. The *collective* motive, the healing of a war-scarred and deranged society through feminine nurturing principles, isn't well understood. No, all that is focused on is the breakdown of marriage, with the men painted into corners by misandrist attack dogs. The gender feminists and their academic meme troops are an aggressive, in-your-face, unprincipled bunch attached to a hate-motivating factor. They have a victimhood obsession, trapping themselves as eternal victims swamped in an inexorably berserk burden of repulsing hate. This is their lifestyle *éclat*. It's because they want it black and white. They are rational, too rational, and want targets.

But the intuition behind the distancing from men and marriage, may come from ultimately solid and well-meaning humanistic intention—the benefits society could derive from a greater female input. But many gender feminist recruits are not aware of their own sisters' underlying quest, and think they simply want to thump out the patriarchy.

Female Psychological Approach

Prior to World War II, while the female was assuming more public and professional recognition and the legal rights of the male, society began to open its bosom to the psychological approach.

This suited women, the psychological type,
Who in psychic relationship realizes her might.

But next off, it's into the abyss of another startling world war, the proof that something dreadful is perturbing western society. When the devastation draws to a halt, the ideology behind war is seen as a *male* creation. Ideology is blamed at fault, pitting man against man. Ideology had brought: belief in master plans for dominance; brought division—someone to blame for suffering; religious spins, nationalistic spins, together with dogma, creeds and doctrines. Here all had aggresively claimed the rules to set the world upright and this rational approach is said to originate in the *male*. And without womanly rectification, it's thought, soon the world shall *fail*.

Woman wants to be involved. The goodness behind that desire accrues to her psychic relatedness, a forte of feminism. She sees the murderous results of traditional society's disregard for what it hypocritically says it values.

The Jesus wars show how brotherly love is only
   window dressing,
That underneath the rhetoric the truth is much more
   distressing.

The moral and ethical principles taught in Christian nations did not divert the disaster of World War I or II. But can that justify totally dumping morals and ethics for subjectivity, a "feelings" approach, a psychic approach unconcerned with laws and principles based on the common good?

To unite under Christian love in the twentieth century was impossible, with Christian countries left by war in catastrophic consequences. But the women's studies courses and the organized women's advocacy organizations could well benefit from putting an ear to the *ground,* from allowing a holy spirit to come in and *surround*, and from allowing angels or spirit or imagination *carte blanche* to help them avoid leaving society in a similar *circumstance*.

Women Try the Masculine

Once an enemy is identified, the job of the leaders is to promote the belief that elimination of the foe will fix society's problems. This foe must be painted with all the people's sorrows, be seen as what is keeping the social body under ailment and assault, and thus belief is glued to the mind that with removal of the enemy the healthy functioning of the society will return intact. The enemy becomes the problem, the only problem, and its annihilation is believed a panacea for the nation.

To try to heal the hunger of their souls and to attempt to end feelings of personal unrelatedness to their society, many women have usurped a masculinity. It's called a "take-chargeness." It is goal-oriented, and it has great social-governmental support. Many books are marketed, dealing with "how to" do it all—yourself. But the radical feminists use masculine tactics, create an enemy—men—and then distribute *information* to win support. This setting up of dualism, right and wrong, good and bad, is too simple. But it works, it gets anger involved, and hot buttons become easy to push.

Many feminists have cross-dressed themselves and come up in the battle dress of the *man,* but here she is dissatisfied and needs a better *plan.* Forever it's been the indirect approach of the woman that has secured her lifestyle. Now does she want to conquer, in gender war, to go direct and *toe-to-toe* with him, the guy, as her recognized *foe?* Sounds masculine. And where do the feminine virtues go? Feminine values, of inclusion, acceptance for all, of care for feelings and of less weight on rationality and more for intuition, these values are finding a barren environment and can't survive under the rule of market economics and the gender war.

Hurling insults at each other, the genders focus on the other as the only problem. Thus they could see victory as simply the other's defeat, while lists of *abuses* only give more *excuses* to punish, *liquidate,* those whom they've come to *hate*. Creating hate, building the women's power organism into a *reactive*, *raging* force, is good for recruiting troops.

> *To think that society may one day recover from*
>   *this one-way street*
> *Will bring deluded believers to their great defeat,*
> *But it is of the utmost importance to remember that*
>   *a woman's gift is often within,*
> *And that her spiritual and communal work doesn't*
>   *have to include many men.*

The masses aren't always aware of the significance around some of their interactions. Those in power have exploited this lack of information by keeping the masses entertained into distraction, only to summon them to do the dirty work—even to die for their bosses. The aristocrats, the owners, the capitalist CEO's and their Pentagon gangs, all preserve confusion (alienation) operating, of course, for a fee in the land of the free. The country is bewitched by football, baseball, NASCAR and hoops, porno and pretend and the Hollywood enemas of antagonistic insight. Then debating, fumbling about trying to be right, taking sides and painting either black or *white*, the poor people exhaust themselves in a sicko "freedom of speech" knife *fight*.

Men Try the Feminine

As women have moved in and appropriated the masculine, men have learned to access the female knowledge. That, too, is claimed to be located somewhere in "his" human genes. The twentieth century came to a close with many a male being engrossed in the *female knowledge*, and understanding mentally and even intuitively this stuff of the psychic relationship: the importance of the individual's healthy relationship to society, to groups, to families and to other individuals—and to himself! And that must have been one of the liberator's tasks—not only to liberate women by achieving the same social and civil rights as men, but to get rid of the male aggressive, war-like rigid ideology and the unfeeling approach.

Women began to use hard language like "victims of men" to inspire floods of particular information to gain government support, to bring in new troops, and to *change* the one pegged as the enemy—the man. So she went mental, she's gone mental, overly mental, to reach to the other she wants so desperately to bring in.

The feminine side of men has been released and is virtually

accepted as fact. Men have also learned that to keep her *up there and at a distance,* as an idealized sex object, could reveal an immature man today. The publisher of *Penthouse* may claim that Viagra will undo the damages of feminism by allowing men to engage in sex without being sensitive, without the personal and emotional factor. But men can become the victim here, just worshiping the physical, and could be put into *her* back pocket, so to speak.

Eventually the masculinity of the female is inferior to that of the male, just as his feminine side—when it's released and gives him much needful insight—is inferior to that of the female. When the push must come to shove, the male's feminine side is not above the woman and her feminine understanding.

The Genders Positive Exchange

It's like nature itself causes the genders to mutate, to assimilate the other's defining characteristics to some degree in the hope for a successful continuation of the species. Both gain from the other gender's modus operandi. She makes gains in independence and the critical judgement obtained from the macho "knowing" of what she wants, and then taking action to get it. He gains in the feminine insight into his own psyche, into his feelings, his body and into his relatedness to society.

Women have backed off from marriage today, a feminine institution to be sure. That is still what woman wants—marriage, but not the traditional marriage where she can't get free and have the right to affect more than her immediate family. Women began to establish a distance between their husbands and themselves, and that *distance* has over the recent past mutated and is now embodied in the modern conception of *relationship*. Each mate is now thought to deserve his or her own "space."

The feminization of western culture has a positive side, away from all the gender feminist lies that carpet-bomb our nation's conscience into a dangerous and dumbfounded psychosis. The process at its best is above and beyond individual or gender conflict.

End the Gender War

Some of the female gender have moved location, in hope to repair the collective's consciousness. The World Wars' damage is deep. So "she's" become responsible for the external, or partly so, even though she may not be best suited for the outside world of politics, and the external sciences of structure and control. But the distance women have brought into their marriages gave them more freedom to influence the healing of society.

But it may be that Freud had a valid point, when he claimed women had a weakened superego and thus a diminished sense of justice. The superego, to Freud, represented socially induced morals and ethics. Maybe that's why many women aren't strongly united behind the effort to improve external society. Although hoping for a more compasionate society, they may lack the drive to strongly unite intellectually for this purpose. Some may primarily seek protection and security for themselves and their children. For many women, being subjectively motivated, the objective perspective that would see justice brought to help men based on the evidence of their demise may be ignored.

Many women had wanted room to expand their compassionate influence on all of society. But unfortunately, many angry and self-interested women have gobbled up the extra room and called it their liberation from men. And thus the hope of marriage programs making a comeback is crashing.

Thus women must call off the attack dogs some of their stepsisters have sent, and get serious about the coming event— male-female agency above corporate control. The goal is getting beyond a society dominated by capitalist imperialism, with its flashy propaganda machines, and overcoming the engineered gender anger used to divide, rule and distract the public.

20
The Bomb

To confront the disposition to elevate the female,
Attention is needed to endure the travail
Of the ego when its fighting assumptions are seen to fail,
But to remove disease and get organic truth into a
  better place
Will take more than just praying for grace,
One may need at first to briefly surrender long-held
  prejudices or belief,
And this usually can't happen without accompanying
  grief,
But to allow these next few words their due
Is recommended so that the soul and its images may
  start to come through.

It is ridiculous. This Information Age produces dummies armed with truth denial. The world they "see" doesn't really exist. They may believe many things (memes—thought groups) about their country and their leaders, or about the opposite sex. But their knowing is not, and they are being done-in. It's about people being in their prison of political correctness, and moreover, the people's *false-consciousness* is stranded hopelessly within society's pervasive marketing propaganda. Just how would a human being truly relate and interact today, without all of the trained behavior and brainwashing propaganda boxing them into the false-consciousness?

Maybe some women haven't a reliable clue as to what a real woman could or should do, because the definition of herself is so varied, so complex and so open to criticism. That's the result of radical feminism getting way too much respect. And that has made the men uncertain and confused. Feminist culture spins the "individual" thing that keeps everyone seperated. There is a rational, argumentative confusion about gender and its role in society. Bits and pieces, sound bites rocket many valid claims through the air, but then they only fizzle out under the continuous assault of politically correct consensus memes. And they call this freedom!

> *Today man and woman, who have they got to thank,*
> *For keeping them isolated and in a holding tank?*
> *They have freedom only for word groups to careen*
>   *inside their brains,*
> *While their organic knowing is interrupted by marketing*
>   *excitation for the insane.*

The chicanery responsible for the present psychological impasse, *psychosis* between the sexes, the root cause of many a wandering psychotic, is found in the past. Present perplexity and mortification need not continue to be passed on from generation to generation. Instead, "major surgery" needs an invitation, as therapy to clear the big picture up. Something must operate on the mind to remove the thought groups (memes) hindering support for organic living. This operation is needed to cure the body from its unhealthy attachments and to allow it freedom.

Worship of Women

The worship of women has been a foundation of western society like a sea bottom, and an ocean of emotion has been poured over this worship.

To keep its converts and for secret purposes, official Christianity had adopted certain Gnostic traditions that displayed themselves in the worship of women. Christians were directed to an intensified worship of Mary, Mother of Jesus. And the heritage of the Magna Mater, Isis and the other mother goddesses, like the Vas Sapientiae, vessel of wisdom from its Gnostic prototype, Sophia, gave Christianity a wide appeal and a connection with the past.

The worship of woman is the keystone prop of western society. But the direction of attention into the worship of women is the *miscue* that has facilitated losses in both gender camps, since women and men have been forced to surrender their gender's individuality.

Meaning their *personal* understanding of the "other" is gone, replaced by impersonal stereotypes. With gender, western society ingrains an imaginary "regard," socializes a lie. So people get stuck on politically correct and feminized images that are difficult to get past. Then the over-rational western mind constantly gets in the way, swamped by mistaken assumptions.

The worship of women has forced both sexes into politically correct behaviors that serve to castrate natural libidinous relationships. It has also interfered with an individual's relationship with common sense. And the only general symptom of insanity, Immanuel Kant said, is the loss of *common sense*. Weakened is the person's *singular* ability to know "grounded" reality and then to be responsible for their understanding, and to take action. Worshiping women set the stage for the gender wars that are so messy and so full of innocent disillusionment.

Influence of Christian Morality

The Christian Church is known to have persecuted the sensual, the erotic, and to have constructed "sin" out of many sexual happenings. A huge morality inundated all of western civilization as Christianity spread throughout Europe during the Middle Ages and then became global in modern times. But demonization of the sex instinct serves to undermine the *distinguishing* aptitudes treasured by both the male and the female. The true unique and creative individual is debased.

It is interesting that humans would allow tampering with pleasure, but the libido encroachment of western civilization and of its church would serve up an amazing solution to protect women from an instinctive backlash from the sexually manipulated, sexually obsessed men. Men would remain victims of their sex drives, but women themselves weren't seen as the ones responsible for men's slavery to sex. By repressing sex, by devilizing sex, women were protected! That is because women were elevated above it all, above sex and base desires. Thus they were *above* responsibility for men's humbling sex drive. From back then until today men are like victims who are trained to worship their tormentors!

In Christian society, many men interested in earthly sex were marginalized, painted as Godforsaken guilty sinners. The *guilt* the church brought insured little hope of men breaking out, and allowed women to be raised higher as a compensation.

Sex then went underground; undercover, the "sinners" had their censured liaisons. Out in the open, women became idealized—as the mother, the source of life, painted angel-like and as custodians of the man's *home and heaven*. Their idealized nature was far removed from that of a sexual conspirator. And the redirection of sexual energy, the libido, towards building the church gave that institution great power to grow and take control in societies all around the world. The Christian church has for a long time now empowered women, has made its chapels sacred for women's marriages and has been closely allied with women's values and needs.

Men and Virtue

Poets from the time of Homer have instructed young men to be virtuous and pious, to restrain their passions and to be good family men and decent citizens. In the past, virtue was portrayed as difficult to develop, while vice was seen as easy and pleasant. To be the ideal man needed great attention, sacrifice and will, and this ideal is what our ancient male ancestors were taught to strive for.

Homer, in *The Iliad*, portrays the Trojan prince torn between his love of his family and his duty to the common good. He must rise above his wife's pleas that he not go into battle and risk leaving her a widow and his son an orphan. But the prince really has no choice—he must fight for his country.

Socrates said if men were to become the guardians of the common good, they must govern their passions, not run endlessly to gratify endless desires. Men were to mirror *rationality* in their behavior and turn their ambitions inward to get control over unruly impulse. For Socrates "courage" unfolds as a quality of soul, mind and will, not as monstrous rankness or fighting prowess.

Marcus Aurelius, the Roman emperor and philosopher, taught that happiness stems from virtue. And this happiness was promised to last for eternity as compared to the rewards of riches and power that vanish with man's mortal body. To Marcus Aurelius true strength comes from inner psychic savvy.

Xenophon in *The Education of Cyrus* amplifies the classical ideal of manhood, as boys were asked: to prefer the common good to their own selfish desires, to control themselves and to keep busy with their duties.

Aristotle thought a *self-contained* man was a proud man, one who had a "greatness of soul," and his pride would stop him from treating others unjustly. Being his "own man" he would be expedient and liberal to others because he needs nothing from them.

The Age of Chivalry. The medieval notion of chivalry was the role a knight encompassed. He was a man that ideally strove for compassion, gentleness, valor, and spiritual knowledge. He was taught to act with moderation, composure and patience in pursuing the woman he loved. She was to love him for his worthy character and for his brave willingness to *define* justice, faith and duty. *By love and through love the man experiences the perfection of his own character*—this sums up the influence of chivalry and was the means given to the man to overcome bad behavior. Romantically trained passion led to moral decency and enabled the chivalrous man to rise above the temptations of lust.

Disastrous results were thought to come through unfaithfulness. This is taught through legends and stories and is reinforced by the church. When Sir Lancelot and King Arthur's Queen Guenevere submit to their passions and commit adultery, they begin transgressing their duty to their King. A massive tragedy ensues for them and for the Kingdom as Arthur's knights will divide and take sides, killing each other for years.

Another of Arthur's knights, Sir Gawain, is the subject of a different tale, *Sir Gawain and the Green Knight* from the twelfth century. Here Sir Gawain's honor is tried by his host's wife, not once but twice as she endeavors to seduce him. He withstands her amorous assault that is later revealed as having been a test her husband orchestrated. Sir Gawain, by rising above temptation, becomes the hero of the times, "the most faultless knight who ever lived; as a pearl in comparison with a dried pea is of greater value, so, truthfully, is Gawain beside other gallant knights."

Medieval tales and legends of knights and heroes supplied role models displaying behaviors a man should emulate toward women. Sir Bohort, a knight who succeeded in his quest for the Holy Grail, once left even his brother in danger in order to rescue an unknown maiden from rape. That spoke loudly to the extent that the female principle ruled over men, and to the connection between dedication to women and the search for the Holy Grail.

The Holy Grail is itself a vessel. It symbolizes women and the womb as bearers of life and represents the worship of the woman. The Holy Grail brought elevation of the "feminine" into the consciousness of the medieval man. Glorifying the feminine brought continuity with the ancient and pagan worship of female goddesses. The *feminine principle* that obsessed Sir Bohort and led him to the Holy Grail was, indeed, the main focus of the noble knight and where he found meaning in his life.

At the height of the Age of Chivalry, Andreas Capellanus wrote the thirteenth-century classic, *The Art of Courtly Love*. Here a man's motivation to improve himself comes precisely through his realization of his imperfections as he looks into his beloved's eyes:

> *"Love causes a rough and uncouth man to be distinguished for his handsomeness; it can endow a man even of the humblest birth with nobility of character; it blesses the proud with humility; and the man in love becomes accustomed to performing many services gracefully for everyone. O what a wonderful thing is love, which makes a man shine with so many virtues and teaches everyone, no matter who he is, so many good traits of character."*[1]

As the Knight's chivalry gave way to a more peaceful luxury, ladies' love was won, not in battle but in courtship rites and rules. A man needed to show himself as adept in conversation, wit and manners. But it is interesting that 700 years ago the code of chivalry demanded that men rise above their here-and-now passions for erotic love. The energizing force of *unattainable* love was believed to provoke finer and nobler passions than an easy conquest. Romantically speaking, the males were taught to idealize love, to raise it above sheer gratification—here celibacy becomes energizing, revving a testosterone engine. It was to be in works, in deeds and in a personal centering of his spirituality that the knight edged closer to fulfillment. Abstinence brought clarity. The knight saved his energy for his higher self, and *here* he expected to welcome his wife. Capellanus states in *The Art of Courtly Love* that "Good character alone makes any man worthy of love."[2]

Later Views. In the mid-eighteenth century Rousseau and the Romantic writers were still promoting the chivalric thoughts of love. In Rousseau's *Emile*, the young man develops and perfects his own character through his devotion to a young woman he admires. The virtues he wishes to develop in himself he sees in her. He wants to be worthy of her, and this stimulates him to strive harder to perfect himself.

And later there is Goethe, the famed philosopher, hitching hope to the *Eternal Feminine* to lead mankind onward. And Nietzsche's *Übermensch,* sometimes called *Superman,* is actually the man who has gotten control of his corrupted and conditioned human nature. This is the man who will make something of himself.

Love Between Man and Woman

Since ancient mythology, the notion of love between man and woman has been exalted and this "love," like that of Isis and Osiris, is given the power to at times overcome even death. Plato attributes the comic poet Aristophanes with the idea that men and women were once single beings that the gods split in half, into male and female, as punishment for human arrogance. Thus when the genders fall in love with each other it is a yearning for the missing half, to make wholeness.

From the ancients, through the chivalry of the medieval times, into the Renaissance, Romantic and Modern periods, there are prevalent themes that have endured steadfastly up until our recent past. These themes have defined masculinity in terms of its relationship with femininity, and have elevated unduly the image of woman into the clouds of make-believe, surrounding her with a reverence due a saint. The themes have served through her image to lead men towards sacrifice and service, and to induce them to the highest "moral ground" and self-restraint. Here men have hoped to realize their potential.

Men want to be the woman's hero and the fighter for common good. Moral limits were set by the church and the ruling authority. These limits were respected and brought erotic constraint. Romantic love could itself civilize a nation, or so it may have been believed.

Feminist Revision of Gender Roles

Is the heat behind the great traditions of intellectual and spiritual guidance dissipating today? Yoga, meditation and therapy suit women, that's for sure. Postmodern women have found refuge in paying attention to mind and body. Many have located their spiritual center in their *hearts*. But where are all the guys? Gyms and workshops filled with females, young and old: that's the America of today. Although many guys also do exercise, it is in the area of ethics where they aren't out front. Spiritual leadership had traditionally been by the male. Has all the male bashing beat the guys, downtrodden and subjugated them?

It's partly a feminist fantasy: that boys and girls, men and women are the same human, just bodies in a different *shape*, that without patriarchal conditioning the genders are intrinsically just the same *ape*. But that idea is abuse of reality. The radical feminists are looking for hoped-for outcomes, but their *revisionism* may have catastrophic potential for the human race.

> *This revisionism is making the masses bitter and mean,*
> *Not happy today with what they are seeing,*
> *Forcing "good ideas" like gender sameness down*
>   *youngsters' throats,*
> *Flings innocents into an ocean in which they can't float.*

Males Seduced by Female Tactics

Being a butthead is being a slave to women's buttocks. And as the male's head turns and cranes, ever mesmerized by the tick-tock sway of the globes sailing by, believe it, to respond is automatic. The woman has great potential manipulative power.

A male *terrorized* by physical obsession emerges from meagre results, his not getting his hands on what political correctness today keeps away and on the shelf. He could figure that she's really to blame for dangling her parts, teasing endlessly, dawn to dusk, making lust her *slave* and really bending his brain, he the butthead forced below, a *knave*. Why doesn't he get mad, take revenge at the gender that's got him nailed, his desires inflamed even while on a whim she may butt him out.

> *Can't he make her take any responsibility,*
> *admit to low crimes under her sail,*
> *And misdemeanors and thus elevate himself above*
> *the travail?*

Is "female" just another way of saying "unaccountable"? Why do most men willingly allow the charade—of woman as a *higher being*, this by the *she* who has him in lustful chains? Why don't men identify the enemy as the one: manipulating and insulting them, holding them emotionally-sexually hostage, assimilating them as penis-heads by dressing to excite sexual responses, demanding so much attention and a subservient attitude; educating all his children with perverse gender feminist beliefs?

Male Sacrifice

The tall towers of metropolis, the downtown buildings reaching up into the sky, they may enable feelings of progress. They beckon to a future society where industry and scientific development will hopefully organize a civilization that will function effectively. But these rigid walls were built for society to continue as it had in the past, and that past has a woman-worshiping history.

So much has been done in the name of helping women that a young male is conditioned to sacrifice even his life to protect her. And without a war to prove the point, still women live six years longer than men, so he is still the sacrificed one. Can anyone imagine the noise and much ado if the woman lived today six years less than the man?

> *Summon up the fury, imagine the storm,*
> *Finger-pointing and her furious and bent way out of form,*
> *If men should have any benefit that is not hers,*
> *that is the norm.*

Governments use the male worship of the female to get recruits. Ad agencies, meddlers in spin, entice sales using the male's protective urge. And to all it's *her* convenience that is catered to. Conditioning from the past, this desire to help and protect the woman is still a high priority. That was where the men found meaning and motivation too, but this desire now comes from a need that is very suspect.

Women Go It Alone—Hillary's Gang

Hillary Rodham Clinton's group of females say they can go it alone. But they are dubious characters, and reality won't match up with their wordy claims. Hillary's got the persecuted male in her house, her own in-home example of the zits covering the patriarchy. He's an obsessive man, brought up without a father. And he is reckless beyond belief. He is even possibly the embodiment of much any woman disdains. So Bill Clinton's presidency sees millions in cash go to feminist organizations, and the ladies turn the other way, "cause, Honey, it's money that's become the savior and the way."

So Hillary's gonna lead all the sisterhood, together with the newly brainwashed and the politically correct, who stand in and relish in the false-consciousness that has been subbing in for too long as reality. She will lead them first over the body of this Bill, trampling him under their work boots while other troopers tear at his neurotic need—maybe leggy feminazis wearing tall spiked and toe-strapped high heels. This is one of their ways of seeking certain knowledge and power.

And there are far too many men who are first brought up on mommy's milk and then stuffed full with their mother's sharp-stinging rebukes about just what is "being bad", and what a good boy should feel, do, think. Then, together with the gentle-mother and angry-mother reminds, it all embeds and soaks into a young boy's gut today. Soon the matriarchy could have the boys in a single line with the girls.

> *Basically school has feminizing hands,*
> *Blending the boys into behaviors that suit some*
> *feminist demands.*

The gender feminists stand ever so near to capturing almost total control. It seems the creature they have built is now going to mutate, and re-create itself through their control of the education system. Their converts will be like those of the Christians earlier last century, who were basically delivered to the church when they were, by law, enrolled in school.

The universities are now female-dominated. And the media follow instructions about what to mesmerize the public with.

*The top guns of the land have decreed
That into the female shall the boys directed be.*

Boys are socialized as if only one gender exists—female, with all the baggage—caring, sharing, sensitive to all feeling, needing constant support and self-esteem building.

But the truth be known, females in general are emotionally obsessed, often perturbed and moody, with perpetually shifting rushes of energy charging through their bodies. Astrological, numerological and psychic solutions are getting too high a ground for explaining all the chaos going on in these bodies. *Soap opera* types of explanations about life keep everyone forced into sympathy and sentiment. Anti-male explanations create an oppressor.

Today a male prioritizes a female agenda for his life—he has no choice, from infancy women have brought him up and trained his behavior. So won't governments get away with murder if the boys become feminized? Women's wishful thinking and their truly desired happy endings and sympathy can't be the males' only guiding principle. "He" can't grok that forever. Trying to bring unrealistic dreams into reality while on his knee, awaiting her new ideas of how society should be run, may eventually provoke a disrupting and impassioned response. The males will become cynical, and angry, but most won't understand why. *Insurance* builds while the neurosis of sorrow torments, as many will blame themselves for her fantasies not coming true. And the masochists, they won't act, won't complain.

Like the gargoyles atop the downtown high-rise buildings put there to drive away evil, there are forces in human evolution that have been set up to protect women. Today these forces may not relate to many of the new female complaints. They may be sent chasing after "fantasy" problems, sent looking for a non-existent psychological security, while society ruptures internally. Dishonest governments just carry on when men tear off to find the solutions to imaginary problems, rather than working in unison with women on the *real* social problems of the day. Women may be on the verge of losing their protectors, so dizzy has the present false-consciousness made man.

Just listen to Hillary and her gang. They now want not husbands, but government to be their *partners!* And to these women that means money, day care, women's separate housing. The trashing and marginalization of males continues. Now women can be "childless by choice." Or they can use artificial insemination to create a pet baby. Hillary's gang and their rally call—*A Woman's Right To Choose*—that says it all. Men are to have no say.

'Rounding the Inferno

The men who now are educated to be like
*   the women*
Will space out, go internal,
Soon to be driven ape by the inferno.
Or they may simply, luckily, begin to focus,
To observe the come around
Of just what does come around,
During his rounding at this time.

21
He, He

> "It is now technically possible to reproduce without the aid of males and to produce only females. We must begin immediately to do so."
>
> Scum Manifesto[1.]

Is it simply a failure to connect with soul mates that's revealed in the dramatic increase in singles, those unattached and unmarried? Warning signals are flashing! In percentage, one-third more adult US women are single in 2000 than in 1960. And recent US Census Bureau stats reveal that by 2007 fifty-one percent of all adult females are rumbling along the road of what would just yesterday have been called spinsterhood. Over fifty million of them! The percentage of unmarried women ages 25 to 34 roughly tripled between 1970 and 1998.[2] And the portion of unmarried women 20 to 24 years old who had never married more than doubled between 1970 and 2003—from thirty-six percent to seventy-five percent. For unmarried women in the 30 to 34 age bracket, the increase between 1970 and 2003 was greater, more than tripling from six percent to 23 percent. Big time changes, wo-man! And in a dramatic Time-CNN poll, 61 percent of single women aged 18 to 49 said "Yes" they *would* raise a child on their own, become single moms. That is almost two out of three, and therefore for a would-be papa who's driven by his mission to procreate—what type of future can he now foresee? The handwriting is on the wall. It's plain to see his limitations are rising.

Women are pleased to choose among possibilities, and many understandably call this freedom. A freedom to shop around, to weigh and consider lifestyles, before they buy in. They've been taught to go for power, and they try to shrug off many external demands, particularly those by a man. Today they see the man's demands or expectations as the big taboo—a *control* over them. So now they want men to fit what's on *their* shopping list.

But women also want *aloneness* to be digestible today. They want to threaten the men by making them face aloneness. Women are wanting to push the envelope, and are distancing from men to give themselves more space to influence society. Many are probably interested to find out if there really could be a full life without traditional relationship and marriage. But by women themselves also learning to accept aloneness, they are basically in training to be away from a husband. So the forces of single motherhood grow. *Women and children, society for the people!* Or the people that courts prefer receive privilege. Being a spinster, well, even that is becoming all right, and can be twisted into an affirmation; it's *OK*. They can adopt babies, or get artificial insemination. Or maybe they will hope to produce the human equivilent of the successfull birth in 2004 that used only two females (mice) to produce a baby. But the implication, of course, is a future in which males will not be required for reproduction.

Can it be that today some women are encouraged to see females as desirous sex objects? Is western society that feminized? Maybe some women have bought right in, and see the feminine as the crown of creation, as the ruler, and they now snuggle right in. Are females beginning to see females as sexual conquests? A society that elevates everything female may get the goal-oriented shoppers seeing females as worthy of acquisition. Even for females themselves!

Many men are nobody's hero. And they desperately agonize about how they will ever be important, happy and powerful—without a woman. They are left with their hard-wired sex drive while the object of their need is now loving its own image. They feel discarded.

Lesbian relationships end up with as much violence as the *straight* couples have to deal with. Lesbian mothers with their insemination specials may haggle in court with same-sex partners over custody of the children. Then lawsuits rocket towards financial assets, and more violence occurs. Just like heteros breaking up.

Western society is corrupted on many levels. Is lesbian sex a revolt against today's society? Do these lesbians think society patriarchal and misogynist, not capitalist?

At the political level there was Bill Clinton surviving scandal after scandal, leaving elected office with approval ratings in the stratosphere. A marvelous spin success. But who knew the president of CNN was Clinton's buddy? CNN president Rick Kaplan, a former employer of Hillary Clinton and a Lincoln bedroom guest, ran what some called the "Clinton News Network." They say that is the only reason Clinton survived—the media image and spin, resulting in his unbelievable poll numbers!

At a gender level, was Kurt Kobain murdered? Courtney Love's father said on TV that she killed Kurt Kobain, and others say so too. The rebel, the leader of teen spirit is offed by his wife? Here's something for the female-only empowerment lobby group to face up to. It's obviously about male defeat, this gender war.

At a personal level, who is taking responsibility for what's invited into their homes? The internet may be the best way to find out what's really going on in the world and get beyond all the media lies. Men use the internet more than women. They could become a threat to those who dish out the spin tacts if they get the "goods" on them from internet sources. Although certain American goverment agencies are increasingly able to control content allowed on the internet, in a preemptive strike to derail men from getting to the truth, there now cascades onto the internet innumerable *free* pornography sites. Thousands and thousands of them! Their purpose is to seduce men. And they keep them distracted, too. Away from the hunt for truth. Trapped in their carnal desire. Detoured on the Internet from their need to set the world right.

Network Television programs people. Manipulation, abuse and lies are lived with. But what about the transmission of subliminal messages—the ones beyond people's normal sight and hearing that some say are now flying around, invading people's home space? What are people being made into, what ideas are becoming accepted as true, and who is writing the script? The media now has a message—but whose?

Notes:

Steinem Quote
1. Gloria Steinem, *Revolution From Within: A Book of Self-Esteem.* (New York, Little, Brown and Company, 1992). p. 261

Introduction:
1. Simone De Beauvoir, *The Second Sex.* (New York, Vintage Books, 1952). p. xxxiii

Chapter 3: Staring Truth in the Face. Eating Popcorn....
1. Ann Douglas, *The Feminization of American Culture* (New York: Farrar Straus & Giroux, 1977)
2. Ibid., p. 8
3. Ibid., p. 8
4. Ibid., p. 8
5. Ibid., p. 6
6. Ibid., p. 12
7. Ibid., p. 13
8. Ibid., p. 12
9. Ibid., p. 13
10. Ibid., p.60
11. Ibid., p.42
12. Ibid, p. 6
13. Ibid., p. 327
14. Ibid, p 327
15. Ibid., p 328
16. Ibid., p xiv
17. Ibid., p xiv
18. Ibid., p xv
19. Ibid., p. xv

Chapter 6: Progress Is Failure
1. J.S. Mill, 1869, *The Subjection of Women* (Indianapolis: Hackett Publishing, 1988, [1869]) p. 69
2. Ibid. p. 63
3. CNN. June/21/02
4. Daniel Bell, *New York Times* (October, 27 1970)
5. Ibid.
6. Ibid.

Chapter 7 Estrus Ardent
1. "Herstory" – Elizabeth Arden
2. D.H. Lawrence, *Fantasia of the Unconscious* (Great Britain: Penguin Books, 1971) copyright 1921, p.100

3. Ibid., p. 98
4. Ibid., p. 99
5. Ibid., p. 99
6. Susan Brownmiller, *Femininity* (London: Collins Publishing, 1984), p. 33
7. Ibid., p. 33
8. Susan Brownmiller, *Against Our Will: Men, Woman, and Rape* (New York: Simon and Schuster, 1975), p.209
9. Ibid., p. 209
10. Ibid., p. 31-114
11. Ibid., p. 64
12. Ibid., p. 182
13. Ibid., p. 182
14. Ibid., p. 182
15. Ibid., p. 182
16. Ibid., p. 19
17. Ibid., p. 19
18. Ibid., p. 126
19. Marshall Berman, *All That's Solid Melts into Air* (New York: Penguin, 1988), p. 121
20. Brownmiller, *Femininity*, p. 34
21. Ibid., p. 122
22. Ibid., p. 124
23. Ibid., p. 123
24. Ibid., p. 123
25. Ibid., p. 124

Chapter 8: Red Mouth
1. 41% figure, 1994 US Bureau of Criminal Justice Statistics of the US Department of Justice's Special report. Survey of family homicides in thirty-three urban US counties
2. 90% victim figure for men
3. Patricia Pearson, *When she Was Bad: Violent Women and the Myth of Innocence* (New York, Viking, 1997)

Chapter 11: Spice and Rodham
1. Warren Farrell, *The Myth of Male Power* (1993), pp. 304-306
2. *Talk* magazine
3. *Talk* magazine
4. In this section all quotes from Mary Wollstonecraft [1792], *A Vindication of the Rights of Women*. (Hammondsworth, UK: Penguin, 1978)
5. Shere Hite, *Women and Love, a Cultural Revolution in Progress*, 1987.

6. Lionel Tiger, The Decline of Males (New York: St. Martin's Griffin, 1999)
7. Shere Hite, *Women and Love, a Cultural Revolution in Progress.*
8. James Petersen, *The Century of Sex* (New York: Grove Press, 1999), p. 489
9. Harper's Index in *Harper's Magazine*, March 2002.
10. All quotes in this section from Elizabeth Wurtzel, *Bitch: In Praise of Difficult Women* (New York: Doubleday, 1998), p. 30
11. Ibid., p. 30
12. Ibid., p. 282
13. Ibid., p. 282
14. Ibid., p. 3
15. Ibid., p. 4
16. Ibid., p. 5
17. Ibid., p. 6
18. Ibid., p. 8
19. Ibid., p. 8
20. Ibid., p. 33
21. Ibid., p. 14
22. Ibid., p. 11
23. Ibid., p. 32

Chapter 12: You've Gone a Long Way Baby
1. Mary Wollstonecraft, A *Vindication of the Rights of Women) (London, Penguin Group), first published 1792.*
2. Ibid.
3. Ibid., p. 103
4. Ibid., p. 103
5. Ibid., p. 284
6. Ibid., p. 289
7. Ibid., p. 316
8. Ibid., p. 286
9. Elizabeth Cady Stanton, "The Seneca Falls Declaration (1. Declaration of Sentiments)" (1848).
10. Ibid.
11. Friedrich Nietzsche, Giorgio Colli and Mazzino Montinari, *Samtliche Briefe: Kritische Studienausgabe (1988, 1999)*, p. 166.
12. Ibid
13. Saul, John R. *The Unconscious Civilization* (Ontario: House of Anansi, 1995) p.14
14. Warren Farrell, *The Myth of Male Power*, p. 134, 385
15. Ibid., p. 125

Chapter 14: Mad Donna
1. MTV—10th Anniversary. 1991
2. Ibid.
3. Betty Dodson, *Liberating Masturbation* (New York: Bodysex Designs, 1974)
4. *The Girlie Show* in Australia, Nov.-Dec. 1993
5. MTV
6. Kate Millet, *Sexual Politics* (New York: Doubleday, 1970)
7. Hadria's lament in: Mona Caird, *Daughters of Danaus* (1894)
8. Andrea Dworkin, *Intercourse* (Toronto, Simon & Schuster, 1987)
9. King, Norman, *Madonna: The Book* (Quill, 1991)
10. *The Girlie Show* in Australia, Nov.-Dec. 1993
11. King Norman, *Madonna: The Book*, p. 14

Chapter 16: 21st Century Foxed
1. Friedrich Nietzsche, *The Gay Science* (Nietzsche 1974) p. 319
2. Cambridge, MA: *Harvard University Press, 1980. Bastardy and Its Comparative History. P.54-85.* In Lionel Tiger's, *Decline* of Males, p. 34
3. Lionel Tiger, *The Decline of Males* (New York: St. Martin's Griffin, 1999), p. 33
4. Ibid., p. 5
5. Ibid., p. 188
6. Paula Kamen, *her way: Young Women Remake the Sexual Revolution* (New York: Broadway, 2002), p. 237
7. Ibid., p. 237
8. Ibid., p. 239
9. Ibid., p. 234
10. Ibid., p. 73
11. bid., p. 73
12. Ibid., p. 75
13. Ibid., p. 78
14. Ibid., p. 81
15. Ibid., p. 77
16. Ibid., p. 78
17. Ibid., p. 234
18. Ibid., p. 234
19. D.H. Lawrence. "Fantasia of the Unconscious" (Penguin, 1977),p.109. (1921)

Chapter 17: The Male Click Experience
1. 41% of spousal murders, from US Bureau of Criminal Justice Statistics, the Department of Justice's Special Report. 1994. Survey of thirty-three urban US counties.

Chapter 18: Lash
1. Lionel Tiger, *The Decline of Males* (New York: St. Martin's Griffin, 1999), pp. 200-201.
2. Stuart Miller and Rich Zubaty, "Reuniting Fathers with their Families," *Washington Times*, December 19, 1995, p. A19.
3. Ibid., p. A19.
4. Ibid., p. A19.
5. Lionel Tiger, *The Decline of Males*, p. 23.
6. Ibid., p. 166.
7. Miller and Zubaty, "Reuniting Fathers with their Families," p. A19.
8. Susan Faludi, *Backlash: the Undeclared War Against American Women* (New York: Crown, 1991).
9. James Petersen, *The Century of Sex* (New York: Grove Press, 1999), p. 442.
10. Naomi Wolf, *The Beauty Myth: How Images of Beauty Are Used Against Women* (Garden City, NY: Doubleday, 1992).
11. Ibid.
12. Naomi Wolf, *Fire with Fire: The New Female Power and How it Will Change the 21st Century* (London: Chatto & Windus, 1993), p. 14.
13. Christina Holy Grail, *Who Stole Feminism?* (New York: Simon & Schuster, 1994), p. 136.
14. Arthur Schopenhauer, "On Women." In D.H. Parker, ed., *Schopenhauer Selections* (New York, Charles Scribner, 1928).
15. Ibid.
16. Ibid.
17. Immanuel Kant, "Observations on the Beautiful and Sublime." J.T. Goldthwait, ed., (University of California Press, 1960).
18. Ibid.
19. Ibid.
20. Ibid.
21. Ibid.
22. Ibid.
23. Rev. S. Thelwall, translator, *The Writings of Tertullian* (Edinburgh: T. & T. Clark, 1869), vol. 1, chp. 2.
24. Friedrich Nietzsche, *Beyond Good and Evil*. Quoted by Arkada Plotnitsky, "The Medusa's Ears: the Quest of Nietzsche, the Question of Gender, and Transformations of Theory." In Peter Burgard, ed., *Nietzsche and the Feminine* (Charlottesville: University Press of Virginia, 1994), p. 244.
25. Ibid., p. 244.
26. Friedrich Nietzsche, *Beyond Good and Evil*. Translated by Helen Zimmern (Mineola, NY: Dover Publications, 1977), p.104. Also: Walter Kaufmann, *Basic Writings of Nietzsche* (New York: Random

House, 1966), 1992 edition, p. 358.
27. C.G. Jung, *Aspects of the Feminine* (New Jersey: Princeton University Press, 1982), p. 63.
28. Ibid., p. 64.
29. Hoff Sommers, *Who Stole Feminism?*, p. 201.
30. Murray Straus and Richard Gelles, *Physical Violence in America* (New Bruinswick, NJ: Transaction Publications, 1991).
30a. Journal of the Americn Medical Association, June 22-29, 1984
31. Lenore Walker, *The Battered Woman* (New York: Harper Colophon Books, 1979).
32. Hoff Sommers, *Who Stole Feminism?*, p. 190.
33. Ibid., p. 207.
34. Ibid., p. 12.
35. Ibid., p. 11.
36. Ibid., p. 13.
37. Naomi Wolf, *The Beauty Myth*, p. 166.
38. Michael Rivero, "Scholarly Articles about Husband Abuse." Jan. 12, 2000 (rivero@kwcc.com).
39. Hugh Nations, "Some Facts about Rape and Accusations of Rape." *Transitions: Journal of Men's Perspectives,* November-December 1994 (published by National Coalition of Free Men, PO Box 129, Manhasset, NY 11030). The data in this paragraph all come from Nation's article.
40. Purdue University study, 1994.
41. Ibid.
42. Hoff Sommers, *Who Stole Feminism?*, p. 210.
43. Ibid., p. 213
44. Ibid., p. 214
45. American Association of University Women (AAUW), "Shortchanging Girls, Shortchanging America." (Washington, DC: AAUW Foundation, 1991).
46. Hoff Sommers, *Who Stole Feminism?*, p. 141.
47. Christina Hoff Sommers, *The War Against Boys* (New York: Simon & Schuster, 2000), p. 111.
48. Hoff Sommers, *Who Stole Feminism?*, pp. 154-155, 160. Data and quotes in this and the following paragraph.
49. Ibid., p. 161.
50. Mary Pipher, *Reviving Ophelia* (New York: Ballantine Books, 1995), p. 27.
51. Hoff Sommers, *Who Stole Feminism?*, p. 161.
52. Kant, "Observations on the Feeling of the Place of the Beautiful and Sublime."
53. Hoff Sommers, *The War Against Boys*, p. 128.

54. Ibid., p. 137.
55. Tiger, *The Decline of Males*, p. 248.
56. Hoff Sommers, *Who Stole Feminism?*, p.239.
57. Ibid., p. 199.
58. Ibid., p. 191.
59. Ibid., p. 195.
60. See "domestic violence" on F.A.C.T. (Fathers Are Capable Too) Canadian web page [www. Fact.on.ca]
61. Hoff Sommers, *Who Stole Feminism?*, p. 197.
62. Warren Farrell, *Father and Child Reunion* (New York: Tarcher Putnam, 2001), p. 104.
63. Ibid., p. 171.
64. Hoff Sommers, *The War Against Boys*, p. 129.
65. Farrell, *Father and Child Reunion*, pp. 29, 85.
66. Ibid., p. 192.
67. Ibid., p. 174.
68. Ibid., p. 198.
69. Ibid., p. 12.
70. Tiger, *The Decline of Males*, p. 161.
71. Ibid., p. 161.
72. Ibid., p. 172.
73. Ibid., p. 161.
74. Farrell, *Father and Child Reunion*, p. 242.
75. Ibid., p. 134.
76. Tasker and Boswell, *Ottawa Citizen*, February 4, 1999.
77. Farrell, *Father and Child Reunion*, pp. 10, 259.
78. Ibid., p.10.
79. Ibid., p. 76-77. (Source of facts and quotation in this paragraph and facts in the following paragraph.)
80. Ibid., p. 32-33. (Source of facts in this paragraph.)
81. K.D. Pruett and R. Litzenberger, "Latency of Children Nurtured by Fathers," *Psychoanalytic Study of the Child*, 1997.
82. Farrell, *Father and Child Reunion*, p. 180.
83. Ibid., p. 144.
84. Ibid., p. 100.
85. Ibid., p. 201.
86. Ibid., p. 79.
87. Ibid., p. 200.
88. Ibid., p. 79.
89. Ibid., p. 83.
90. Ibid., p. 78.
91. Ibid., p. 48.
92. Ibid., p. 72.

93. Ibid., p. 106.
94. Ibid., p. 48.
95. Ibid., p. 72.
96. Ibid., p. 61.
97. Ibid., p. 33-37.
98. See "domestic violence" on F.A.C.T. (Fathers Are Capable Too) Canadian web page [www. Fact.on.cal]
99. Ibid.
100. Ibid.
101. personal communication. Keith Harris, Dec. 31, 1999 (keithnharris@canada.com). "Family Homicide: Family Violence in Canada." Statistics Canada, Cat. No. 85-224.
102. personal communication. Keith Harris, Dec. 31, 1999 (keithnharris@canada.com).
103. Stuart Miller. American Fathers Coalition web page, September 1997. His sources: FBI, Uniform Crime Reports 1994-1995; *Murder in Families,* Bureau of Justice Statistics, US Department of Justice, July 1994; Warren Farrell, *Myth of Male Power* (New York: Simon & Schuster, 1993), p. 281.
104 Ibid.
105. Murray Straus, Richard Gelles and Suzanne Steinmetz, *Behind Closed Doors: Violence in the American Family,* (Garden City, NY: Anchor Doubleday, 1980).
106. M. Brinkerhoff and E. Lupri, "Interspousal Violence," *Canadian Journal of Sociology* 13, no.4 (1988):407-434.
107. Tiger, *The Decline of Males,* p. 3.
108. Pipher, *Reviving Ophelia,* pp. 17-44.
109. Andrea Dworkin, *Intercourse* (London: Arrow Books, 1987), p.182.
110. Ibid., p. 33
111. Ibid., p. 71.
112. Ibid., pp. 66-67.

Chapter 20: The Bomb
1. Andreas Capellanus, *The Art of Courtly Love* (13th century)
2. Ibid.

Chapter 21: He, He
1. Valerie Solanas, *Society for Cutting Up Man* (London, Olympia Press, 1971)
2. Campbell, Kim, *Beyond Bridget, a fuller view of single women.* Staff writer of *The Christian Science Monitor*. April 2001. (Campbell cites 1998 Census figures)

Bibliography

Bakan, Joel. The Corporation, *The Pathological Pursuit of Power*. Toronto, Canada: Penguin Group. 2004.

Berman, Marshall. *All That Is Solid Melts Into Air*. New York: Penguin, 1988.

Brandt, Dr David. *Everyday Masochists: Don't Stop Now, You're Killing Me*. New York: Poseidon Press, 1986

Brock, David. *The Real Anita Hill*. New York: The Free Press, 1993.

Brownmiller, Susan. *Femininity*. London: Paladin books, 1986.

Burgard, Peter, editor. *Nietzsche and the Feminine*. Charlottesville: University Press of Virginia, 1994.

Chomsky, Noam. *Power and Prospects*. Boston: South End Press, 1996.

Chomsky, Noam. *9-11*. New York: Seven Stories Press, 2001.

Clack, Beverley, editor. *Misogyny in the Western Philosophical Tradition*. New York, 1999.

Denfeld, Rene. *The New Victorians*. New York: Warner Books, 1995.

Dineen, Dr. Tana. *Manufacturing Victims, What the Psychology Industry is Doing to People*. Montreal, Canada: Robert Davies Publishing. 1996.

Dobbin, Murray. *The Myth of the Good Corporate Citizen*. Toronto: Stoddart Publishing, 1998.

Douglas, Ann. *The Feminization of American Culture*. New York: The Noonday Press, 1977.

Dworkin, Andrea. *Intercourse*. New York: Free Press Paperbacks, 1987.

Eatwell, Roger. *Fascism*. London: Vintage 1996.

Eisenstein, Hester. *Contemporary Feminist Thought*. Boston: G. K. Hall & Co., 1983.

Ensler, Eve. *The Vagina Monologues*. New York: Villard Books, 1998.

Eszterhas, Joe. *American Rhapsody*. New York: Alfred A. Knopf, 2000.

Faludi, Susan. *Backlash, The Undeclared War Against Women*.

New York: Doubleday, 1991.

Farrell, Warren. *The Myth of Male Power*. New York: Simon an Schuster, 1993

Farrell, Warren. *Father and Child Reunion*. New York: Penguin Putnam, 2001.

Fillion, Kate. *Lip Service*. Toronto: Harper Collins, 1996.

Frank, Lisa and Smith, Paul, editors. *Madonnarama, Essays on Sex and Popular Culture*. Pittsburgh: Cleis Press Inc., 1993.

Gamble, Sarah, editor. *Feminism and Postfeminism*. Cambridge: Icon Books, 1999.

Hitchens, Christopher. *No One Left To Lie To*. New York, 1999.

Hoff Sommers. *Who Stole Feminism*. New York: Touchstone, 1994.

Hoff Sommers. *The War Against Boys*. New York: Simon & Schuster, 2000.

Hutchison, Michael. *The Anatomy of Sex and Power*. New York: William Morrow and Company, 1990.

Johnson, Chalmers. *Blowback, The Costs and Consequences of American Empire*. New York: Henry Holt and Company, 2000.

Jung, C.G. *Aspects of the Feminine*. New Jersey: Princeton University Press, 1982.

Kaufman, Walter, editor, translator. *Basic Writings of Nietzsche*. New York: Random House, 1992.

King, Norman. *Madonna: The Book*. New York. William & Morrow & Co. Inc. 1991

Krishnamurti, J. *On Love and Loneliness*. New York: Harper Collins, 1993.

Lapham, Lewis H. *Gag Rule*. New York: Penguin Group. 2004

Lasn, Kalle. *Culture Jam, The Uncooling of America*. New York: Eagle Brook, 1999.

Lawrence, D.H. *Apocalypse*. London: Penguin Books, 1931.

Lawrence, D.H. *Fantasia of the Unconscious*. Great Britain: Penguin Books, 1971.

Mill, John Stuart. *The Subjection of Women*. Indianapolis: Hackett Publishing, 1988.

Mitroff & Bennis. *The Unreality Industry*. New York; Oxford

University Press, 1989.

Moore, Michael. *Stupid White Men*. New York: Regan Books, 2001.

Morris Desmond. *The Naked Ape*. London: The Trinity Press, !967.

Newell, Walter R. *What is a Man?*. New York: Harper Collins, 2000.

Newton and Rosenfelt. *Feminist Criticism and Social Change*. New York: Methuen, Inc, 1985.

Norris, Christopher. *Uncritical Theory, Postmodernism, Intellectuals and the Gulf War*. Amherst: University of Massachusetts Press, 1992.

Nietzsche, Friedrich. *Twilight of the Idols*. New York: Oxford University Press, 1998.

Nietzsche, Friedrich. *On the Genealogy of Morals*. New York: Oxford University Press, 1996.

Nye, Andrea. *Words of Power, a Feminist Reading of the History of Logic*. New York: Routledge, Chapman and Hall, 1990.

Orwell, George. *Nineteen Eighty-Four*. London: Penguin Books, 1989.

Paglia, Camille. *Sex, Art, and American Culture*. Toronto: Random House, 1992.

Patton, Paul, editor. *Nietzsche Feminism & Political Theory*. London: Routledge, 1993.

Petersen/Hefner. *The Century of Sex*. New York: Grove Press, 1999.

Pipher, Mary. *Reviving Ophelia*. New York: Ballintine Books, 1994.

Reich, Charles A. *Opposing the System*. New York: Random House, 1995.

Ross, Andrew. *The Chicago Gangster Theory of Life, Nature's Debt to Society*. London: Verso, 1994.

Sayers, Osborne, editors. *Socialism, Feminism and Philosophy*. New York: Routledge, 1990.

Saul, John Ralston. *Voltaire's Bastards*. Toronto: Penguin Books, 1992.

Saul, John Ralston. *The Unconscious Civilization*. Concord,

Ontario: House of Anansi Press, 1995.

Saul, John Ralston. *On Equilibrium*. Toronto: Penguin Books, 2001.

Schippers, David. *Sellout, The Inside Story of President Clinton's Impeachment*. Washington: Regnery Publishing, 2000.

Solanas, Valerie. *Society for Cutting Up Men*. Olympia Press, London, !971.

Steinberg, Milton. *Basic Judaism*. New York: Harcourt, Brace & World, 1947.

Tannen, Deborah. *Gender and Discourse*. Oxford: Oxford University Press, 1994.

Tiger, Lionel. *The Decline of Males*. New York: St. Martin's Press, 1999.

Wolf, Naomi. *The Beauty Myth*. Toronto: Random House,1990.

Wollstonecraft, Mary. A *Vindication of the Rights of Woman*. London: Penguin Group, 1972.

Wurtzel, Elizabeth. *Bitch*. New York: Doubleday, 1998.

Ventura, Jesse. *Do I Stand Alone?*. New York: Pocket Books, 2000.

Index

"insurance", 19-20, 57, 218, 237 238, 254-256, 273, 277, 283, 300
    collective guilt, 221, 277
    rape, 56, 58, 113-114, 166, 234, 240-242, 266
"lace curtain", 263
"learned helplessness", 113
"One in Four", 240, 242, 262
"Pink and White Tyranny", 13
"rule of thumb", 236-237
"Sexual Politics", 166
AIDS, 87, 117, 122, 168, 189
Air Polution, 41
alcohol, traffic deaths, prohibition
    boys, 249
Allen, Woody, 191
androgyny, 50, 192
Arden, Elizabeth, 51-55, 62
Aristotle, 84, 230, 294
army, gender equality, 139
athletes, 76, 188, 191
battery of men, 252, 270, 277
battery of pregnant women, 239
Bell, Daniel, 31-32, 35
biology, gender, 49, 51
    Wellesley College, 96
bound foot, 90
Brownmiller, Susan, 56-60, 62-63
Buel, Sarah, 277
Calvinism, vi, 14-15
capitalism, vi, 11-12, 14, 16, 19-20, 42, 52, 57, 72, 105, 122, 130, 146, 152, 155, 158, 168, 179, 193, 217, 249
celebrities, 1, 95, 109, 170, 174, 187, 189
children
    abuse by mothers, 219-220
    burden of, 130
    child support, 266
    custody, 199, 258-260, 266
    Germaine Greer, 202
    humanism, 141
    murder, 261, 269
    outside marriage, ix, 92
    protection, 48
    sexual abuse, 265
    suicide, 249
chivalry, age of, 294
Christianity, 18, 184, 199, 281-282, 291-292
cigarette, deaths, 41
Clinton, Bill, viii, 4-6, 23, 30, 92, 96-97, 100-101, 103, 120, 138, 140, 184, 221-222, 239, 264, 304
Clinton, Hillary, 17, 95-101, 103, 105, 111, 116, 140, 222, 272, 299, 301
CNN, 22, 31, 72, 100, 302, 304-305
consensus, x, 24, 27, 49, 61, 86, 89, 101, 108, 126, 158, 195-196, 199, 236, 238, 246, 262, 265, 281, 291
counter culture, vi, 135, 153-155
de Beauvoir, Simone, x, 272
Diana, Princess, 121, 181-183, 185-192

disco, 178
disestablishment of the church, 13
dissimulation, vi, 19, 93, 197, 220, 226-228, 247
divorce, 92, 107, 111, 113, 129, 132, 150, 210, 256, 258, 265, 267
    children, 220, 256-259, 265
    custody, 199
divorced
    Wallis Simpson, 188
domestic violence, 214, 233-235, 240, 252-253, 261, 267-268, 270, 311-312
doubt, 30, 33, 59, 138-139, 182, 185
Douglas, Ann, 10
Dworkin, Andrea, 117, 274-277
Dylan, Bob, 135, 156
Elvis, 22, 150, 172
extra-marital pregnancy, historical, 200
fall from grace, 230
Faludi, Susan, 221-224, 242, 273, 277
Farrell, Warren, 258, 261, 263
female
    moral superiority, 6, 49, 100, 117, 164, 175, 178-179
    protection and privilege, 118, 220, 258
feminism, communal, 12
firemen, NY-9/11, 69
Forrest Gump, 86
fourth-wave feminism, 196
Freud, Sigmund, 136, 208, 231
Gelles and Straus, 233, 252-254, 270, 310, 312
gender feminists, 48, 58, 77, 96-97, 100, 109, 115, 126, 129, 137, 140, 172, 182, 200, 216-220, 222-226, 232, 234-239, 241, 243-249, 252, 256, 259, 264, 268, 273, 275, 277, 283-284, 288, 298-299
General Motors, 72
Gilligan, Carol, 245, 249-250, 269, 271, 273-274, 277
GM, 35, 116, 134, 136, 141, 214, 251
Greer, Germaine, x, 159, 202-203
Hill, Anita, 5, 96-97, 121, 221
Hite, Shere, 112-113, 115
Hoff Sommers, Christina, 225, 244-246, 250
Holy Grail, 274, 294, 309
Homolka, Karla, 78
homophobia, 93, 176
humanism, 30, 33, 86, 108, 127-128, 132, 135, 141, 158
IMF, 4, 108
Ireland, Patricia, 239, 279
Jagger, Mick, 210
Jung, Carl, 233
Kant, Immanuel, 226, 228-229, 249, 292
Koss, Mary, 114, 242, 277
Lawrence, D.H., 54-56, 131-132, 211, 282, 305, 308, 314
life expectancy, males/females, 298
Lilith Fair, 115-116
longhairs, 4, 17, 41, 88, 94,

97-98, 106, 110, 183-184
Madonna, 124, 152, 160, 177, 180, 209, 308, 314
Mantle, Mickey, 148
market economics, 4, 11, 30, 36, 43, 86, 105, 107, 116, 134-136, 274, 286
marriage, ix, 6, 16, 24, 53, 91-92, 96, 112-113, 128-129, 147, 157, 166, 169, 172, 186, 188-190, 193, 196, 200-205, 209, 213-214, 222, 228-229, 233, 259, 277, 279, 281, 284, 288-289, 293, 303
Master's degrees, gender, 251
memes, 33-34, 36-37, 39, 91, 194, 199, 234, 252, 264, 271-272, 280, 283, 291
menstrual cycle, 49, 141
Mill, J.S., 28-29, 136
ministers, 12-15, 17-19, 107
monopoly
    Adam Smith, 136
Moore, Michael, viii
Morisette, Alannis, 126
Mother Teresa, 181, 183, 185
Mother's Day, 16
Ms magazine, 97, 114, 234, 240, 242, 245
Mussolini, 248
Nader, Ralph, 248
Nation, Carrie, viii
Nietzsche, Fredrich, 131, 194, 204, 231-233, 296, 307-308
Novak, Bob, 31
NOW, ix, 133, 237, 239, 279-280
Orwell, George, vii
Pipher, Mary, 249, 271-274, 277
Plato, 84, 230, 296
political correctness, vii, 20, 43, 126, 200, 217, 223-224, 232, 280, 290, 297
Potter, Harry, 218, 247
Prince of Wales, 181-182, 187, 192
psychologist, vi
psychology, 23, 26, 34-35, 58, 78, 101, 103, 106, 114, 139, 235, 247
rape, 38, 56-58, 65, 68, 78-79, 95, 113-114, 123, 129, 166, 219, 234, 240-242, 266, 275-277, 282, 294
reproductive freedom, 164, 257, 259-260
Revelation, 169
Rivera Live, 98
schadenfreude, ix
Schopenhauer, Arthur, 226, 230
sentiment., vi, 1, 10-11, 13-15, 17, 19, 21, 56, 87, 93, 97, 110, 120, 129, 179, 300
sexual abuse
    false accusations, 265
    of children, 113, 175, 264-265
    of males, 265
sexual harassment lawsuits, 97
Simpson, Wallis, 188
single fathers, 263
single mothers
    access to father blocked, 266
    births to, 257, 259
    boyfriends and children, 220
    crime of children, 269

drug use of children, 219
feelings of victimization by children, 263
mental illness of children, 266
number of, ix, 259
schooling of children, 262
Spice Girls, 124-126
spinsterhood, 91, 302-303
spousal murder, vi, 64, 213-214
Stanton, Cady, 129-130
Starr, Ken, 97
Statistics Canada, 267-268
Steinem, Gloria, xi, 114, 159, 234-235, 238-239, 242, 245, 252, 277
stock market, 4, 86, 248
suicide
    divorce and, 257
    gender, 249
    Wollstonecraft, 119
Sunday, Billy, 18

Super Bowl Sunday, 235
tacts, 9, 216, 218, 223, 234, 237, 244-247, 268, 273, 304
talk shows, 17, 78, 99, 198
The Simpsons, 216-217
Thomas, Clarence, 5, 96, 221
Tiger, Lionel, 260, 271
Twiggy, 61
unmarried women, 113, 302
    births, 259
value, 33
Walker, Lenore, 277
Wolf, Naomi, 222-224, 238-240, 242, 273, 277
Wollstonecraft, Mary, 109-110, 119, 125, 127-128, 140
Wurtzel, Elizabeth, 118-119, 121-122
X-rated rentals, 115
Yates, Rusty, 270

To order **Operation: Gender War**

visit

Chi Publications
bond@culturebuster.com
www.culturebuster.com